Reconstructing the Slave

Frontispiece. Attic red-figure kylix by the Dokimasia Painter, *c.* 490 BC.

Reconstructing the Slave

The Image of the Slave in Ancient Greece

Kelly L. Wrenhaven

B L O O M S B U R Y

LONDON · NEW DELHI · NEW YORK · SYDNEY

Bloomsbury Academic
An imprint of Bloomsbury Publishing Plc

50 Bedford Square	1385 Broadway
London	New York
WC1B 3DP	NY 10018
UK	USA

www.bloomsbury.com

Bloomsbury is a registered trade mark of Bloomsbury Publishing Plc

First published in 2012 by Bristol Classical Press
Reprinted 2013
Paperback Edition first published 2013

© Kelly L. Wrenhaven 2012

British Library Cataloguing-in-Publication Data
A catalogue record for this book is available from the British Library.

ISBN: HB: 978-0-7156-3802-6
PB: 978-1-4725-0442-5

Library of Congress Cataloging-in-Publication Data
A catalog record for this book is available from the Library of Congress.

Printed and bound in Great Britain

Contents

List of Illustrations

Acknowledgements

I would first like to thank Tom Harrison and Jon Hesk, who provided me with support, advice and encouragement when this project was at its earliest stages. I would also like to thank Paul Cartledge and Mark Golden, both of whom kindly took the time to read and comment upon drafts of Chapters 1 and 2, gently correcting errors and offering advice for further reading (any remaining errors are, of course, my responsibility). I am further grateful to Nick Fisher, who has kept me up to date on his own work related to slavery and provided me with some useful information regarding a particular Attic tombstone; Timothy McNiven, who provided me with some useful images of comic slaves; François Lissarrague, who many years ago directed me towards the only known figure identified as a 'slave' on a Greek pot; and Christopher Smith and Sian Lewis, who encouraged me to think more about the provenance and audiences of Greek pottery. I would also like to express my appreciation to my colleagues at Cleveland State University for allowing me the funds, time, space and encouragement I needed to complete this book, and to the National Archaeological Museum at Athens for their quick responses to my requests for the rights to images of Attic tombstones, which were sent to me free of charge (an unfortunate rarity today). I would also like to acknowledge a personal debt to my parents, who have given me limitless and unquestioning support throughout many years of studies and research.

Finally, I would like to thank the one person to whom I am most indebted: my husband, who has been a constant source of friendship and support over many years, and without whose firm and unconditional encouragement I would never have considered going this far. Thank you for never letting me take the 'easy way out'. I dedicate this book to you, with all my love.

To Steven Wrenhaven

Introduction

In 422 BC, during the Gamelion (January/February), an audience of primarily Athenian residents (citizens and non-citizens) gathered to celebrate the Lenaia.[1] As part of the festival, they were entertained by some of Attica's leading dramatists, among them Aristophanes, who produced a comedy that year entitled *Wasps*, which cast a satirical eye upon Athens' jurors and political demagogues. Characteristic of Aristophanes' plays (and quite likely of those of other comic writers; see below), the audience was first presented with two slave characters, Sosias and Xanthias, whose task it was to guard the door of their owner Bdelycleon's house in order to prevent his father, Philocleon, from escaping. The play opens with Sosias scolding Xanthias for sleeping on the job and warning him that he 'will owe a great penalty to (his) ribs', meaning that he will be roundly flogged if his master catches him (3). Sosias himself then promptly falls asleep. Both slaves blame their drowsiness upon the Thraco-Phrygian god Sabazios, whose function, in this context at least, was to bring sleep, perhaps in the form of a drunken stupor.[2] Once fully awake, the slaves share with each other their dreams, which are peppered with an amusing mixture of omens and commentary about contemporaneous Athenian political figures. Finally, Xanthias focuses the audience's attention upon the issue at hand, namely Philocleon's seemingly insurmountable addiction to jury service (hence his 'imprisonment' in the house). After explaining the premise of the play, the slaves are reprimanded by Bdelycleon for sleeping and ordered to run to the house to keep an eye on his father, who is threatening to slip out through the drain in the kitchen sink.

This is just one example of Aristophanes' use of slave characters for initial, attention-grabbing comic relief and plot introduction – *Peace* and *Knights* begin in much the same way, with two bungling slaves narrating the action and explaining the plots to the audience. The way in which Aristophanes represents these slaves, however, is not unique to his plays. Not only does he reflect and manipulate representations of comic slaves from the plays of other dramatists (as Xanthias suggests when he warns the audience that he will not resort to the lowbrow tactics of other comedies, such as throwing basketfuls of nuts into the audience), within just over one hundred lines, he manages to draw upon

1

what was by this time a well-established series of ideas about slaves found in sources as varied as historiography, philosophy, tragedy and the visual arts. One of the most readily apparent stereotypes is his representation of barbarian slaves, which reflects the tendency in Greek sources to associate barbarianism with slavery.[3] Aristophanes does this, in part, through the slaves' names. Although neither name is exclusive to slaves, 'Sosias' is likely a Hellenized version of a Thracian name (cf. Xen. *Ways* 4.14), and always marks a slave in Attic comedy. Similarly, the name Xanthias means 'golden' or 'reddish' hair, which was likewise associated with foreigners. Xanthias' name might also have been reflected by his costume, which perhaps included the red-haired slave mask. The slaves' reference to Sabazios further connects them with barbarianism. Although there was a contemporaneous Athenian cult to Sabazios, the god was adopted from the East, most probably from Phrygia or Thrace, and was associated with a lack of moderation in the form of corybantic revelry.[4] These characteristics, or weaknesses, were likewise connected with slaves and barbarians in a variety of sources. Moreover, since it appears to have been primarily women who worshipped Sabazios in the Athenian version of the cult, the god was linked to effeminacy, which by Aristophanes' time was considered characteristic of slaves and barbarians.[5] The slaves are also characterized by a general shirking of their duty, since both spend more time sleeping than guarding, and when they are awake (and unwatched by their master), they chat and gossip about the citizens of Athens and divulge a great deal about the goings-on in their master's household. When their master gives them orders, however, they quickly jump to attention, no doubt from fear of being flogged.

Aristophanes' depiction of these slaves would have come as no surprise to the members of the audience, who were already accustomed to seeing slaves stereotyped as lazy, untrustworthy and prone to excessive behaviour and gossip. As this book will show, these ideas were essential to the slave-owning society of the ancient Greeks. Indeed, judging by the frequent inclusion of slave characters in comic scenes on Greek pots, and the relatively numerous terracotta figurines of slave characters produced between the late fifth and the second centuries BC, these types of characters appear to have been amongst the most popular and collectible, perhaps in the same way that people later collected (and continue to collect) black Americana items such as rag dolls of black slave Mammies, rotund Aunt Jemima cookie jars, tea pots and salt and pepper shakers in the form of Aunt Jemima and Uncle Moses (Fig. 19). Although in both the ancient and modern contexts such items were considered amusing and entertaining, at least by their intended audiences, both also draw upon an ideology of slavery which aimed to justify the enslavement of certain people by 'Othering' them, typically through the attribution of characteristics which were considered non-ideal, such as laziness, barbarianism, servility, and mental and moral inferiority. Indeed, these types of amusing, likeable, even childish slaves are constructions which had the effect of making slavery, an intrinsically cruel and contradictory institution, seem as agreeable, acceptable and justifiable as the slave characters themselves. By emphasizing the slave's perceived barbarity and lack of intelligence, or 'Otherness', a hierarchy of power was established between the master and the slave, making the former appear superior and deserving of dominion and the latter inferior and deserving of domination. In this way, representing slaves both aided in the construction of identities and, through repetition, in perpetuating ideas which were important to maintaining these identities.

It is clear that these kinds of representations are caricatures of slaves, in the same way that Philocleon is a caricature of an elderly Greek male citizen and Bdelycleon is a caricature of a Greek youth. Yet, while studies of Greek comedy generally recognize the generic distortion of non-slave characters (we can hardly assume that Aristophanes provides a mirror image of the real Cleon), in an effort to determine the historical reality of slavery in the Greek world, studies of Greek slavery tend to underestimate the power of generic distortion as it applies to slaves. To use the same example, because slaves are so often represented as barbarians in Greek comedy (and in other sources) it is often assumed that *the majority* of slaves in Greek city-states were, in fact, barbarian. While this might represent the real situation, it can hardly be proved definitively; in fact, there is at least as much evidence of Greek as barbarian slaves in epigraphic and historiographic sources.[6] On the other hand, the value of the *idea* of the barbarian slave, whether for comic effect or for some other purpose (such as connecting slaves with the innate moral and intellectual deficiency associated with barbarians), is underestimated or even overlooked altogether.

The issue of the selectivity of our source material is further compounded by the fact that the majority of the evidence, not only for Greek slavery but for Greek culture in general, is provided by a small segment of society, namely the literate, *polis*-dwelling elite. As has often been noted, particularly in studies of Greek women, this poses challenges for any socio-historical examination of ancient Greece; however, it is a particular challenge for the topic of slavery. For instance, it is often assumed, based upon the impression given by our sources, that slaves were to be seen virtually everywhere and that virtually everyone owned at least one slave. This has, in turn, led to the general assumption that slave ownership was common amongst all but the most impoverished levels of Greek society. Moses Finley, for instance, argued that 'the fact (of slave-ownership) is taken for granted so completely and so often in the literature that I strongly believe many owned slaves even when they could not afford them'.[7] While the 'fact' of slave-ownership might have been true from the point of view of members of the upper class who owned slaves and were therefore surrounded by them, it has the potential to distort our view of Greek society, and quite possibly the real situation of slavery in the Greek world. Lysias' speech *On the Refusal of a Pension* is sometimes cited as an example that even average men of middling means (i.e. tradesmen) were expected to have at least one slave. In this speech, the speaker is trying to demonstrate that he suffers such abject poverty that he is unable to afford even one slave to help him in his trade (24.6). This might indicate that it was considered unusual not to have at least one slave; however, it should be stressed that the speaker is responding to the argument that he has an affluent trade and so should be able to afford to support himself and, presumably, purchase slave help. More importantly, perhaps, he clearly expected the jury to believe that there were, indeed, some men who were so poor that they could not afford slaves. The idea that not all Greeks owned slaves is further suggested in Aristophanes' *The Assembly Women*, when Praxagora aims to correct the inequality of a society in which some men have many slaves and some none at all (593).

Although such poverty might have seemed virtually unimaginable to the wealthy, surely most Greeks did not fall into the category of being able to afford the luxury of slaves, who, if epigraphic documents such as the Attic Stelai are accurate measures of their cost, did not come cheap.[8] A comparison might be made here between the possible situation in Greece and that of the slave-holding American South, where modern historians generally assume that slave-holders made up 'a relatively small part of the southern population'.[9] This assumption is based, in part, upon census data from 1860, which indicates that only about 25 per cent of the population of the fifteen states owned slaves.[10] Therefore, even though southerners seem generally to have *identified* with the institution of slavery insofar as it helped to define their own rights and freedoms, most did not directly partake in it as slave-owners. Although the extent to which average Greek citizens identified with slavery is not so easy to determine, there is a strong possibility that the presence of slaves in Greek society similarly helped the Greeks to define themselves appositionally, as free Greeks with political, civic and legal rights, especially over their own bodies.

Another area where our sources often conflate slaves and the lower levels of Greek society is in the context of labour. Because poor free persons often performed the same type of work as slaves, members of

4

the elite made little or no social distinction between them. This, in turn, raises questions regarding what exactly our sources mean when they describe someone as a 'slave'. According to the Erechtheion accounts, slaves and citizens worked side by side on Pericles' building project, and even earned the same wages.[11] The powerful polarity Greek literature makes between the concepts of slavery and freedom, therefore, is likely more reflective of an elitist ideology, such as that demonstrated by Plato, Aristotle and the so-called Old Oligarch, all of whom wished to see labourers excluded from politics. In short, the pervasiveness of the concepts of slavery and freedom in broader Greek society is questionable; it is not something which should be taken for granted. As Andreau notes: 'Not infrequently, there is a certain gap, sometimes a quite large one, between social practices and the way they are thought about.'[12]

Even though the elitism of Greek sources has long been recognized by scholars, the tendency to underemphasize the selective nature of representations of slaves is particularly strong because, unlike in later historical contexts, there simply exists no evidence from the slaves themselves, or any other type of documentary information (e.g. photographs or voice recordings). In the same way that examinations of women in Greek society must utilize sources which 'see them only through the screen of their use by men', if we are to discuss ancient Greek slavery, we must make use of the evidence as presented by slave-owners for slave-owners.[13] Because of this, representations of slaves yield much less than we might like about the experiences and lives of actual slaves; they do, however, reveal a great deal about Greek *ideas* about slavery, as well as how the Greeks conceived of their own identity and culture through an antagonism with the image of the slave.

The aim of this book is not to rectify, dispute or challenge other examinations of Greek slavery in an attempt to piece together any sort of historical reality, but rather to embrace the representational, selective and ideological nature of literary and artistic images of slaves in order to reconstruct the *ideology* which informed and constructed them; hence the title, *Reconstructing the Slave*. Almost thirty years ago Finley recognized that it is 'the psychology and ideology of slavery which seems to me most urgently in need of continued inquiry'.[14] Since then, a great deal of scholarship has been produced on the ideology of the 'Other', which includes slaves and barbarians (see especially Cohen, 2000; Harrison, 2002; Wiedemann and Gardner, 2002), yet there has been no extensive study on the ideology of Greek slavery. By extensive, I mean one that is cross-genre, bringing together a wide variety of material in an effort to illustrate the pervasiveness of certain ideas about slaves, which although distorted by genre are not defined by it; for instance, the slave nurse is depicted as loyal and loving, almost to a fault, in epic, tragedy, comedy and the visual arts (i.e. pottery, sepul-chral imagery and terracotta sculpture). It is hoped that this book will make a useful contribution to the topic of the ideology of Greek slavery, and further, that it will be of use not only to Classical scholars and students but also to anyone interested in how the Greeks attempted to naturalize and justify the institution of slavery, which was not only taken for granted but viewed as intrinsic to Greek identity, culture, and, indeed, the Greek way of life. While this book is not intended as a comparative study of slavery through the ages, parallels will be at times be drawn between Greece and other slave-holding societies, such as the eighteenth- and nineteenth-century American South. The reader might be surprised at how little human society changed over the time in its effort to justify and naturalize an intrinsically unnatural institution.[15]

Since the elusive term 'ideology' will be seen repeatedly in this book, I should clarify what exactly I mean when I use it.[16] My understanding of ideology in this context is most closely aligned with that of Barbara Goff, who defines it as: 'All the sources, discourses, practices, and institutions that seek to eliminate or disguise the conflict by naturaliz-ing the unequal distribution [of power and resources]. What is socially determined, to the advantage of one identifiable group and at the expense of another, is said to be natural, and moreover, to benefit all groups rather than simply the overtly advantaged one.'[17] In the ensuing study, the conflict is, of course, between free and slave. As with gender ideology, the naturalization of slavery (or the attempt to do so) was done through stressing the alleged natural inferiority and inevitable subju-gation of certain people. In actuality, 'if such inequities *were* natural, little ideological effort would have to be expended in claiming them so'.[18] As we shall see, the Greeks expended a great deal of effort in differen-tiating free from slave, typically characterizing slaves as naturally physically and/or mentally inferior to free persons – in Greek thought, slaves were *naturally* suited to slavery.

Yet the term 'slave' and its cognates cannot be as neatly defined as one might like. Because slavery is not only a reality but also a concept, slave ideology is fluid and could apply to more than just legal slaves. My examination of slave representation therefore considers not just slaves but slavery as an analogy. This is evident, for instance, in Greek terminology, which allows for the application of slave-like qualities to non-slaves. Although, as we shall see, any free person might be deemed 'slavish', the most prevalent application of this terminology was to barbarians (*barbaroi*). Obviously most barbarians were not slaves, but Greek ideology perceived barbarians as slavish due to factors such as differing customs, language and government – this was the case par-ticularly (but not exclusively) after the Persian Wars.

6

The idea of 'slavishness' could also be utilized in a more general, metaphorical context. People might be described as 'enslaved' to love, food or drink. This use is most common in the philosophical and rhetorical contexts and is related to the view that slaves lack control of themselves and are therefore subject to being controlled. A good example is when Socrates asks Xenophon: 'What do you think will happen to you if you kiss an attractive boy? Won't you immediately become a slave, become unfree, spend a great deal of money on harmful pleasures, have very little leisure to cultivate what is *kalokagathos*, and be forced to pursue what only a madman would pursue?' (Xen. *Mem.* 1.3.11).[19] By examining how and why slaves were perceived in certain ways, we can gain some insight into what Greeks meant when they applied the concept of slavishness to non-slaves.

It is my contention that if we are to determine the ideology which informed Greek slave representation, it is necessary to examine as much data as possible. This is further necessary in view of the fact that no treatise on slavery exists from ancient Greece. This book, therefore, makes use of representations from philosophy, oratory, drama, historiography and material sources. While I recognize that by using a variety of data in one study I run the risk of ignoring a genre-specific context, the very fact that images of slaves in different sources map onto one another suggests that the ideology of slavery transcends genre. That is, although genre can distort and refract ideas, common patterns can be found amongst the genres and it is these common patterns which attest to the pervasiveness of slave ideology across mediums. This, in turn, reflects the omnipresence of slavery in Greek thought.

Since the bulk of the evidence for Greek slavery was produced between the fifth and fourth centuries BC, the Classical period will be the primary timeframe for this book. In order to trace the history of ideas about slaves, however, there will be some discussion of the Mycenaean and Archaic periods, particularly in my examinations of slave terminology, Greek law and the image of the nurse. Because Athens is our richest source for literary and material evidence for perceptions of slaves, most of the material examined will necessarily be Athenian. However, concepts such as environmental determinism and physiognomy, both of which contributed to perceptions of slaves and are therefore important to this examination, are not restricted to Athens but can be found in non-Athenian sources, such as the Hippocratic *Airs, Waters, Places*, Herodotos' *Histories* and Aristotle's *Politics*.[20] Moreover, the concept of *kalokagathia*, which is so prevalent in the Athenian context, is related to the more general connection Greeks made between a person's physical form and character. As we shall see in Chapter 2, this connection, which is most thoroughly revealed by the

Aristotelian *Physiognomics* and the Hippocratic *Airs, Waters, Places*, can be found, with variations, in several other contexts, including Athenian comedy and art.

In order to emphasize the pervasiveness of slave ideology across genres and to avoid excessive repetition, this book is arranged around themes. In the first chapter I consider how slaves are represented through language, that is, through the terminology for slavery, the way in which slaves are represented as speaking, and how slaves are spoken to and of (e.g. slave names). The variety of terms the Greeks used to describe slaves is an ideal representation of their multi-faceted conception of the slave as simultaneously many things (e.g. child-like, animalistic and property). Chapter 2 will consider the body of the slave, with a specific focus upon how Greek ideas about the relationship between the body and the soul map onto ideas about slaves and the slavish (such as labourers) as they are expressed in Greek literature and art. While the first two chapters focus primarily upon the more prevalent derogatory ideas about slaves, the third chapter concentrates upon what ostensibly appear to be more positive representations, or what I call the 'good' slave. Although these types of representations have sometimes resulted in the perception that they recognize the humanity of slaves, this chapter contends that the good slave is no more realistic than the bad slave. Since he (or more often she) embodies precisely the characteristics slave-owners wanted in their slaves, such as loyalty, obedience and even love, these representations were just as useful to the justification of slavery as more negative portrayals. The final chapter examines the ideas of conventional and natural slavery as expressed by Euripides and Aristotle. Perhaps because of their own experience and fear of enslavement, the Greeks made a strong distinction between those who were naturally suited to slavery and those who were only slaves in name. At least a century before Aristotle provided a definition and discussion of the two types of slaves in the first book of his *Politics*, Euripides explored the ideas of natural and conventional slavery through Trojan war captives, who lament and reject their enslavement, largely on the grounds that their nobility remains intact regardless of their change in status. It was not until Aristotle wrote his 'theory' of natural slavery, however, that the range of ideas about slaves previously found scattered across the sources were brought together into a concise and comprehensive treatment of natural slavery.

1

The Language of Slavery

1. The terminology

A good place to begin this examination is with the vocabulary the Greeks used to describe 'slaves' and 'slavery', since it is essential to our understanding of how slaves were perceived in Greek society. The terminology is also one of the most powerful illustrations of the complexity of Greek slavery and slave ideology. Scholars have often noted the range of words and their uses, calling it 'astonishing', 'extremely complex' and 'ambiguous'.[1] This is, in part, because in Greek literature, from comedy to historiography to the forensic speeches, we find several words for 'slave', frequently in the same text and even referring to the same individual. In Aristophanes' *Frogs*, for instance, the slave Xanthias is referred to as both a *doulos* and a *pais* and in the Xenophontic *Athenian Constitution* the terms *doulos* and *andrapodon* are used interchangeably (1.11).[2] Thucydides, likewise, refers to the same group of slaves as both *douloi* and *oiketai* (3.73). The tendency of Greek writers to use a variety of terms for 'slave' is also found in oratory: Demosthenes, in his speech *Against Timotheus* calls Aischrion an *akolouthos*, a *doulos* and an *oiketês* (49.55-7) and Lysias likewise refers to the same group of slaves as *therapontes, douloi* and *oiketai* (7.16-17).

As a result of the fluidity of the lexicon for slavery, Greek writers are sometimes accused of being 'frequently loose and inconsistent in [their] use of slave terminology', because they seem to employ different words for slaves with little 'rhyme or reason'.[3] Kyrtatas has found that 'the ancient Greeks were neither rigorous nor consistent in their use of terms denoting social categories', particularly in the very early (e.g. Mycenaean and Homeric) sources.[4] Similarly, Garlan notes that most words can even be seen as 'generic' because they need not always refer to slaves but were sometimes applied to free persons who were deemed in some way slavish.[5] The metaphorical use of slave terminology, however, need not detract from its meaning – in fact, as we shall see throughout this book, by considering what made a free person appear slavish, we can clarify which qualities were considered intrinsic to slaves.

This section will argue that the range of slave terminology is in fact a compelling illustration of the Greeks' multifaceted conception of the

9

slave. For the Greeks (as for many slave-holding societies) the slave could be many things, sometimes simultaneously: he (or she) is unfree; an article of property; connected to the *oikos* (whether private or the state 'household'); and considered both animal- and child-like. Throughout, we shall see how each of these concepts contributes to and reifies the image of the slave in a wide variety of sources. The four primary words for slave will be examined: *doulos, oiketês, andrapodon* and *pais*.[6] By understanding the parts, here the actual terminology, we can better understand the whole.

Doulos

The most common and the oldest word found in classical sources for 'slave' is *doulos*, or in the feminine, *doulê*, and its derivatives (e.g. *douleia, douliskos*, etc.). The term is generally agreed to have been derived from the Mycenaean word *doero/-a*, which is preserved in the Linear B tablets. There have been various studies of the etymology of *doero/-a*, notably by A. Tovar (1972), D.J. Kyrtatas (2001), and most recently by K. Raaflaub (2004). There is general agreement that the word has an Indo-European origin. Tovar narrows this down to the easternmost subgroup of Indo-Iranian, contending that the root **dem* is probably related to the Sanskrit *dasah* and *dasyuh*, meaning 'to tame' and 'servant' or 'slave'. This might be further compared to the Persian *dah*, meaning 'servant'.[7] The issue here, however, is not so much the word's geographical origin, that is, whether it was a foreign loan-word, but rather its original meaning in Bronze Age Greece and its subsequent relationship to the later term *doulos/-ê*. While the meanings of *doero/-a* and *doulos/-ê* cannot be equated, a consideration of how the word was used in Late Bronze Age Greece can provide some insight into the development of slavery and slave ideology.

The way in which the term *doero/-a* should be understood is closely connected with the social and economic structure of the palace-society of the Mycenaeans, which thrived between 1600 and 1100 BC. While neither its meaning nor form remained the same after the fall of the Mycenaean civilization, the word does appear to have indicated some type of subjugation, if tenuously, and is found in both social and religious contexts. Raaflaub cautions that the term should not be mistaken for the later conception of 'slave' but contends that it denoted some sort of dependence and function vis-à-vis the palace.[8] Austin and Vidal-Naquet similarly reject the idea that the *doeroi/-ai* can be equated with slaves: 'The lowest grade [in Bronze Age Greece] was not the position of the slave, but that of the *thês*, or free man but with no resources or property of his own.'[9] As both Raaflaub and Beringer point

10

out, the *doeroi/-ai* were not without rights, since some are connected with land allotments – yet, they do not appear to have belonged to the more privileged group because they were required to 'render tribute or service' to the palace, whether in the form of produce, such as textiles, or religious service.[10] In contrast, the *ereuteroi*, which is understood to be an early form of the word *eleutheroi* (free men), seem to have been exempt 'from specific quotas of product deliveries' and appear 'in connection with economic or fiscal matters.'[11] Some of the *doeroi* who are connected with land allotments are preceded by the word *teojo*, which is understood to be the genitive form of the later *theos* (*theou*, 'of the god'). It was perhaps the case that those who are described as 'servants of the god' enjoyed some sort of privileged status. While some of the *doeroi/-ai* might have been slaves, therefore, not everyone designated by this word was bereft of all rights and privileges. As Raaflaub concludes, 'the variety of categories of persons designated (or not designated) by this word precludes a unified and simple use of the term.'[12]

Due to the differences between the Late Bronze Age and Classical Greek society, we must avoid anachronistically associating the concepts of freedom and slavery with Bronze Age Greece. It is likely that at this early date these concepts, at least as they came to be understood later, did not exist. It is not until the Archaic period that a concept of slavery seems to have developed. This is apparent from the Homeric usage of the term, as well as from that found in the laws of Gortyn and Solon. In Homer, the term is rare (the archaizing word *dmôs* is much more common, see below), but it is found as an adjective, a personal noun and an abstract noun.[13] In Gortyn's Code, moreover, status distinctions are clearly evident, and free men and slaves are treated differently under the law.[14] Similarly, if we are to assume that Solon's wording has been exactly preserved by Aeschines, Solon used the term *doulos* in his law excluding slaves from exercising in the gymnasion or anointing themselves with oil (1.138; cf. Chapter 2.2). At this time also the terms *doulos* and *eleutheros* were used as opposites and were often paired with each other, a practice which continued into the later periods of Greece.[15]

Before moving on to how *doulos* is used in Classical literature, it is worthwhile to note a related word, *dmôs*, which might also stem from the root **dem*. This word occurs relatively frequently in the works of Homer and Hesiod. By the Classical period, however, it seems to have gone largely out of style. When it does appear it is usually in the works of the tragedians, who favoured archaic language for their poems set in the distant mythical past (Aeschylus' *Persians*, which was set in the near, historical, past, is an exception). Out of the three tragedians

11

whose works have come down to us whole, the term appears by far the most often in Euripides, where it is found forty-three times. In contrast, it is used seven times by Aeschylus and three times by Sophocles. While this might be due to a word-preference on the part of Euripides, or because we have more extant from Euripides than other tragedians, its frequency might be connected to the fact that slavery is a common trope in Euripides' extant plays, as are slave characters. In fact, Euripides' tendency to include many lowly characters is mocked by Aristophanes when Dicaiopolis accuses Euripides of dressing his characters, and even himself, in rags (*Ach.* 410-17). As Chapters 3 and 4 will demonstrate, Euripides is by far the most useful tragedian for the study of representations of slaves as well as the lower classes in general.[16]

Turning back to *doulos*, in Classical sources it is the only word for 'slave' which appears as the semantic opposite to *eleutheros*. As such, it is frequently used as part of the proverbial slave-free dichotomy, appearing in phrases like 'whether *eleutheros* or *doulos*' (e.g. Thuc. 4.118.7; Xen. *Anab.* 2.5.32). The word is most often used to refer to someone who is literally a slave or when the writer does not have a particular slave in mind. This is illustrated, for instance, by Demosthenes when he delineates 'the difference between being a *doulos* and an *eleutheros*' (24.167). The generic sense of the word is demonstrated also by the nouns *douleia* and *doulosunê* ('slavery') and *douliskos* and *douloprepês* ('slavish'), although the latter adjectival use is also found for other words for slave, such as *andrapodôdês*, a derivative of the noun *andrapodon* (see below).

Due largely to its generic nature and to its opposition to *eleutheros*, the word was also frequently used in a broader metaphorical sense to describe someone who was in some way (or ways) perceived of as being slave-like. The condition of being *like a slave* is often used in philosophical and dramatic contexts and is applied to those who are controlled by their passions. Socrates claims that some men are *douloi* because they are 'enslaved' to gluttony, lechery, drink or to foolish and extravagant ambitions (Xen. *Oec.* 1.22). Similarly, Hecuba in her eponymous play reasons: 'No mortal is free; he is either a *doulos* to money or to fate' (Eur. *Hec.* 864-5). Euripides also employs this use in *Heracles*, when Amphitryon states that 'the hoplite is the *doulos* of his arms' (190) and later when Heracles claims that he 'must be a slave (*douleuteon*) of good fortune (*tuchê*)' (1357).

The term *doulos* was also used metaphorically to describe barbarians. The association between barbarians and slaves began very early in Greek history and might even be linked to the meaning of *doero/-a*. As discussed above, Tovar contends that the stem **dem* is related to the Sanskrit *dasah* and *dasyuh*, both of which can refer not only to slaves but, more generally, to barbarians, or foreign enemies.[17] Certainly, by the Classical period the concepts of barbarianism and slavery were inextricably linked. While the Greeks were well-acquainted with non-Greek people and cultures, largely through their extensive and longstanding involvement in trade and warfare, and there was clearly an appreciation, perhaps even an admiration, of foreign cultures, Greek literature and art frequently express the barbarian as the slavish antithesis to the freedom-loving Greek.[18] After the Greco-Persian Wars, it was the Persians in particular who tended to be depicted as slavish, cowardly and effeminate. This type of representation is connected not only with a general perception of superiority over all barbarians but is one of the ways in which the Greeks tried to make sense of their seemingly impossible victory over the Persians. While Herodotos provides several reasons for this, including superior equipment, organization, skill and the will of the gods, his *Histories* ends with the implication that the Persians, by eventually choosing an easier life, had become subjects, the 'soft' inhabitants of a 'soft' land (9.122).[19] As we shall see in Chapters 2 and 4, the Greeks made a strong connection between not only barbarianism, but also between the way in which people lived, their form of government, and the land in which they were born and raised. Considered from a broader perspective, the connection that the Greeks made between barbarians and slavery must also have had something to do with the presence of foreign slaves in many Greek city-states.

In short, the broad applicability of the term *doulos* and its long history help to explain why it is so pervasive in Greek literature. While it was used to describe actual slaves, it could also be used metaphorically to describe someone who was considered in some way slavish. Due to its semantic opposition to *eleutheros*, moreover, it was often used as a standard term to describe anyone who might be seen as being in a state of unfreedom.

Andrapodon

While *doulos* can refer both to slaves and to anyone who was considered in some way slavish, the word *andrapodon* seems more straightforward in that it was used specifically in the context of slavery (the same cannot be said of the adjective *andrapodôdês*, however, which is a general term referring to slavishness). Due to its relationship with *tetrapodon*, literally 'four-footed thing' (livestock), *andrapodon*, or 'man-footed thing', is by far the most potent illustration of the conception of the slave as animal-like. As Paul Cartledge writes, the term 'provides as perfect an illustration as could be hoped for of the norma-

tive Greek construction of slaves as subhuman creatures'.[20] The fact
that *andrapodon* appears most often in the military context points to
this as its probable origin. It is especially common in the works of
Xenophon, where it tends to refer specifically to war captives, usually
non-Greek women and children who were intended either for sale or for
personal use as slaves. Like the *tetrapoda*, the *andrapoda* (slaves) were
part of the live plunder. In his *Anabasis*, Xenophon frequently mentions
andrapoda in conjunction with baggage animals. For instance, he
relates that at one point 'many of the baggage animals (*hupozugia*) and
andrapoda perished' (4.5.4). He later describes how the Greeks set off
with 'their baggage animals (*hupozugia*) and *andrapoda*' (6.6.1) and
also how Greek soldiers had secured 'many *andrapoda* and sheep'
(6.6.38).[21]

The relationship between the word *andrapodon* and the military
context, and more specifically its connection to war-captives, is also
expressed by the noun for 'slave-trader', *andrapodistês*. This word was
also used for 'kidnapper' (e.g. Lys. 10.10). There was, however, little
difference between the two, since a kidnapper might also be a slave-
trader (Strabo 14.5.2). Since other words for 'slave' do not have similar
derivatives, this term associates slave-traders with the context of warfare. Traders would follow in the wake of armies, hoping to purchase
war-captives to sell in the slave-markets located around the Mediterranean. There were also traders who worked 'hand in glove with the
pirates', who are known to have raided settlements and kidnapped
people to sell into slavery.[22] While the Greeks made use of such traders
and kidnappers as important sources of slaves, ironically they had a
negative view of people who made their living selling human beings.
Aristophanes uses the word as an insult in his plays (e.g. *Thesm.* 818,
Wealth 521-6) and both Plato and Aristotle refer to 'kidnappers' in the
same breath as thieves, swindlers and clothes-stealers (Pl. *Rep.* 1b;
Arist. *Ath. Pol.* 52.1). There are other less common words similarly
derived from *andrapodon*, such as *andrapodokapêlos* ('slave-dealer')
and *andrapodokleptês* ('slave-stealer'). Again, no such derivations exist
for other terms for 'slave', not even for *doulos* (there is no *doulokapêlos*,
for instance).

It is noteworthy that in the context of warfare the Greeks drew a
distinction between *andrapoda* who were free (that is, those who were
newly enslaved) and those who were already slaves (presumably, those
who were slaves prior to the Greek victory). This is expressed by
Thucydides in his description of the Peloponnesians' capture of the
people of Iasos (8.28), whom he describes as *ta panta andrapoda, kai
doula kai eleuthera* ('all the captives, both slave and free'). This use is
likewise seen in the *Hellenica* when Xenophon describes the sale of the

14

1. The Language of Slavery

Methymnaean captives who were already slaves (1.6.15) as *ta an-drapoda ta doula panta* ('the captives who are all slaves').

While the term surely originated in the military context, where war-captives were herded away along with the farm animals, in time *andrapodon* came to be used as a general word for 'slave'. Regardless of how a person might have fallen victim to slavery, the word was appropriate for all slaves as it expressed the ideological connection that Greeks made between slaves and animals. Thomas Wiedemann's claim that 'it does not follow that the Greeks saw their slaves as analogous to four-footed beasts' is not borne out by the evidence, which often connects the two.[23] This is argued at length by Keith Bradley, who found after examining both Greek and Roman evidence that 'the ease of association between slave and animal ... was a staple aspect of ancient mentality'.[24] Xenophon's Ischomachos provides an example of this when he suggests that wild animals and slaves benefit by the same type of training, as both can be taught obedience by feeding them the food they like as a reward for good behaviour (Xen. *Oec.* 13.9). This connection is also found several times in the works of Plato. In his *Statesman*, slaves are classified with 'tame animals' (289c), in the *Laws* the Athenian claims that some men believe that their slaves have the same nature as wild animals (777a), and in the *Republic* Glaucon explicitly compares *andrapodôda* to wild beasts (430b).[25]

The connection between animals and slaves is also found in drama. Hippolytos, for instance, asserts that slaves should be kept away from women and instead given as companions to brutish wild beasts (Eur. *Hipp.* 646). The satyrs in Euripides' *Cyclops*, moreover, who in this play typify the perceived character of slaves and are even kept as *douloi* by Polyphemos, exemplify by their hybrid form the conception of slaves as animal-like (24, 78). As we shall see in the next section, analogies are also drawn between the sounds made by animals, barbarians and slaves. As stated above, however, there are few examples of the word *andrapodon* or its derivatives in the extant works of the tragedians. This is puzzling – it is possible that the tragedians found this term too unpalatable for the slave characters of their plays, with whom the audience was often intended to empathize. The term, however, is also rare in the plays of Aristophanes, where it is only found twice (*Birds* 523, *Ecc.* 593), yet, as in tragedy, the idea that slaves are animal-like is not. Slaves in comedy are typically expected to be at the beck-and-call of their masters and are often depicted as human beasts-of-burden. The beginning of Aristophanes' *Frogs* even parodies this when the slave Xanthias complains about carrying his master's baggage even though he is the one riding the horse (1-25).

The term also recalls the reality that slaves were the living property of their masters and were enumerated along with the livestock. This is made explicit by Ischomachos' statement that his slaves are not allowed to breed without his permission (Xen. *Oec.* 9.5). While there was some recognition that slaves were not seen as interchangeable with animals, they were generally viewed in terms of and often treated like 'animal-like property'.[26] In both Greek and Roman society, any defects of slaves and animals had to be divulged prior to sale. Both were treated in the same way in the markets in that they were put on display and subject to being poked and prodded by potential buyers.[27] In Roman law, the first provision of the *Lex Aquilia* includes both slaves and animals in the same sentence, assuming that both were the property of their owner. Centuries later, the *Digest* states that dealers of animals and slaves are required to divulge any defects before a sale can take place (21.1.38.2-3).[28]

Although late, one of the most comprehensive Greek examples of the conception of the slave as animal-like is provided by the *Life of Aesop*. The extant text dates to the tenth century AD but it is thought to be based upon a second-century version.[29] Because of references by Herodotos (2.134) and Aristophanes (*Wasps* 1446, 566; *Peace* 129; *Birds* 470), it is evident that the story of Aesop existed at least as far back as the mid to late fifth century, perhaps earlier depending on the date one accepts for Herodotos.[30] Aesop is frequently portrayed as animalistic, which is in line with other representations of slaves found in the Classical period. The slave dealer at first refuses to take him, calling him 'the trumpeter in the battle of the cranes' (14).[31] Similarly, when one of Xanthos' female slaves first sees Aesop, she asks him, 'Where's your tail?' (31) and makes fun of his 'dog's head' (31). Even after Aesop regains his speech, he continues to be considered animalistic, as his first master asks: 'Who will want to buy him and have a baboon instead of a man?' (11). Indeed, the paradoxical image of Aesop, a beast on the outside but a man on the inside, personifies the genre of fable itself, which typically portrays animals with human characteristics.

The analogy between slaves and animals is not, of course, restricted to the ancient world but has been a persistent characteristic of all slave-holding societies. An essential component to the successful enslavement of another human being, relatively speaking, is to construct for the slave a persona of animalism. This helps to justify the treatment of the slave, which is akin to that of a domesticated beast-of-burden in that it lowers him or her to a subhuman status. The animalization of the slave must have had a significant impact not only upon the psychology of the slave-owner and, more broadly, the slave-owning society, but also upon the slave himself, whose obedient subjugation was essential to the success of the institution. In the plantation accounts of slave-

16

holders in eighteenth-century Jamaica, for instance, slaves were enumerated together with the livestock.[32] There will be much more to say about the animalization of the slave in subsequent chapters.

Oiketês

While *andrapodon* stresses the treatment and the conception of the slave as animal-like, the word *oiketês* expresses the idea that the slave is inseparable from the *oikos* (household). The term *oiketês* is usually translated as 'household slave'. Fritz Gschnitzer has argued that the word literally means 'inhabitant of a house' and functioned much like *dêmotês* ('member of a community').[33] The Homeric form of the word, *oikeus*, is usually translated as 'servant', since it is often unclear whether the person (or more usually people) referred to is unfree or whether he or she simply worked and lived within the master's household.[34] This need not overly concern us here, since, as discussed above, the conceptions of freedom and slavery were not fully developed at this period. While the word *oiketês* need not denote slavery, however, by the Classical period it was almost always used in relation to slaves and took either a feminine or a masculine article depending upon its subject. The Hellenistic poet Theocritos has been identified as an exception, since he used the feminine form *oiketis* to describe a housewife (18.38). This form, however, is uncommon and is found only once in the Classical sources, where it is used by Euripides nonspecifically to refer to any 'serving girl' (*Elec.* 104). Although Theocritos could have used *oiketês* with the feminine article, he chose not to, probably because by this time the term had long been associated with slaves.[35]

The word *oiketês* identifies the slave not only as part of the *oikos* (household) but also as 'the performer of various tasks of everyday life'.[36] While it might be used of any slave, it is typically used of domestics, who lived and worked within their masters' *oikoi*. The proximity of this type of slave to his or her master might explain why *oiketês* is the most common word for 'slave' after *doulos* (found 366 and 801 times respectively). Domestic slaves would be the most likely to witness or to figure in household events. It is almost certainly no coincidence that Xenophon in his *Oeconomicus* (*Treatise on Household Management*), which focuses primarily upon the domestic sphere, used it more often than any other word for 'slave'.[37] *Oiketês* is also relatively common in the works of Aristotle, where it occurs 39 times, and in Aristophanes' plays, where it occurs 22 times. While Aristotle uses the term more loosely to refer to any type of slave, Aristophanes uses it mainly for domestic slaves, who appear frequently in his comedies. The term, however, is most prevalent in oratory, which is usually personal in nature and accordingly tends to centre upon events of the *oikos*. *Oiketês* is found 115 times in the Attic speeches. Demosthenes was particularly fond of the word and used it a total of 62 times, only four of which occur in his political speeches.

Due to the domestic slave's proximity to the household and to the master, there were frequent attempts to summon slave testimony in court, which could be provided only under torture (see Chapter 2.2 for a discussion of *basanos*, the 'evidential torture' of slaves). Antiphon claims that if victims of foul-play are unable to tell friends or relatives who attacked them before they die then they will call their *oiketai* to witness the charges (1.30). Demosthenes, moreover, argues in his speech *Against Aphobos III* that his *oiketai* knew well that Aphobos was selling goods out of his home (29.38), and there are many other such examples in the forensic speeches.[38] It should be stressed that the households under discussion are typically those of wealthy individuals who would have owned at least one domestic slave. Virginia Hunter, in her tally of the extant references to slaves in the forensic speeches, notes that 'as far as numbers go, speakers in the forensic orations assume that everyone had a slave or slaves'.[39] Yet, it is important to keep in mind that our sources do not provide a cross-section of Greek society. While domestic slaves were commonplace in wealthy households, where their presence was taken for granted and is thus reflected in the sources, many more did not have the luxury of slave labour.

Of course, slaves could belong to an *oikos* without being domestic slaves *per se*. The word *oikos* does not refer strictly to the master's dwelling but is inclusive of all of the members of the *oikos* as well as the movable and immovable property. It might even be used of temples, the dwelling places, or *oikêmata*, of the gods. In this sense then, the term *oiketês* might describe any slave, regardless of his or her duties. It might even be correctly used for public slaves if we are to consider the *oikos* in the broader sense as being the household of the collective citizenry. Aeschines in his speech *Against Timarchos* describes Pittalakos as an *anthrôpos dêmosios oiketês tês poleôs,* 'a man who is a public slave of the city' (1.54). Moreover, there was a variety of uses for slaves and many worked in industry. Since Greek *ergasteria* ('workshops') do not appear to have been separate from but were extensions of the *oikos*, even an artisan slave could still be viewed as belonging to the *oikos* of his or her master.[40] The shoemakers in Aeschines' first speech are referred to as *oiketai,* even though they lived separate from Timarchos, paying him *apophorai* (dues) from their earnings while presumably keeping the rest for their own maintenance (1.97).

1. The Language of Slavery

In short, *oiketês* does not necessarily imply the occupation of the slave so much as the perception of the slave as simultaneously a possession and thus bound in some way to the *oikos*, whether that of an individual family or collectively of the *dêmos* ('citizenry'). The term expresses the fact that Greek writers could no more conceive of an *oikos* without a slave than they could conceive of a slave without an *oikos*.

Pais

The connection between slaves and the *oikos* is further demonstrated by another word for 'slave', *pais*. Its meaning is flexible and may connote descent, age and/or condition. It could be used to describe a son or a daughter, biological or adopted; it could be used for a boy or a girl; and it could be used for a slave of any age. Other forms of the word might also be used for slaves, such as *paidion* (e.g. Ar. *Clouds* 132) for both male and female slaves, and *paidiskê* for female slaves (e.g. Lys. 1.12).[41] Although late for the scope of this book, Athenaeus uses a derivative of *paidiskê* for 'brothel', *paidiskeion*, probably because brothels were largely composed of female slaves (*Deip.* 10.437f.). The word was also occasionally used for *erômenoi*, the junior partners in male sexual relationships, and is sometimes seen on pots depicting idealized youths who are referred to with the words *ho pais kalos* ('the boy is beautiful').[42] One of the primary factors that each use has in common is the idea of subordination or dependence, such as a child in relation to his or her parent; the *erômenos* in relation to the *erastês* (male lover); or a slave in relation to his or her master.[43] This is also apparent in the metaphorical use of the word, sometimes seen in the context of myth ('Echo, child of the rocky mount', Eur. *Hek.* 1110; 'Child of the vine', Pindar *Nem.* 9.52). The word *pais* for 'slave' is particularly common in Attic comedy. While this might reflect the actual sociolinguistic situation of Athens, as much of the language of comedy does, it was doubtless also funny for the audience to hear an old tottering slave like Daos called 'boy' (Men. *Aspis* 305) or to see the servant of the god War, *Kydoimos* ('Uproar'), respond to such a call (Ar. *Peace* 255).

When used in the context of slavery, *pais* is particularly demonstrative of the perception of the slave as interminably puerile. This is because the word was applied indiscriminately to slaves of all ages, much as 'boy' was applied to male slaves of any age in the slave-holding American South. The idea that the slave is forever child-like is expressed by the Greek sources, which often depict slaves as lacking the intellectual and moral potential to advance to maturity.[44] Socrates in Plato's *Lysis* compares the treatment of children to that of slaves when he contends that Lysis is maintained in a state of 'constant servitude to someone' (*aei tôi douleuonta*) and is prevented from being happy and doing what he pleases (208e). Yet Socrates also notes that while Lysis' body is managed by others (e.g. his parents), certain tasks are entrusted to him, such as writing letters and stringing his lyre. When Socrates asks Lysis why he is not given the management of his own body but is permitted to manage some tasks himself, Lysis replies that it is because he understands some things but not others (209c). This interchange evokes not only the Greek perception of the child but also that of the slave. While the slave's body is in the power of his master, he is also given the responsibility of certain tasks which are considered within his ability to achieve. Aristotle will later recall this idea in the *Politics* when he argues that slaves partake in reason (*logos*) enough to apprehend it, but not enough to possess it (1254b23-4; see Chapter 4.2 for a discussion of Aristotle's theory of natural slavery).

The word also makes a connection between the child's 'susceptibility to desire, pleasure, and pain' and the slave's perceived lack of *sôphrosynê* ('self-moderation/control').[45] Plato makes this comparison in the *Republic*, where it is stated that appetites, pleasures, and pains are found primarily in children, women and slaves (431c). The idea that slaves were susceptible to their desires because they lacked self-control is particularly evident in Aristophanes' plays, which include a number of memorably loquacious and lascivious slave characters. *Wasps* opens with two slaves who are so drunk they can hardly stay awake, *Knights* opens with two slaves vociferously complaining about being beaten, and, several lines down in the same play, masturbation is presented as a common pastime of male slaves (*Knights* 24-5). Slaves in comedy are also particularly prone to gossip, as demonstrated in *Frogs* when Xanthias and Aiacos joke about babbling their masters' secrets to anyone who will listen (745-53). Chapter 2 will discuss how the slave's penchant for gossip is graphically illustrated by the trumpet-mouthed masks worn by slave characters.

The word *pais* also recalls how slaves were subject to physical violence, particularly for disciplinary reasons. This is made explicit in Aristophanes' *Wasps*, when the Chorus Leader tells Xanthias that 'it is just to call anyone a *pais* who takes beatings, even if he is an old man' (1297-8). While an Athenian man could be prosecuted for injuring or killing another man's child or slave, this was primarily because both were considered the property of the father or master. Yet a man could treat his own children or slaves in any way he pleased with legal impunity. The only possible exception was an act of *hubris* ('deliberate infliction of shame or dishonour'), which might make him susceptible to prosecution if one of his fellow citizens saw fit to bring a *graphê hubreos* (charge of *hubris*) against him.[46] Aristophanes further expresses the

connection between slaves and violence by making a pun on the onomatopoeic verb *paiein* ('to beat') with the word *pais*. The slave Xanthias,
for instance, complains that Kleon 'beat me violently (*neanikôs*), shouting *pai pai*' (*Wasps* 1307).[47] Corporal punishment, particularly beating
and whipping, also importantly served to identify the slave as an
outsider who was typically not subject to protection under the law (see
Chapter 2.2 for a discussion of slaves, *hubris* and Greek law).[48]

It is noteworthy that the perception of slaves as child-like is also
expressed in the art. Female slaves are sometimes shown wearing
kandys, a long-sleeved garment adopted from the Persians and typically worn by children.[49] Slaves are also sometimes depicted as smaller
than free persons, even free children. Due to these similarities, slaves
in iconography are often mistaken for children. If we were to take these
visual representations as accurate depictions of reality, however, it
would appear that many slaves were abnormally small. There are a
number of grave reliefs, for instance, which show slaves attending to
free children who are almost twice their size (see Chapter 3.1; cf.
Chapter 2.3). It has been suggested that slaves might have been prone
to an early death or to stunted growth due to malnutrition.[50] There is,
however, no way to prove that this was the case. On the contrary, there
is very little evidence for slave children in Greek city-states, where
slave breeding appears to have been restricted and under the tight
control of the master (cf. Xen. *Oec.* 9.5).

It is more likely that the art, in much the same way as the literature,
reflects an ideology of slavery which perceived slaves as child-like.
Their small size is representative of their lowly position in society, in
much the same way that mortals are inferior to gods and heroes and so
are often depicted as smaller in the imagery. It must also be stressed
that by depicting slaves as smaller than free persons, even free children, the artists could draw a stark visual contrast between free and
slave. As in life, although slaves were expected to be present, they were
also expected to fade into the background. In this way, the iconography
reflects both the conception of slaves as *paides* as well as the inferior
social position of actual slaves. While the child, however, has the
potential, indeed the expectation, to obtain status, whether as a citizen
or a wife, the slave does not have this same expectation; as long as a
slave remains a slave, he or she will be forever without status and thus
will never 'grow up'. In this respect of social exclusion and expectation,
and in the broader conception of the slave as perpetually in a mental
and moral state of puerility, it was perfectly suitable to apply the word
pais to all slaves, regardless of their age.

2. Speaking slaves

Like slave terminology, the ways in which slaves are represented as speaking can reveal a great deal about Greek perceptions of slaves. Since the stereotypical slave was barbarian, a consideration of how the Greeks perceived foreign languages, and by extension the people who spoke them, is crucial to an examination of slave representation. This section will begin by considering the broader topic of Greek perceptions of non-Greek languages and will then focus more specifically upon how this applies to representations of slaves.

Greek views of non-Greek languages

Before considering the popular conception of *barbaroi* (non-Greeks, barbarians), it is important to consider briefly the importance of language to Greek identity. A famous definition is given by Herodotos, who lists *homoglôsson* ('same language') second only after *homaimon* ('common blood') in his description of *to Hellênikon* ('Greekness') (8.144).[51] Herodotos' story of the so-called 'Attic deeds' even makes a specific connection between cultural superiority and Attic Greek. In this story, Herodotos claims that when half-Pelasgian children were taught Attic Greek by their Athenian mothers, they were unwilling to mingle with the fully Pelasgian children but rather 'deemed it right to rule over the [other] children and were much stronger [than they]' (6.138). The idea that Greekness, in part, resided in the language, however, is not restricted to Herodotos. Thucydides expresses the same idea when he writes that some of the Amphilochians were hellenized when they adopted the dialect of the Ambraciots, while those who did not remained *barbaroi* (2.68).[52] Similarly, Plato's *Menexenos*, in a speech attributed to Aspasia and relayed by Socrates, states that the Athenian naval operations against the Persians following the Persian Wars were waged against the *barbaroi* on behalf of 'all the other *homophônoi*' ('homophones', or 'Greek-speakers') (242a).[53]

These kinds of examples illustrate that the criteria the Greeks used in defining their self-identity favoured language over many other factors, including geographical location, political systems and physical differences. Because the Greeks were dispersed widely and did not all share in the same type of social or political structure, they had to look elsewhere for ways to define themselves as a single people.[54] When faced with foreigners, who often did not look any different from themselves and who might even have shared a similar political or social structure, the most obvious way for the Greeks to contrast, and thus define, themselves was to focus upon differences in language. The importance of language to self-identity is expressed by the very word the Greeks used for a foreigner, *barbaros*, which is, as Moses Finley put it, 'the ancient antonym of Hellene'.[55] This word is usually understood to be onomatopoeic, expressing the linguistic perception of foreign languages as *barbar*, or 'babble' as we say in English. Strabo claims that the word initially referred to people who spoke Greek badly, that is, to those who spoke Greek with a thick, harsh accent, and then eventually it came to be 'misused' as a generic term for anyone who was not Greek (14.2.28).[56]

In contrast to another word for 'foreigner', *xenos*, the word *barbaros* was sometimes used pejoratively and is indicative of how foreigners were often perceived in Greek society. After the Greco-Persian Wars, the word *barbaros* became synonymous with Persians (or Medes, whom the Greeks identified with the Persians). In Aeschylus' *Persians*, Xerxes' army is referred to as a *stratos barbarôn* ('army of barbarians') (255). The word also became synonymous with the idea of brutishness and ignorance. Socrates in Aristophanes' *Clouds* uses *barbaros* as an adjective when he describes Strepsiades as *amathês kai barbaros* ('ignorant and barbaric') (492). The word is also often used in conjunction with *phonê* ('language') to describe non-Greek languages or even non-human communication. Tereus in Aristophanes' *Birds* claims that before he taught the birds language, they were *barbaroi* (199). The idea that barbarians did not even speak a real language is further reflected in Sophocles' *Women of Trachis* when Heracles draws a contrast between Hellas and the rest of the world, the latter of which he calls *aglôssos* ('without speech') (1060).

These examples provide evidence of the hellenocentric view that the only true language is Greek. Other languages were seen as the products of a less developed, slavish people. Agamemnon in Sophocles' *Ajax* insinuates this when he accuses Teucer of being unfree and claims that he is unable to understand Teucer's *barbaros glôssa* ('barbarian speech') (1260-3). While this is clearly meant as an insult, since both heroes shared the same Greek father, Ajax's words draw a connection between slavery and barbarian languages. The idea that Greek is the only true language can be connected with the perception that the Greeks had surpassed the barbarians in civilization. Thucydides claims that Asiatic barbarians still have customs that the Greeks had long since abandoned, such as wearing loin-cloths during athletic competitions (1.6). Moreover, when Theseus in Euripides' *Suppliant Women* praises god for rescuing humans from their 'brutish state' (*thêriôdês*) by giving them speech, he is likely referring to Greek society in particular (202). The perception that foreign languages are inferior might help to explain why there is so little evidence of Greek polyglots. Even

Herodotos, who travelled widely and utilized many foreign sources of information does not appear to have had a working knowledge of any language other than Greek.[57] As we shall see, the often negative perception of foreign languages provided fodder for Attic comedy. While non-Attic dialects are also ridiculed, all Greek dialects were considered intelligible. Barbarian languages, on the other hand, tended to be portrayed as a nonsensical mix of human and animal sounds.[58]

Comparisons between barbarian speech and animal sounds are found in both prose and poetry and date at least as far back as Homer, who approximates the Trojans' battle cry to the bleating of sheep (*Il.* 4.433-6). Herodotos provides several further examples. For instance, he compares the language of the Garamantes, a Libyan tribe, to the sound of squeaking bats (4.183). In line with the Greek tendency to represent barbarians as the semantic opposite to Greeks, he also claims that the Garamantes ploughed their fields backwards due to the backward-facing horns of their oxen.[59] He makes a similar comparison between foreign language and animal sounds when he writes that the priest-esses of Dodona are said to have spoken a language which sounded like the cries of doves and suggests that these priestesses were called *Peleides* (doves) after the sound of their barbarian language (2.57). This type of comparison is also found in drama. Clytaimestra in Aeschylus' *Agamemnon* indicates that Cassandra's language is unintelligible like a swallow's (1050-1), and the Triballian god in Aristophanes' *Birds* is likewise said to be 'twittering like the swallows' (1681).[60]

It is further noteworthy that Herodotos applies the verb *ôruesthai* ('to howl') only to wild animals and barbarians. For instance, he claims that the Persian subjects settled around the Aces River go 'howling' to the King when they run out of water (3.117) and he later describes the Skythian men as 'howling' with joy during their vapor baths (4.75).[61] This might be compared to Orestes' fear that the Phrygian slave will raise a cry (*kraugê*) and thwart Orestes' plans (1529). The word *kraugê* typically describes the baying or barking of dogs. The Greeks were not alone in comparing unfamiliar languages to the sounds of animals. Pliny describes a tribe called the Choromandae who he claims are not only covered in fur but also shriek because they lack a proper voice (*sine voce*) (*Nat. Hist.* 7.2.24). This type of impression is also seen in later historical accounts of foreign peoples. Christopher Columbus, after coming into contact with the natives of America, is said to have desired to bring some of them home 'so that they may learn to speak'.[62]

The Greeks also made a general association between outlandish language and outlandish customs. Herodotos claims that the Troglo-dyte Ethiopians not only sounded like screeching bats, they also feasted on serpents, lizards and reptiles (4.183). This dietary peculiarity was worthy of mention since reptiles were hardly culinary delights in Greece.[63] An even more potent example of the connection between linguistic skills and culture is given by Ktesias in his description of the Indian tribe of the *Kunokephaloi* (Dog-Headed People) who, among other peculiarities, are said to have had sufficient capability to understand speech but could themselves only bark like dogs (*Indika* FGrHist 688 F45.37). Even Greeks who spoke a dialect far removed from Attic Greek were subject to the same types of prejudices normally reserved for non-Greeks. Thucydides remarks that the Eurytanians, an Aetolian tribe of central Greece, speak the most unintelligible *glôssa* ('dialect') and are also *ômophagoi* ('eaters of raw flesh') (3.94).[64]

Barbarian slaves in Attic drama

The frequently depreciatory view of foreign languages and the people who spoke them was doubtless a factor in negative perceptions of slaves. As will be demonstrated throughout the course of this book, representations of slaves are partially contingent upon views of barbarians, and it is difficult to discuss one without considering the other. Attic drama is a particularly rich source of representations of both. Since there already exist a number of useful studies on barbarians, this section will focus primarily upon two barbarian slave characters of particular interest to the present discussion: the Phrygian slave in Euripides' *Orestes* and the Skythian Archer in Aristophanes' *Women at the Thesmophoria*.[65]

While barbarians are commonplace in Greek tragedy, it was unconventional for tragedians to portray characters speaking with foreign accents or in a foreign language.[66] This was surely due primarily to the austere nature of the genre, where accents might have rendered the speech awkward and even unintentionally humorous. Outside of foreign clothing, barbarianism was instead stressed through references to foreign speech, as well as by acoustic effects, such as cacophony and occasional non-Greek vocabulary.[67] A good example is Euripides' Phrygian slave, who is simply called *Phryx* ('Phrygian').[68] While this character does not speak with an accent, he utters the barbarian cry *ailinon*, which he identifies as Asian (*Orestes* 1395). He also refers several times to his barbarian/Phrygian origin. Early on in his lengthy lament he mentions his 'barbarian slippers' (1369-70), Ilion, the 'Phrygian city' (1381-2), and the *barbaroi* with their *Asias phônê* ('Asian sound') (1396-7). These self-conscious and rather unnatural references ensure that the audience is well-aware of his non-Greek origin.

The Phrygian slave is also excessively boisterous and verbose, which are characteristic qualities of tragic slaves. This is evident from his frequent cries which punctuate his description of the tragic events unfolding in the palace. While such cries are suitable for tragedy, the boisterousness of this slave might be further due to the idea that barbarians were noisy. Foreign languages evidently sounded coarse to the Greek ear.[69] The connection between boisterousness and barbarianism probably also had something to do with the idea that barbarians were considered less civilized, lacking in self-control, and that Asiatics in particular were prone to fearful flight. These characteristics by extension were considered intrinsic to slaves. Often the shouting of slaves precedes news of an event. This is evident in *Orestes* when the Phrygian slave bursts onto the scene preceded by the clanging bars of the palace (1366-7). What follows is the slave's rather choppy description of the attack on Helen, punctuated by cries of *ômoi moi, otototoi, aiai* and the above mentioned *ailinon*.

The vociferous, frightened and cowardly barbarian slave character is certainly not restricted to Euripides' *Orestes*. There are a number of references in other plays to the shouting of the household slaves. For instance, the Messenger in Euripides' *Heracles* describes how 'the throng of *oiketai*' shouted when Heracles went on his rampage (976) and Theseus in Euripides' *Hippolytos* remarks on the shouting of the palace slaves (790-1). This idea is reflected and parodied in comedy when Chrysis says to the brazen slave Parmenon: 'Why are you shouting, you scoundrel?' (Men. *Samia* 69).[70] This quality is also applied to free barbarian characters and had the same exotic effect. The cacophonous speech of the Egyptians in Aeschylus' *Suppliants* is a good example (825-902). While the manuscript is defective at this part of the play, there are enough words extant to conclude that Aeschylus gave the Egyptians lines in broken Greek: e.g. 'Hurry, hurry to boat as fast as feet! Then not, then not hair pulled out, hair pulled out, and tattoos, bloody murderous chopping off head?' (836-41).

The clangour of slaves and foreigners in tragedy is further illustrated by their often excessive mourning, behaviour which by the Classical period the Athenians characterized as effeminate and barbaric. This impression is likely coloured more by Asiatic funeral customs than those of non-Asiatic barbarians.[71] In Aeschylus' *Persians*, when the Chorus of elderly Persian men hears that the Persian army has been destroyed, they abandon themselves to grief and lack any measure of *sôphrosunê*. After the Messenger delivers his news, the Chorus punctuate their words with cries of *aiai, otototoi* (256-89), expressions of mourning more suitable for women and slaves. It is noteworthy that the Chorus consists wholly of Persian men, which illustrates the Greek view of Persians and old men as effeminate.[72]

While vociferous mourning accompanied by tearing at one's own

26

head and body was also customary for Greek funerals, at Athens these practices evidently went out of favour as early as the sixth century. It was during this period that Solon is said to have instigated reforms banning excessive mourning, promoting milder rites in contrast to 'the harsh and barbaric practices in which most women had previously indulged' (Plut. *Sol.* 12.5).[73] It is possible that Demosthenes refers to this same law when he states that Solon had limited the number and the age of women permitted to be mourners at funerals (43.62). This view, however, might be Atheno-centric, since these practices had evidently not been outlawed everywhere in Greece. Herodotos compares the Spartan mourning customs to those of the Asiatic barbarians when he claims that the Spartans also mourned their kings through vigorous wailing, physical defilement (tearing at their bodies and muddying their garments) and clamour (6.58).[74]

As for Euripides' Phrygian slave, he is not only depicted as vociferous, he is also somewhat incoherent. This is made explicit when the Chorus Leader asks him to speak more clearly (*saphôs*) (1394). Gradually the slave begins to make more sense but his speech continues to be halting. Even though Euripides stops short of giving him a foreign accent, his stilted phrases and repetitive use of vocabulary give the overall impression that his language is to some extent forced and over-emphasized. Stephen Colvin has suggested that the slave's repetitive use of vocabulary might be a play 'on a prejudice about Asiatic excess in the repetitive nature of dirges'.[75] While this might have been a factor in how he is represented, his linguistic portrayal more strongly suggests that he does not have the comfort-level or the experience with the Greek language that a native speaker would have. By using short phrasing and repetition, Euripides could delineate the slave's tenuous grasp on the Greek language while avoiding the linguistic awkwardness which might result from poor pronunciation and foreign accentuation. Once again, this might be compared to Aeschylus' representation of the Egyptians (above).

In contrast to tragedy, foreign accents are portrayed with some frequency in Old Attic comedy.[76] This is conceivably due to the opportunities for humour presented by non-Greek accents as well as to the fact that Old Comedy is more firmly rooted in contemporaneous locations and time. While this is most evident in the work of Aristophanes, the only poet of Old Comedy whose plays have survived intact, the portrayal of foreign accents was certainly not an Aristophanic invention. This comedic technique dates at least as far back as the sixth century and is found in a fragment attributed to the iambic poet Hipponax in which a female character sings a rude incantation mixing Lydian, Phrygian and Greek words, all languages which would have been spoken in Hipponax's home city of Ephesus (fr. 92 West).[77] Aristophanic comedy, however, furnishes the richest material and preserves the everyday Greek of the time, including accent and idiom. This was later noted by the first-century AD Roman rhetorician Quintilian, who writes that Attic comedy almost exclusively preserved *sinceram illam sermonis Attici gratiam* ('the genuine quality of Attic speech') (10.1.65).

As stated above, several of Aristophanes' barbarian characters reflect the myriad foreign accents which many Athenians must have heard regularly throughout their cosmopolitan city (cf. Ps.-Xen. *Const. Ath.* 2.8). There is evidence to suggest that Aristophanes had a good ear for 'foreign noises' and attempted to reflect barbarian accents accurately.[78] The best example of this appears in the *Women at the Thesmophoria*, which includes the lengthiest portrayal of a speaking barbarian in Attic comedy. While some of Aristophanes' barbarian characters merely utter foreign-sounding gibberish (e.g. *Birds* 1628-9, *Acharn.* 100, 104), the Skythian Archer actually speaks a 'cacophonous pidgin Greek'.[79] It has been noted that Aristophanes is remarkably consistent in his depiction of the Skythian Archer's pronunciation. The Skythian does not use aspirates and he often mistakes the letter *s* for *x*. He also makes frequent grammatical errors and has problems using the correct gender and case, issues which are still common amongst modern students of ancient Greek.[80]

Aristophanes' representation of the Skythian Archer is a parody of the real archers who formed Athens 'police' force at the time. In the period following the Persian Wars, Athens purchased three hundred Skythian slaves (Aesch. 2.173; Andoc. 3.5). These public slaves, or *dêmosioi*, would stand guard at public events and meetings. Their main function appears to have been crowd-control, although they also assisted magistrates by helping with arrests and 'manhandling prisoners' (Ar. *Ach.* 54, *Knights* 665).[81] They were clearly distinguished from Athenians by their Skythian attire and bows, hence the name given to them, the *toxotai* (archers). They also used whips or sabres, which are referred to in the play and were doubtless part of the Skythian Archer's costume (*Thesm.* 933, 1125, 1127, 1135). The Archers would have been a familiar sight to all Athenians and so provided a rich subject of humour for Aristophanes. They also appear in some of his other plays, such as *Lysistrata*, where they are similarly depicted as overly zealous and completely inept. In this play they are silent, but there is a particularly humorous scene in which four bumbling Skythian Archers unsuccessfully try to tie up a group of women, who refuse to let the barbarian *dêmosioi* come anywhere near them, let alone lay a hand on them (*Lys.* 387-462).[82]

In an effort to convey the effect that the Skythian Archer's words must have had on the Greek ear, scholars sometimes render the translation phonetically. Alan Sommerstein, for instance, uses a non-specific accent in his translation: 'Now you gan 'owl 'ere in de oben air' (1001). It is interesting to note that this kind of phonetic rendering has also been found in literature from later slave societies when the words of slaves are recorded. In a typical example, an early eighteenth-century West African slave, simply called 'Jin, native of Guinea', is recorded to have said: '... and we nebber see our mudders any more'.[83] There are other similarities in the ways in which ancient and more recent slave speech have been depicted. In both, noun and verb endings are sometimes dropped. The Skythian Archer tends to drop the *n* before a consonant (e.g. 1096). An eighteenth-century American slave is similarly recorded as saying: 'His master live [*sic*] in a tall house on Broadway.'[84] In the nineteenth-century American novel *Uncle Tom's Cabin*, moreover, Harriet Beecher Stowe uses phonetic spelling almost exclusively for slave speech. A notable exception is the slave trader, whose words are also rendered phonetically. In this novel, the hero Tom introduces himself with the words: 'My name's Tom; the little chil'en used to call me Uncle Tom, way back thar in Kentuck.'[85] While Tom's pronunciation can be ascribed to the Southern accent and dialect of the time, it is noteworthy that Stowe does not depict free persons from the very same region speaking this way unless they are social inferiors (such as the slave trader).[86]

By depicting slaves and barbarians with a distinct way of speaking, the writers were able to illustrate both the inferiority of these characters in relation to the other characters as well as their social exclusion, or Otherness. Aristophanes' parody of the Skythian Archer's accent not only differentiates him from other (Greek) characters, but also emphasizes his buffoonery. And Aristophanes evidently enjoyed the joke; the goddess Echo mimics the Skythian's words for a lengthy fourteen lines (1082-96). It is significant, however, that the Skythian Archer makes fewer syntactical errors than phonological or morphological ones and so can always be understood. He repeatedly mispronounces Artemisia's name as *Artamuxia* (1201, 1213, 1217). While this makes him appear ridiculous and thick-skulled, it also reflects a mispronunciation which was conceivably common amongst Skythians, whose names seem often to have included the letter *x*.[87] The Skythian Archer's especially wide vocabulary of vulgar words further adds to his buffoonery.[88]

Slaves, however, are not supposed to speak well. Eloquence was considered a characteristic of the well-born and was certainly not something expected, or even desired, of slaves. As Plato's Socrates tells Theaitetos: 'He who speaks beautifully (*kalôs*) is both beautiful and good (*kalos te kai agathos*)' (*Th.* 185e). As will be discussed in more

29

detail in the next chapter, the quality of *kalokagathia* ('beauty and goodness') was considered an attribute of the elite, that is, of well-born, free Greek males. Slaves, by contrast, were considered to be naturally inferior, so those who spoke well might be considered unnatural. This is made explicit in Euripides' *Andromache*, when Hermione's slave nurse describes her own barbarian words as *phauloi* ('humble, common') and implies that allowing oneself to be swayed by the words of a barbarian slave is demeaning (807). Hippolytos' servant likewise prays to Aphrodite 'as befits slaves to speak' (Eur. *Hipp.* 115). This idea is also found in comedy when Chremylos accuses his slave Carion of asking a question 'in a clumsy (*skaiôs*) and harsh (*chalepôs*) way' (Ar. *Wealth* 60). Aristophanes' choice of the word *skaios* is interesting as it suggests that the slave is 'on the wrong side', or 'cack (left)-handed'. This could be taken as an indication of the slave's foreign origin, which is further indicated by his name. It also implies that the slave is in opposition to his master, who is a free Greek. The other word, *chalepôs* literally means 'difficult', which could refer to a poor grasp of Greek, as well as to the slave's uncivilized way of expressing himself. Similarly, in Menander's *Dyscolos* Sicon accuses the slave Getas of asking a question 'like a dung-eater' (*skatophagôs*) (488).[89] On the other hand, when a slave does manage to speak well, the listeners appear surprised. This reaction is expressed by Deianeira in Sophocles' *Women of Trachis* when she says, referring to the Nurse: 'So even words from the low-born can fall out well (*kalôs*); this woman is a *doulê* but the words she has spoken are free' (61-3; see Chapter 3.1 for a discussion of slave nurses).

A parallel might also be drawn between the manner of speech of slaves and children. Callicles in Plato's *Gorgias* suggests that slaves are like well-spoken children or, alternatively, that children are like lisping adults (485b-c). This latter idea is reflected in Aristophanes, when Strepsiades remarks that his son was once 'a lisping six-year-old' (*Clouds* 862). Some slaves might have sounded like children due to a lack of education or conversational experience. As will be discussed in the next section, slaves are usually just given orders. If they were non-Greek *paidagôgoi* or nurses, moreover, they might have learned Greek largely from the children they cared for. The view that slaves are child-like was undoubtedly further reinforced by the Greeks' experience of barbarian slaves and their elementary grasp of Greek.

Slaves are also frequently presented as overly verbose blabbermouths who are unable to control their gossiping. As discussed above, this representation is, in part, due to ideas about barbarians and their perceived lack of self-control. This representation could also have something to do with the connection Greeks made between children and slaves, who were considered to be child-like, an idea further expressed

30

by slave terminology (i.e. *pais*). In Menander's *Misoumenos*, the slave Getas shows a lack of restraint when he interrupts his master like an excited child (98). The clamour associated with slaves in the literary sources is also reflective of the behaviour of children. In a fragment attributed to Menander, Slave A, who is intoxicated, smashes on a door using both his fists and feet (*Fabula Incerta* 8.66-70). As discussed above, moreover, both children and slaves were subject to beating. In comedy, slaves are frequently shown howling during or after being beaten (e.g. Ar. *Peace* 263, *Wealth* 111). We even find metonymic references to shins and doors howling like beaten slaves (Ar. *Wealth* 275-6, 1098-9).

In short, the ways in which slaves are represented as speaking typically reflect the broader conception of them as degraded people, or 'socially dead'.[90] The slave's social and ethnic disassociation from and opposition to the idealized Greek taps into social and ethnic prejudices against slaves. These prejudices, in turn, are the very same ones contained in the terminology in which the slave is represented as the non-ideal Other: as a barbaric, animalistic and childish person lacking in self-control and intellect. There is, however, much more to say about slave characters in the Attic tragedies, which also include intelligent, eloquent and noble slaves. This topic will be revisited in Chapter 3.

3. Addressing slaves

The ways in which slaves are addressed also inform an examination of Greek perceptions of slaves. The final section of this chapter will examine the types of slave names found in literary and epigraphic documents. It will also consider what these names can tell us about Greek perceptions of slaves; whether there is a correlation between the names found in the literature and epigraphic documents; and finally how slaves were spoken to and how they spoke (or were expected to) speak) to others.

Name-changing: a ritual of enslavement

When a slave was first brought into his or her master's *oikos* ('household'), a ceremony called the *katachusmata* took place which was analogous to that of a new bride entering her husband's *oikos* (Ar. *Wealth* 768-70, cf. 788-95; Dem. 45.74).[91] This ceremony, which consisted of 'showering' nuts and dried fruit such as figs over the new bride or slave, was intended to bring good fortune, presumably to the *oikos* or, more specifically, to the husband or master.[92] Aristophanes indicates that this custom took place at the hearth, where the new slave or bride

31

would conceivably kneel or crouch to receive the offering (*Wealth* 795).[93] While the bride would keep her given name, however, the slave would be provided a new one. This is expressed, for instance, by Hermogenes in Plato's *Cratylos* when he states that 'we change [the names] of our *oiketai*' (384d). Hermogenes' matter-of-fact statement suggests that changing slaves' names was standard, at least in Athenian society. While it is risky to try to determine a person's status based solely upon their name, there are certainly names which are suggestive of slavery. Moreover, name-changing was not limited to ancient Greece but has persisted as a 'major feature of the ritual of enslavement' for millennia.[94]

Since slaves were typically imported, often from non-Greek areas, it might appear initially that names were changed simply to make them more familiar to the owners. Slave-owners, however, have historically changed their slaves' names even when they come from the same region or linguistic group and this also appears to have been the case in ancient Greece.[95] Since names have value and can signify a person's kinship ties or tribal affiliations, an essential part of the process of enslavement was to remove the slave's former identity by imposing upon him or her a new identity. When a person's name is changed, their former name is made obsolete and so, in theory, is the life they knew prior to enslavement. In ancient Greece, free persons were identified with at least two names, a given name and a patronymic (father's name) in the genitive, which expressed their familial connection. After the Cleisthenic reforms of the late sixth century, Athenian citizens were also identified by their demotics (deme names). Pericles' full name, for instance, was *Perikles Xanthippou Cholargeus,* which means 'Pericles [son] of Xanthippos of [the deme] Cholargos'. Slaves, on the other hand, were usually identified only by their first names. In inscriptions, slaves might also be identified by an occupation (e.g. 'Pyrrhias, retailer'; 'Paideusis, nurse') or by their masters' names in the possessive genitive (e.g. 'Nicon [slave] of Cimon').[96] While the full names of Athenian citizens therefore stress their familial and political connections, slave names, in their brevity, stress the slaves' lack of such connections.

Names were important to the Greeks and so presumably also had meaning in the context of slavery. This is made explicit when Socrates contends that the giving of a name 'is hardly a trivial matter' (Pl. *Cratylos* 390d). Herodotos was intrigued by the origins of certain names, notably those of the continents (4.45), Heracles (2.43) and some Greek gods (2.50-2).[97] Plato's *Cratylos,* moreover, is wholly committed to examining onomastic correctness (*orthotês onomatos*). The primary question here is whether there is 'some kind of innate correctness in names' (383a-b), or whether their correctness is due simply to 'convention and agreement' (384d). Socrates concludes that correct names are, like paintings, imitations of the object's nature and therefore should reflect the nature of the thing named (430d). While incorrect names do occur, he contends that these are either given in honour of a relative or are wish-names, 'such as *Eutychides* ("good-fortune"), *Sosias* ("saviour") and *Theophilos* ("god-loved or -loving")' (397b).[98]

To use Plato's terminology, we shall find that the Greeks gave their slaves both 'correct' names, that is, names presumably intended to reflect the perceived nature of the person, and 'incorrect' names, that is, names indicating desirable but not necessarily the actual characteristics of slaves.

Slave names

Since some slave names are also relatively common for free Greeks, determining status based solely upon a name can be problematic. The Erechtheion Accounts list slaves with names such as Aeschines, Apollodoros and Timocrates, which were also those of prominent Athenian citizens.[99] There are, however, a number of names which appear to have been associated specifically, though perhaps not exclusively, with slaves, and it is with these that this section is primarily concerned.[100]

Demosthenes, in his speech *On the Crown*, implies that not all names are equal when he accuses his rival Aeschines of having changed his parents' names from Trometos and Empousa to the more respectable Atrometos and Glaucothea (18.130). Although this is a baseless accusation designed as an attack upon Aeschines' allegedly slavish lineage, it nevertheless suggests that there were 'free' and 'slave' names.[101] Trometos actually means 'Trembler', which is fittingly slavish since, as we have seen, cowardice was considered a non-ideal characteristic and was associated with barbarians and slaves. On the other hand, the antonym Atrometos means 'Not-a-Trembler' and is fitting for a free Greek man who should ideally be brave. The name Empousa, similarly, 'Others' Aeschines' mother by associating her with the eponymous shape-shifting hobgoblin of Greek mythology. This name also draws a humorous contrast with Aeschines' father, the 'Trembler', and further 'Others' Aeschines' parents by insinuating that their relationship is the inverse of the accepted patriarchal relationship between a man and a woman (barbarian society, by contrast, was sometimes viewed as topsy-turvy, e.g. Hdt. 2.35-6). Aeschines' mother's 'new' name Glaucothea, on the other hand, means 'gleaming/grey goddess' and is perhaps a reference to Athena, whose epithet is 'grey/gleaming-eyed'.[102] While their 'old' names therefore associate Aeschines' parents with negative characteristics more suitable for slaves, their 'new' names associate them with positive characteristics and were presumably considered more suitable for free persons.

Yet, in contrast to the negative way in which slaves are often represented, names denoting negative character traits were rarely given to slaves.[103] Much more common were those formed from ethnics, such as Asia, Scythes, Lydos, Carion and Thratta. Taking into account both the literary and the epigraphic evidence, the *ethnikon*-type name is found 104 times for slaves in the Classical period alone.[104] As Victor Ehrenberg remarked with reference to Aristophanes' plays, it is this type of name which reflects 'the multicoloured picture of Attic slavery most clearly'.[105] In the absence of more direct source material, *ethnikon*-type names have often been used by scholars as evidence for slave origins. It is questionable, however, how accurate these names are or even whether they were intended to be. Just as in modern Western society where an English woman may be called Michelle, a non-regional name need not indicate that a person is foreign. Some Greeks also had non-Greek names, probably because they were fashionable at the time. Braund and Tsetskhladze point out that Colchos was a popular name for Greek citizens, although they also note that this name was especially common amongst Greeks residing in the region surrounding the Black Sea.[106] Names like Gerys, Iasos, Carion and Croisos, moreover, identify Greek citizens in the Erechtheion Accounts.[107] Even the name Skythes, which is found four times for slaves, occurs five times for Athenian citizens.[108]

That said, these types of names were not nearly as common for Greeks as they were for slaves. Strabo's comment that Athenians 'tended to call their slaves by the same names as those of the nations from which they were brought' is corroborated by the evidence (7.3.12). Names denoting non-Greek regions or adopted from barbarian cultures appear relatively often for slaves in both the literary and epigraphic evidence (although not as often as Greek names). Demosthenes suggests that the names Manes and Syros were stock slave names when he urges the jury: 'Do not consider that they are Syros or Manes or whatever while this man is Phormion. The matter is the same, they are slaves and this man was a slave' (45.86). The idea that there were stock names for slaves is also reflected in comedy. Aristophanes used the Phrygian name Manes for slave characters in five different plays (*Peace, Birds, Lys., Thesm., Frogs*). Menander similarly used the name Daos, which was perhaps Phrygian or Eastern European, in at least nine plays (*Aspis, Per., Dysc., Her., Col., Carch., Epitr., Georg., Peric.*) and the name Syros in at least three (*Phasma, Dis. Ex., Georg.*).[109]

While it is risky to assume that evidence from comedy reflects a historical reality, epigraphy indicates that the dramatists were in fact reflecting a real situation. The name Syros was relatively popular for slaves and occurs ten times in epigraphic documents, seven of which are found in the Naval Catalogue.[110] The name Thraix/Thratta was also relatively common for slaves and is found fourteen times in epigraphic documents. It also appears in four plays by Aristophanes (*Acharn.*, *Wasps, Peace, Thesm.*) and once in Demosthenes (59.35). The name Manes, moreover, appears fifteen times in epigraphic documents, seven of which occur in the Athenian Naval Catalogue alone.[111] Strabo mentions that this is a common slave name and claims that it is Phrygian (7.3.12). While, in contrast to Strabo's claim, the name does not appear to have been popular in Phrygia, in Greece it seems to have become a moniker for the clichéd Eastern slave.[112] To a Greek audience this name was especially fitting for a slave, since in Greek the word *manês* might also refer to a person who is dull-witted (cf. Ar. *Frogs* 965). Aristophanes plays upon this when Manes is scolded for being lazy and slow and also when Peisetairos comments that 'Manes is worthless (*deilos*)' (Ar. *Birds* 1329, 1323-8).[113]

Even if slave-owners did sometimes name their slaves after their presumed place of origin, however, the average Greek probably had little detailed knowledge of exact geographical locations. If a slave-owner thought that a slave came from the North or looked like a northerner, he might simply have assumed that the slave was Thracian or Skythian. If the slave came from the East or, looked eastern, the owner might have concluded that the slave was Syrian, Phrygian, or Lydian. It should also be kept in mind that slave dealers themselves might not have known exactly where a slave came from and so might have misidentified the origin to potential buyers. Based upon stereotypes about people from certain regions, dealers might even have purposely misidentified a slave's origin in order to make their wares more attractive. For instance, if a potential buyer was looking for a man he could put to hard labour, he might have wanted a Thracian slave, while another might have wanted an Asiatic slave as a *paidagôgos* for his son. The waiter's comment in Menander's *Aspis* suggests that Thracian slaves were considered physically rugged and therefore useful for hard labour. Similarly, Aristophanes' intellectually blunt and bossy Skythian Archer also fits the stereotype of a boorish northerner. On the other hand, people from places such as Phrygia were considered meek and effeminate (Men. *Aspis* 242-4). Aristotle expresses a similar kind of stereotyping when he suggests that Asiatics, because of their warm climate, have skill and intelligence but lack spirit and so have a 'predisposition to live slavishly' (*Pol.* 1327b24-8; see Chapters 2.1 and 4.2).

Some slave names suggest physical attributes not characteristic of Greeks and so might also indicate barbarian origin. For instance, the names Xanthias ('Ginger' or 'Blondy'), Pyrrhias ('Fiery') and Chrysis ('Goldie') might have referred to hair colour. The connotations of such names are unclear, but red-hair does appear to have been associated with the Thracians. This is expressed by Xenophanes of Colophon in the early fifth century, who claims that Thracians have red hair and blue eyes (Fr. 16). Pollux in his list of comic masks, moreover, associates red-hair with a type of slave mask (*Onomasticon* 4.143-56), and the red-haired mask has been identified in comic scenes on Greek pots.[114] Some images also show tattooed figures with light-coloured hair and may represent barbarian slaves (see Chapter 2).

In short, although onomastic evidence alone is hardly a precise measure of slave origins, what is clear is that there was a desire amongst some slave-owners to give their slaves names suggesting foreign origin. It is also clear that, while Greeks may not always have identified correctly the geographical origins of their slaves, they do seem to have considered it plausible that slaves came from areas such as Thrace, Skythia and Phrygia, all regions with which the Greeks had trade networks.[115] Given the often derogatory view of barbarians expressed in Greek literature, moreover, the use of such ethnic names for slaves was probably not due solely to a lack of imagination. These types of names both relegated slaves to a barbarian origin and at the same time eradicated their identity as individuals. To many of us today, names like Thratta or Skythes might not sound any more foreign than other Greek names. Imagine, however, calling a person The African or The American and it is easier to put them into perspective. In the Greek context, these types of names stress the slave's 'Otherness' in all its connotations and make a literal and very public association between barbarians and slavery. They also relegate an individual to a collective identity, which includes all of the collective traits associated with that identity.

Many slave names also draw upon personal characteristics and reflect the anxieties slave-owners must have felt over the possibility that their slaves might exhibit poor behaviour, such as stealing, running away, or even that they might die young, before their usefulness was fully realized. Fragiadakis calls these types of names 'Wunschnamen' because they refer to the types of characteristics one can imagine owners would wish for in their slaves.[116] Along with names suggesting foreign origin, 'Wunschnamen' form one of the most identifiable groups of slave names and are particularly suitable for the institution of slavery. Some describe good workers, such as Dexios ('Dexterous/Skilful'), Ergasion ('Workman'), or Ergophilos ('Lover-of-Work'), and others refer to loyalty, such as the names Menon ('Steadfast'), Parmenon ('Standing By'), or Pistos ('Loyalty'). With the exception of the name Parmenon, which appears six times in the Classical period (four times in epigraphic documents and twice in the literature), these names are not particularly common.[117] Names with the prefix *Sô-*, however, are found forty-three times. This prefix is almost surely a derivative of the adjective *sôs,* which is a positive word denoting preservation and wholeness and so may be categorized with the other 'Wunschnamen'. The name Sosias appears fifteen times in inscriptional and literary sources. Menander was particularly fond of the name and used it for slave characters in at least three plays (*Per., Kol., Perik.*). Because comedy uses the name exclusively for slaves, Ehrenberg has suggested that it 'was perhaps invented by a comic poet'.[118] At any rate, the application of this name to slaves implies that it was one of those slavish-sounding names referred to by Demosthenes (above).

While few of the 'Wunschnamen' are found more than two or three times each, when considered together they form an impressive list of some of the most desirable slave characteristics. Xenophon's Ischomachos provides a similar list when he states that the principal female slave of his household should be temperate, mindful of her duties, agreeable and kindly disposed (Xen. *Oec.* 9.11-13). The desire for slaves to be agreeable is further reflected by Heracles in Euripides' *Alcestis* when he warns Admetos' slaves: 'It is not fitting for a servant to be sullen to guests, but rather to welcome them with a courteous spirit' (773-5).

What is more difficult to explain, however, is when qualities typically associated with free persons are applied to slaves. This is expressed by names such as Aristoboulos/-e ('Best Counsel/Deliberation').[119] This name is a composite of two words strongly connected with Greek males and citizenship: *aristos,* a virtue often associated with the upper class and morality, and *boulê,* which in the Attic context recalls Athens' Council of 500, an essential democratic advisory body.[120] Since *aristos* was also used occasionally to describe animals (e.g. horses, boars and rams), its use for slaves should not cause too much pause.[121] The word *boulê,* however, is surprising considering the evidence that slaves were typically portrayed as dull-witted, certainly not people to go to for advice. Perhaps even more surprising is that the feminine form, Aristoboule, is also found. These types of names suggest that there might have been a more fluid use of names in practice than that which is found in the literary sources. The application of typically male Greek virtues to women and slaves, however, should be understood within their appropriate context. Although slaves were perceived to be inferior to Greek citizens, they were considered able to think or to control themselves only relative to the capacity possible for citizens. A slave who could not think at all would have been useless to his or her master, as would a slave who was completely unable to control himself. This is precisely why Aristotle allows the natural slave a measure of reason (*Pol.* 1254b23-4). Although the slave is considered incapable of

37

living the good life, he is capable of just enough reason to allow him to perform his functions as a slave. Therefore, the perception that slaves could practice some independent thinking is not incongruent with slave ideology and in this context such characteristics can be appropriately applied to slaves.

In his study of slave naming patterns in eighteenth-century Jamaica, Trevor Burnard makes several points which are worth mentioning briefly for their comparative value. In eighteenth-century Jamaica, estate managers were responsible for submitting annual reports enumerating 'the whites, slaves, and livestock on their properties'.[122] While whites are listed with two and sometimes even three names, 'negroes', here synonymous with 'slaves', were usually listed with only one name, and sometimes 'a modifier referring to age, occupation, or ethnicity'.[123] Slaves and cattle, moreover, were enumerated together and sometimes even shared the same names (although slaves were always named and cattle only rarely).

Burnard notes that slave names were much more imaginative than those of whites, which suggests that white owners exercised significantly more freedom when naming their slaves than they did when naming their own children. While about 90% of names for whites were chosen from a pool of about twenty-five, slave names were derived from a greater variety of sources, frequently Africa, the Bible, geography and Europe. When European names were used for slaves, these names tended to be in the diminutive (so, Johnny instead of John, Billy instead of William, etc.), which expresses the idea of the slave as child-like and inferior. In line with the Greek evidence, names denoting ethnicity were popular; however, only a few African names were in common use, and these eventually became generic slave names (such as Quashie, Cuffee and Mimba). A comparison might be made here with Manes and Daos, which became generic slave names in Greek comedy. Similarly, while demeaning names, such as Whore and Monkey, are found in the plantation lists, positive names, such as Love, Hopeful, Fairplay and Fortune, are much more common and seem to express qualities that masters desired in their slaves. Since surnames were associated with free persons, when a slave was freed, he or she would also take a surname. In short, in both the Greek and the Jamaican evidence slaves were given names by their owners; slaves were seen as child- and animal-like; names tended to denote ethnicity or qualities useful to slave-owners; and having only one name was a sign of slavery. Although the slave-holding societies of ancient Greece and Jamaica could hardly be more separate in culture, time and space, they were both chattel slave societies, and the similarities between their naming practices provides some insight into how slave ideology can transcend historical differences.

1. The Language of Slavery

Addresses to and from slaves

As we shall see in more detail in the next chapter, the line between the lower classes and slaves is sometimes obscured in literary and artistic sources, which often makes it difficult to delineate between free and slave. This is also expressed by the way in which free and slave servants are addressed by free persons. As Eleanor Dickey argues in her detailed study of Greek forms of address, 'there were similarities between the addresses used to slaves and those used to free men acting in the role of servants'.[124]

While there are a number of examples, addresses to servants are not found nearly as often as addresses to people of higher social status, since addresses, specifically the use of names and/or titles, were often omitted if the addressee was considered to be inferior. Consequently, when free persons speak to slaves, the slaves' names are often omitted and the slaves are just given simple commands. The Athenian in Plato's *Laws* makes this explicit when he states that 'an address to an *oiketês* should be nothing but a command' (777e). Examples of commands to slaves are particularly abundant in comedy, where slaves are frequently ordered to do things such as carry bags, light fires, cook meals and answer doors. While these types of commands are part of circumscribed comic routines and were doubtless included because of their potential to create humorous situations (e.g. slaves grumbling about following orders, not following orders properly, etc.), simple orders also illustrate that the primary function of the slave was to be an object of command.

Although slave characters are not always addressed by name, relative to other genres, comedy furnishes the most extensive evidence for named addresses to slaves. This is doubtless because slaves in comedy 'can be major characters in their own right, rather than the nameless, shadowy figures which often appear in other genres'.[125] It might also reflect the real historical situation in which masters conceivably called upon their slaves by name in order to gain their attention and also, perhaps, to differentiate one slave from another. There are, for instance, a number of minor comic slave characters who are addressed by name but who do not say a word themselves. An example is Xanthias in Aristophanes' *Clouds*, of whom the reader, if not the audience, is unaware until he is addressed as part of a command: 'Come here, here, Xanthias, and bring the ladder and the mattock!' (1485-6).

Named addresses to slaves, however, are notably rare in other genres. Dickey finds that slave names are never used in this way in tragedy and only infrequently in epic.[126] Sometimes there is even an absence of a name where we might expect one. In Plato's *Meno*, Socrates speaks to Meno's slave at length, yet the slave remains nameless throughout their entire exchange (82b-85b). In fact, with the exception of comedy, it is difficult to find an instance in the literature where a master uses a slave's name in an address. Dickey gives the example of Darius' groom, whom Darius calls Oibares, but it is unclear whether this man was a slave and, at any rate, this is a Persian example and does not necessarily reflect Greek custom (Hdt. 3.85).

What is evident is that Greek literature expresses a reluctance on the part of free persons to address slaves by name. There are several possible reasons for this. For example, the use of a first name might indicate a friendly, familiar relationship between addresser and addressee, which for obvious reasons is unsuitable for the master-slave relationship. The Athenian in Plato's *Laws* warns that masters should not joke with their slaves or foolishly indulge them (777e-778a). His general contention here is that masters should not become too familiar with their slaves by treating them like free persons, which, he claims, will only make life more difficult for both master and slave. Aristotle seems to reflect this idea when he contends that there can be no friendship between master and slave, although there might be friendship with him as a human being (*Nic. Eth.* 1161b5-6; see Chapter 4.2 for a discussion of slaves as simultaneously human and animal). More importantly, perhaps, choosing to address or not to address one's slave by name is indicative of the power the master has over his slave. Just as the master has the authority to impose a new identity onto his slave by replacing his or her original name with a name of his choice, he also has the authority to deny his slave any name at all. By not acknowledging a slave's name, the slave is deprived of an individual identity and is relegated, a nameless entity, to a subhuman status.[127]

In view of the fact that slaves are not usually addressed by name in the extant literature, it is worth considering whether there might have been a further reason for the relatively common use of such addresses to slaves in comedy. Since slave names in comedy are frequently indicative of barbarianism, the use of named addresses might have been intended to exploit further negative perceptions of barbarians for comic effect. In addition to the red-haired slave mask, barbarian accents and barbarian costume, the repeated use of non-Greek names was just another way for the comic poet to stress the barbarianism of his slave characters. In this regard, by having free characters address slaves by names such as Xanthias or Thratta, the comic poet can express not only *who* a character is, but *what* they are. The use of slave names in addresses may therefore be more reflective of the requirements of the comic genre than of the real historical situation.[128]

Slaves might also be addressed by words other than their names and these are further indicative of the ways in which slaves were perceived. One of the most common examples is a word we have already examined, *pai*, which is the vocative of *pais* ('boy/child'). For instance, in a humorous parody of the way in which free men speak to slaves, Getas, a slave character in Menander's *Dyscolos*, bangs on Knemon's door shouting: '*Pai, paidion, paides kaloi, pai, paidi!*' ('Boy, little boy, beautiful boys, boy, boy!') (911, cf. 912). Likewise, although Socrates does not call Meno's slave by name, he does address him as *pai* or *pai Menônos* ('Meno's boy') (Pl. *Meno* 82b, 83c, 85b). The closest equivalent for female slaves is *grau*, which is the vocative of *graus* ('old woman'). While *pai* is used indiscriminately for slaves of any age, *grau* appears to have been used only for elderly female house slaves and is therefore more selective. For instance, Smicrines addresses Sophrone, his old nurse, as *grau* (1064). Dickey contends that such 'titles' are not insulting but, as we have seen earlier, calling a slave 'boy' without taking into account his age reflects the perception of the slave as mentally and morally inferior.[129] Since old age was also considered non-ideal, it is reasonable to assume that addressing an old female slave as *grau* had similar connotations. This word, moreover, is cacophonous and unappealing to the ear, recalling images of bent, old, wrinkled slave-nurses (these will be examined in the next chapter). In tragedy, on the other hand, we do not find slaves addressed as *pai* or *grau*, perhaps because these words were considered too colloquial, or vulgar, for the tragic genre. Instead, the poets use addresses such as *dmôes* or *dmôai* ('slaves') and *amphipoloi* ('attendants'), archaizing words which are uncommon outside of the context of tragedy.[130]

When slaves address free persons, they use either first names or titles. If the slave is addressing his master or mistress, the title *despota* ('master' in the vocative) or *despoina* ('mistress' in the vocative) is often used in place of a first name. It is not surprising that slaves are represented as addressing their owners in this way. It is perhaps a little more unexpected that slaves frequently address free persons who are not their owners by their first names. Recalling once again the exchange between Meno's slave and Socrates, the slave addresses Socrates by name a number of times (82d, 82e, 84a, 85b) while Socrates repeatedly refers to the slave only as 'boy'.

We must remember, however, that free-thinking Greeks did not customarily use formal or deferential titles and so do not seem to have expected to be addressed by a title, even by slaves.[131] There is no Greek equivalent of titles familiar to us today, such as 'Mr', 'Mrs', 'Dr', 'Sir', etc., or, more archaically, 'Madam', 'Lord' or 'Lady'. As discussed above, however, the Greeks could demonstrate the inferiority of addressees by omitting their names. In Plato's *Meno* the slave's repeated use of

41

Socrates' name draws a clear contrast with Socrates' lack of use of the slave's name. While Socrates is therefore represented as an individual, the slave appears to be a mere tool, a means to end, and so remains a nameless, shadowy figure, much like slaves were meant to be in real life. Put more simply, by not using the slave's name, Socrates implies that the slave is unimportant. On the other hand, when there is an exchange between two slaves, each normally uses the other's first name because they are both of equal status (e.g. Ar. *Wasps* 1).

2

The Body of the Slave

Introduction

The relative disinterest in the moral justification of slavery in Greek antiquity often confounds modern students and scholars, who find it difficult to believe that a civilization as progressively intellectual as that of ancient Greece could have accepted such a manifestly brutal and inhumane institution with so little reservation. Yet, in ancient Greece, as in later slave societies, people could hardly imagine a world without slaves. Harriet Martineau's statement is as true for antiquity as it was for her own period (1830s) that 'the greater number of slaveholders have no other idea than of holding slaves'.[1] As Isaac notes, however, even though 'the existence of slavery as such was not a relevant topic of discussion in antiquity ... there were arguments about specifics'.[2] The focus was not so much on whether slavery as an institution was justifiable but on what terms. The tendency was to try to demonstrate specific differences between free persons and slaves and these were generally sought at the fundamental levels of body and character. The importance of the body as the central location for ideas about slaves rests, in part, 'on the principle of property in man – of one man's appropriation of another person as well as of the fruits of his labor'.[3] While the importance of the physicality of the slave and of perceived corporal differences between slaves and free persons had consequences upon the physical treatment of slaves in daily life and under the law, they are also reflected in the art, where artists developed ways to distinguish between free and unfree bodies, or 'a hierarchy made visible on the body'.[4]

As with slave representation in general, perceptions of the slave's body were not restricted to the context of slavery but were part of a wider milieu which aimed to explain a person's character by their physical features, geographical origins, and their socio-economic status. This chapter will begin with an examination of how the concepts of physiognomy, environmental determinism, and *kalokagathia* are interwoven with the ideology of slavery. How this ideology was played out in other respects, that is, in the law and the treatment of slaves, will then be examined. The final section will consider how verbal ideas about slaves were expressed in the visual arts.

1. Judging a book by its cover: physiognomy and environmental determinism

Physiognomy

At least some ideas about slaves were informed by the belief that a person's features and comportment are reflected by their emotions and characters. Much like the ideology of slavery, which sought to rationalize and justify the institution, the concept of physiognomy was another 'tool developed to rationalize and classify such ideas'.[5] By the Classical period, the Greeks had a well-developed 'physiognomic consciousness', dating at least as far back as Pythagoras, who lived between the mid-sixth and early-fifth centuries.[6] There is some indication that it may be traced even further back to Homer. This is demonstrated by the Thersites scene in the *Iliad* in which the abominable body of Thersites, who is described as bow-legged and hunched, with a pointy head and shrill voice, seems to reflect his character, which is also ugly and irritating. These shortcomings were particularly evident to his social and physical better Odysseus, who silences him by striking him on the back with Agamemnon's royal sceptre (2.211-77). As Thalmann points out in his detailed discussion of this scene, Thersites was 'evidently a common soldier' because, unlike the majority of characters mentioned in the text, he is 'given neither a patronymic nor a place of origin'.[7] Since Thersites is the only common soldier treated individually in the text and his treatment is negative, the usual assumption is that Homer was reinforcing a class ideology which was intended to illustrate what would befall such a man if he were to forget his place. Thalmann views this explanation as 'reductively simple' and convincingly argues that the context of the scene and the relationship between the nobles and the commoners were much more complex.[8] What is straightforward, however, is that Homer draws a direct correlation between Thersites' ugly body and his correspondingly ugly character. It is further noteworthy that these negative characteristics are applied to someone of the lower class, a point I shall return to in my discussion of *kalokagathia*, below.

The best source for the pseudoscience *physiognomonika* (physiognomy) is a fourth- or third-century handbook on the subject, which most scholars agree is not the work of Aristotle, even though earlier authors attributed it to him (Ps.-Ar. *Physiognomonica*).[9] This work reflects the beginning of the 'theory' of physiognomy, whereby men began to 'set down in an orderly fashion what had long been informally observed and practised'.[10] It is clear from the outset that the author of this work is not the first physiognomist but that he intends to build upon and to clarify earlier theories (805a19). This treatise argues that the body and soul are in a reciprocal relationship, each affected by the other. Indeed, the author of the *Physiognomonica* asserts that 'no animal has ever existed such that it has the physique of one animal and the mental disposition (*dianoia*) of another' (805a12-3).[11] The second part of this work, which was perhaps written by a different author, likewise argues that the body and soul affect each other equally; if the body is altered, so is the soul, and vice versa (808b12-15).

The *Physiognomonica* begins by detailing three tools used in physiognomics, one of which is of particular interest to the present study. Using analogies with animals, the physiognomist categorizes people according to their ethnicities (*ethnê*) and attributes different appearances and characters to people from different regions (e.g. Egypt, Thrace and Scythia) (805a 27-8). Although the author notes that the physiognomist draws data from a number of physical characteristics, he begins with those he presumably views as the most important (which are also the most conspicuous): the colour of the eyes and skin, and the colour and texture of the hair. He contends that people and animals with soft hair are cowardly (e.g. men in the southern climes and sheep), while people and animals with coarse hair are brave (e.g. men in the northern climes and wild boars) (806b7-11). He also claims that people with 'very fiery hair' (*agan purrhoi*) are 'rascals' (*panourgoi*). Although he does not state exactly which regions are south and which are north, he must be envisioning the Thracians as northerners and the Egyptians as southerners. It is noteworthy that these ideas play into stereotypes of Thracians as tough and brutish and Egyptians as soft and effeminate, ideas which were familiar by this period (see below). It is not exactly clear, however, whether he considered the Scythians northerners or southerners.

This is not the place to discuss in detail every type of physical characteristic or disposition examined by the author. One of the elements of particular interest here is that the treatise expresses a strong inclination to idealize characteristics which were considered masculine (e.g. stiffness, strength, great size, muscle, low voice) while portraying as negative characteristics which were considered feminine (e.g. softness, weakness, small size, pallor, fleshiness, high-pitched voice). The conflation of slaves, women, and barbarians here is certainly not novel but is a feature of ancient literature.[12] Although the ancients did not see the three as perfectly analogous (Aristotle, for instance, saw slaves and women as two different types of human beings), each fell 'short of the full virtue of the free man in its own way'.[13] Barbarians were viewed as slavish, due to their degenerate culture and subjection to tyrants, and both women and slaves in patriarchal Greek society were subordinate to men. Similar to barbarians, 'women and slaves were ... distinguished from free men by their social subordination and their imagined otherness'.[14] What is also significant and is likewise a feature of Greek thought is the inclination to view extreme characteristics as negative, such as very dark or very light hair, skin, and eyes (807b 4-5). Those whose skin is 'very black' (*agan melanes*), such as the Egyptians and the Ethiopians, are said to be cowardly (*deiloi*), while those whose skin is 'very white' (*agan leukoi*) are likewise considered cowardly (812a13-4). Similarly, those who have very dark or very light eyes are also considered cowardly (812b1-5). The ideal is somewhere in the middle: medium-coloured hair, skin, and eyes (e.g. 812a14-5; 812b1-4).

As might be expected, the ideal characteristics are the ones which the Greeks associated with themselves. Although the author does not make it explicit that he is thinking about Greeks, the iconography does envision a genetic homogeneity for the Greeks which reflects these traits: wavy hair, dark eyes, and tanned-colour skin. In the *Physiognomonica*, medium-coloured (or tawny) hair, skin, and eyes and hair which curls at the ends are all associated with bravery. Anyone who does not have these characteristics tends to be connected with affectations which were deemed negative.

Not surprisingly for a work based largely upon 'stereotypes and value judgments', this treatise has several inconsistencies.[15] To some extent, the author himself recognizes that physiognomy is not a perfect 'science' when he states that one should search for several physical signs which agree rather than rely upon only one to make a judgment about a person's character (although it is questionable to what extent he keeps this in mind) (806b39-807a1-3). At one point the author states that stiff-haired men are brave (806b8-9) and then later he (or a different author?) claims that 'those having stiff hair on the head are cowards' (812b28-9). In the earlier instance, however, the author is referring to men from the north, who he claims are courageous. In the latter instance, on the other hand, the author may be thinking of Ethiopians who he notes just below are cowardly due to their woolly hair. Moreover, sometimes both negative and positive characteristics are applied to non-Greeks. People from the north are said to be brave due to their stiff hair, yet this is offset by their pale skin colour which makes them cowardly, and their fiery hair, which makes them untrustworthy.

Since slaves were connected with barbarianism, these kinds of stereotypes overlap with representations of slaves, and it is the negative ones which were most often applied, such as cowardice, weakness, and roguishness. It is especially noteworthy that there was a red-haired slave mask. While we cannot know whether all slave characters in

Greek comedy wore this mask or, if not, exactly which ones did, it is certainly conceivable that it was worn by at least the more knavish slave characters, such as Xanthias in Aristophanes' *Frogs*. His name might also indicate that he had reddish hair. The possible connection between the grotesque mask of comedy and physiognomy will be revisited in my discussion of the art, below.

Although the *Physiognomonica* is frequently cited by scholars, the idea that people of different *ethnê* have particular physical characteristics which are reflected in their disposition is certainly not confined to this text but was already a feature of Greek ideas about barbarians. Such stereotypes seem to have been taken for granted; the *Physiognomonica* was simply an attempt to explain why these differences exist. As we shall see, there were also attempts to explain why people from different geographical locations looked and acted differently and these ideas often overlap, and are sometimes inconsistent with 'observations' made in the *Physiognomonica*. Such theorizing was certainly popular in the ancient world and continued to be into the Middle Ages. As Isaac observes, the popularity of physiognomy 'lies in its presumption of scientific objectivity, which provided a rationalization and reinforcement of social prejudices'.[16]

Before moving on to the topic of environmental determinism, it remains to consider some non-ethnic physical features which were similarly deemed negative and were also connected with slaves. As will be discussed in more detail below, physiognomy also reflects an elitism, which associates certain characteristics with people of a certain economic, social, or political class. Notwithstanding the fact that no group of people will have identical characteristics, the physiognomist is not only concerned with differentiating between *ethnê*, he is also concerned more generally with characteristics which might apply to members of any population, including the Greeks. As Jon Hesk points out, 'physiognomy was clearly a strategic resource for the fourth-century litigant', whose adversary was almost always a fellow Greek.[17] For instance, the *Physiognomonica* states that shameless people (*anaidous*) do not stand upright (*mê orthos*) (807b32). Later on, the stooped figure (*tapeinos*) is similarly associated with being spiritless or fainthearted (*athumos*) (808a12). The word *tapeinos* can also connote being humbled or abased in power or pride.[18] Similarly, in the *Politics*, Aristotle differentiates between slave and free bodies by arguing that freepersons stand upright (*ta ortha*) while slaves do not (1254b30; see Chapter 4.2). This might be compared with Socrates' analogy of the soul in Plato's *Phaedrus*, which he divides into three parts: two different kinds of horses and a charioteer. One of the 'horses' has an upright body (*orthos*) and is connected with honour, temperance, modesty and glory. The other is crooked (*skolios*) and is connected with *hubris* and false pretensions (253c-e). In short, crookedness, or a stooped body, was clearly viewed as a negative physical characteristic and is indicative of the kinds of qualities associated with, though not necessarily restricted to, slaves. In the physiognomic consciousness, this posture was seen as reflecting the debased nature of the soul. This perspective, however, may also be based upon prejudicial ideas about labourers. As will be discussed below and again in Chapter 4, menial labour was thought to produce inferior bodies, which resulted in inferior souls and this idea was applied not only to slaves, but to anyone who performed such work for a living.

Environmental determinism

We have already considered ethnological physiognomy as illustrated in the *Physiognomonica*, which connects body, character, and ethnicity. How and why a person's geographical and climatic environment were thought to have such an effect, however, is not fully explained, presumably because such 'explanations' had already been in circulation for at least a century in medical essays. This section will examine the concept of environmental determinism with a specific focus upon how the characters of barbarian populations were thought to be dictated by their physical (geographical and climatic) environments. How this concept may have mapped onto representations of slaves will then be considered.

Airs, Waters, Places is the earliest detailed examination of the idea of environmental determinism, which is a modern designation for the ancient concept.[19] This work is conventionally attributed to Hippocrates, who lived between the late fifth and early fourth centuries. Traces of this concept, however, are found in other roughly contemporaneous sources, notably in Herodotos' *Histories*. Perhaps Herodotos was even influenced by the work of Hippocrates, who was from the nearby island of Cos.[20] Herodotos contends, for instance, that people from the region of the Pontus are 'the most ignorant' (*amathestata*) of all (4.46). This statement hints at a familiarity with the idea that this region does not produce the best people, yet Herodotos does not make it explicit that they are ignorant *because* of their environment. In Book 9, however, Cyrus contends that 'from soft earth are born soft men' and that fertile land does not produce good soldiers (122). This is an early instance of an idea which was to become more common in the fourth century, when the concept of Asiatic, and especially Persian, *malakia* ('softness') was frequently used to explain the Persians' defeat by the Greeks in the Greco-Persian wars.[21]

2. *The Body of the Slave*

Although Herodotos is clearly aware of environmental theory, there is some dispute as to whether he was using it to draw a distinction between Greeks and barbarians, or even how much emphasis he placed upon such ideas at all.[22] Aside from Cyrus' observation, which appears at the end of the text, there is little evidence of a determinist correlation between a person's environment and their character.[23] Rosalind Thomas argues that Herodotos gives *nomoi*, which she defines as 'customs, habits and laws, written and unwritten', more importance in determining the 'ethnic character' of a population, as well their 'political systems'.[24] There is no doubt that Herodotos places significantly more emphasis upon customs when considering a population's character. This does not mean, however, that he did not conceive of character, and by extension *nomos*, as having been formed, in the first instance, by the physical environment. Certainly, Herodotos makes a strong contrast between the luxury-loving Asiatics and the poverty-stricken Greeks, most notably in his description of the Persian and Spartan tables (9.83). Therefore, while he does not fully explore the idea that the environments of Greece and Asia produce different types of people, throughout the text he hints 'at the theme of poverty nourishing a people's warlike spirit', while also hinting at Asia's tendency to produce 'soft', luxury-loving individuals.[25]

Much more explicit is *Airs, Waters, Places* (henceforth *Airs*), which has been described as 'a significant milestone in the rationalization of discriminatory thinking'.[26] In antiquity Hippocrates was credited for having invented the 'science' of physiognomy, although upon closer examination he appears to have been more interested in 'correlations between *mental activity* and *physiology*', which is not exactly the same as the later physiognomist's interest in the relationship between a person's character and their physical appearance.[27] That is, while physiognomy, as a branch of philosophy, aims to judge moral character by means of the condition of the soul, the medical writer is more concerned with 'psychological phenomena'.[28] What is clear, however, is that later physiognomists were greatly influenced by earlier ideas of environmental theory, such as those found in the Hippocratic corpus and other early medical texts.

After considering the changes of the seasons, the author of *Airs* makes clear his intent to connect geographical location with the bodies of the inhabitants. He also draws a bold line between Asia and Europe: 'I want to show how Asia and Europe differ from each other in every way and how the forms of their people (*ethneôn*) are entirely distinct from one another' (12). He contends that the people of Asia, although they are tall and finely built, lack courage, endurance, industry and high spirit, which he attributes to the region's consistently temperate

49

climate and fertile land. That is, Asiatics, who the author sees as relatively homogenous, reflect the homogeneity of their native region and climate in their mild and gentle disposition. A little later, he adds that the political climate, characterized by monarchy, further contributes to their supposed 'feebleness', or 'unwarlike' nature (*analkes*) (16). While he allows for some variation amongst the few Asiatic populations who are not ruled by despots (i.e. some of the Greek colonies of Asia Minor), the vast majority of inhabitants are considered mild and unwarlike, which is in line with how they tended to be represented in other sources, particularly in comedy and oratory.

The author then considers the Europeans and, like Herodotos, singles out the Scythians for special consideration (Hdt. 4.16-31, 103-17).[29] Due primarily to their damp and cold environment, he claims that the Scythians, like the land of Scythia itself, have low fertility, are small in stature, and have flabby and weak bodies (19). Above all, the damp environment of Scythia is blamed for the Scythians' poor physical health and constitution, which he claims results in physical weakness, flabby physiques, low fertility, and male effeminacy (20).

Other European populations, on the other hand, fare better. It is tempting to think that the author had the Greeks in mind here, although he is not explicit about this. In contrast to the Scythians, whom he sees as homogenous, he describes a great variation amongst the other inhabitants of Europe, which he attributes to their variable climate and the geography of the land (in contrast to Asia). This variability was also thought to affect the inhabitants' character, which is likewise said to be wild, unsociable, and fierce. For these reasons, he surmises, most Europeans are less tame and more courageous and independent than the inhabitants of Asia, and are not governed by kings (23). Since some European populations did, in fact, have monarchies, such as the Thracians, who were also well-known to the Greeks, this latter statement seems to reflect a hellenocentric view of the Greeks themselves.

These ideas permeate other classical sources. Although the details sometimes vary from author to author – there was, after all, no formalized theory of environmental determinism which everyone adhered to – there is plenty of evidence that the Greeks associated particular characteristics with particular populations, and that negative characteristics were typically associated with barbarians and, by extension, slaves. In the *Politics*, Aristotle makes a strong distinction between the inhabitants of cold climates, such as the regions of northern Europe, and those of warmer climates, such as the western and southern regions of Asia. While the former are said to be full of spirit but rather deficient in intelligence and skill, they retain 'a measure of freedom';

the latter, on the other hand, are said to be intelligent and skilful but lacking in spirit and so are in a perpetual state of subjection and slavery (1327b). Unlike the author of *Airs*, however, Aristotle is explicit about which people are ideal and why; the Greeks, because they are located between these regions, have a share in both in that they are spirited and intelligent; they are also perpetually free and have the best political institutions, to the extent that they could not can rule over everyone else (1327b). Such ideas are also found in Plato's *Republic*, when Socrates states tha there is the belief that the populations of Thrace and Scythia, and generally all those in the northern regions, are high-spirited, whereas a love of knowledge characterizes the people of Greece, and a love of money those of Phoenicia and Egypt (435e-436a). This type of thinking is also reflected in tragedy. In Euripides' *Medea*, for instance, the Athenians are said to 'feed upon wisdom' and their ideal climate ('the brightest air') is connected with wisdom and love (824-45).

Not surprisingly, since the Greeks associated barbarians with slavery, these kinds of ethnic stereotypes also played a role in how slaves were represented. A good example appears in Menander's *Aspsis*, when the Thracian waiter, who is presumably either a current or former slave, contrasts himself with the Phrygian slave Daos when he accuses him of being an *androgunos* ('man-woman') because he did not escape with the slaves and money but returned to his master's house. On the other hand, the Waiter boasts that he is one of the 'real men' because he is a Thracian of the Getic tribe, and further emphasizes this by clarifying: 'That is why the mills are full of us' (242-4). In a few brief words, the Thracian Waiter demonstrates the very same types of characteristics we have already seen associated with northern Europeans, and their appearance in comedy illustrates that such ideas had by this time become part of the popular consciousness. The Thracian Waiter is depicted as physically strong when he boasts about being a 'real man' in contrast to the effeminate and spiritless Asiatic slave. At the same time, he exhibits a stereotypically northern European spiritedness combined with a lack of intelligence when he boasts about working in the grain mills, which was in fact a punishment for poorly-behaved slaves (the Scythian Archer examined in the last chapter similarly demonstrates this combination of high spirit and dull wits).[30] The Asiatic Daos, on the other hand, exhibits a significant measure of wit and intelligence, particularly when contrasted with Smicrines, yet he might also be said to lack spirit insofar as he voluntarily returned to slavery (which, Aristotle would argue, is his natural state). Because of this, the Waiter calls Daos a 'senseless fool'; he is unable to believe that Daos returned to slavery when he had charge of 'so much money and slaves', and attributes his foolishness to his effeminate, Phrygian eth-

51

nicity (239-45). As discussed above, both intelligence and lack of spirit were associated with barbarians from warmer climates.

In short, the association Greeks made between body, character, *nomos*, and environment was clearly important in Greek thought and this influenced the ways in which slaves were represented. In view of the perceived link between geography and physical and moral character, Bradley's statement that in the ancient world 'there was no physiological or physiognomical imperative to drive [slavery]' should be qualified.[31] Unlike slavery in early American history, when racial difference was a major imperative, the institution of slavery in the Greek world was driven by racial, ethnic and environmental imperatives. Negative character stereotypes were regularly applied to barbarians and it is no coincidence that they were likewise applied to slaves. As we shall see later on, it was also no coincidence that Aristotle's ideal slave was barbarian. Aristotle's contention that all barbarians are slaves and Asiatics more so than Europeans implies that in the Greek imagination the bodies and characters of slaves were closely connected with what the Greeks thought was their inferior native environment.

Reversed kalokagathia

Kalokagathia, which is a composite noun (*kalos kai agathos*) meaning 'beauty and goodness', is also connected with the idea that a person's body and soul are affected by their environment. Unlike physiognomy and environmental determinism, however, the term was often employed in a moral sense and, by the fifth century, tended to be associated with the elite members of Greek society, although it was also sometimes used less restrictively of entire populations (e.g. the Athenian demos).[32] Demosthenes, for instance, contrasts Athens' *kalokagathia* with Philip of Macedon's *kakia* ('baseness') (18.93). Even when used more broadly, however, the concept embodies physical and moral characteristics normally associated with the elite, such as handsomeness, decency, and respectable behaviour. Aristotle states on two occasions in the *Politics* that it is the wealthy who are *kaloi kagathoi* (1293b, 1294a). In Xenophon's *Memorabilia*, moreover, *kalokagathia* is explicitly connected with the cavalry and the hoplites, the latter of whom, although not exceedingly wealthy, were certainly not poor (3.5.19). While *kalokagathia*, as a virtue of the 'better born', may therefore appear to have nothing to do with a consideration of slave representation, it was part of a 'discourse of difference' and helps to contextualize and organize the oppositional representation of slaves and others who were considered to be socially similar to slaves (i.e. the slavish).[33] This section will begin with a brief consideration of the development of *kalokagathia* as an elite ideal and will then examine more specifically how it functioned in opposition to characteristics considered more appropriate to slaves.

The ideal of *kalokagathia* may have originated in the context of the gymnasion, where the youthful, nude male body was on display.[34] Gymnasia, which included athletic spaces such as *palaistrai* ('wrestling schools'), and athletic competitions more generally, were aristocratic in nature, promoting the traditional aristocratic values of physical beauty, heroic excellence, individual glory and immortality in the form of everlasting fame.[35] In democratic Athens, however, there were no laws barring non-elites from taking part in competitive sport and using athletic facilities. Following Cleisthenes' reforms, increasing levels of participation were required for the athletic competitions, which were important components to many Athenian festivals.[36] Yet, while this might have resulted in a wider variety of citizens using gymnasia, only the wealthier classes (i.e. liturgical and hoplite) had the economic resources and the leisure to train on a regular basis, and certainly to the level required to compete in the major athletic competitions. The so-called Old Oligarch provides some evidence of this when he claims that the common people criticize the wealthy for spending so much of their time in the gymnasia because they are unable to do so themselves (Ps.- Xen. *Ath. Pol.* 1.13). Moreover, serious competition required a high-protein (meat) diet, out of reach for most Greeks, as well as often extensive travel and up to thirty days of on-site training prior to the games, which would further restrict who was able to take part.[37]

The very complexes where athletics took place embodied the strong connection Greeks made between the body and the mind. Characterized by shady groves and baths, and by the fourth century sometimes even auditoriums and libraries, gymnasia encouraged not only rigorous physical training resulting in a *kalos* body but also leisurely discourse and academic instruction. It is certainly no coincidence that Plato's and Aristotle's philosophical 'schools' were located in gymnasia (the Academy and the Lyceum) and that Socrates was a well-known haunt of Athens' Lyceum and the Academy.[38] Teachers knew that they would find eager young students in such places, many of whom would be able and willing to pay a premium for academic instruction. Even if instruction was free, however, those who regularly utilized such spaces must have had the leisure time to do so.[39] The gymnasion, therefore, was the ideal place for elite youths to develop *kalokagathia*.

Just as there were people who were associated with 'beauty and goodness', there were also those who were considered lacking in these qualities. Correspondingly, the spaces and the behaviour associated with non-*kaloi kagathoi* were considered suited and even conducive to

53

their allegedly deficient bodies and minds. The reversal of this ideal is what Ingomar Weiler terms 'inverted *kalokagathia*'.[40] While the Greeks did not develop a single word or concept to oppose *kalokagathia*, the concepts of *ponêria* and *kakia* come close.[41] *Ponêria*, often thought to correspond to 'badness' or 'depravity', is the noun-form of the verb *poneô*, which itself is related to the intransitive verb *penomai* ('I am poor') and the noun *penia*, meaning 'poverty'.[42] When a slave asks the Sausage Seller in Aristophanes' *Knights* if he comes from 'good stock' (*kalôn kagathôn*) he replies: 'No, by the gods! I'm from low stock (*ponêrôn*)!' (185-6). Likewise, Isocrates on two occasions opposes the *kaloi kagathoi* with the *ponêroi*. In the first instance, *ponêroi* has a moral sense and describes men who are corrupt (15.100); in the second instance, however, the word is used to refer to men who are base-born and unworthy of the power they hold (15.316).[43] Bad character, poverty and low-status were therefore part of the same 'package-deal'.[44] It is tempting to consider that the classical meaning of *ponêros*, which tended to connote worthlessness, low birth and knavishness, is also an extension of an earlier use of the word, which had the sense of being 'oppressed by toils'.[45] Hesiod describes Heracles' toils (*erga*) as *ponêra* (West & Merkelbach Fr. 302.20).

Similarly, the feminine noun *kakia* was sometimes used in opposition to *kalokagathia*, as seen above where the *kalokagathia* of Athens is differentiated from the *kakia* of Philip of Macedon. *Kakia*, however, is more typically associated with the common masses who are sometimes referred to collectively as *kakoi*, which may be considered cognate with the Latin *vulgi*. *Kakos* is semantically opposed to *kalos* and both are hypernymic due to their flexibility of meaning. As with *kalos*, which might refer either to physical or inner beauty (in the sense of 'noble' or 'honourable'), *kakos* could refer to outer or inner ugliness or badness. The word *kakos* also appears as the binary opposite to *agathos*. This is expressed early in Greek literature when Telamonian Aias complains that the Trojans' spears always hit their mark regardless of whether the spearman is *kakos* or *agathos* (Hom. *Il.* 17.632). Although it is unclear whether Aias meant to distinguish between members of differing social and economic strata or, more simply, between more and less skilled fighters, in the *Odyssey* the word *kakos* does appear to connote the common people. This is evident when Menelaus contrasts the *kakoi* with the 'race of men who are sceptred kings cherished by Zeus' (4.63-4). By the sixth century, Theognis uses the terms *kakoi* and *agathoi* to describe the common or baser people (literally 'the bad') and the nobles or better-born ('the good').[46]

In the Classical period, anyone who was perceived as lacking in 'beauty and goodness' could be considered *kakos*, that is, in some way morally and physically corrupt, and this could include not only slaves but anyone who was deemed in some way slavish. The ideal of *kaloka-gathia* could therefore serve 'as an instrument for the exclusion of non-citizens, foreign ethnic and social-fringe groups'.[47] As stated earlier, our sources sometimes conflate actual slaves and those considered socially similar to slaves. Free persons who worked at occupations considered menial, such as crafts, retail and any other pursuit which required continuous paid work under the same employer, were at the greatest risk of suffering a similar type of stigma as slaves. Herodotos claims that the Greeks adopted a negative view of craftsmen from the Egyptians, who do not permit them to be warriors, and argues that 'nearly all barbarians' view craftsmen in the same way. He further claims that amongst the Greeks this idea was particularly strong in Sparta, whereas the Corinthians apparently found crafts the least contemptible (2.167).

The general aversion to labour found in Greek sources seems to be related to the idea that it was important 'to maintain an independence of occupation ... and at all costs to avoid seeming to work in a "slavish" way for another'.[48] Aristotle notably defines a free man as one who does not live under the control of another (*Rhet.* 1367a33) and Isocrates sees no difference between a person who is hired for work and a slave (14.48). It is worth noting once again, however, that such comments are reflective of elitist ideology and attitudes and do not necessarily reflect the views of the greater number of free persons, many of whom would have had to take paid employment on a regular basis.[49] Indeed, potters and painters sometimes signed their work and even competed with each other, which reflects the pride that some artists had in their work. Although rare, some tombstones also include reference to the occupation of the memorialized person, such as an Athenian stone depicting Xanthippos, the shoemaker. This topic will be revisited in Chapter 3.1, where tombstones for slaves and metics are discussed in more detail.[50]

The word commonly connected with menial labour or the labourer himself was *banausos*. Although *banausos* and its derivatives could simply refer to crafts, or *technai*, it also had derogatory connotations and could describe a person or a type of work which was considered in some way menial or vulgar. To be sure, in the mind of a wealthy citizen, there was little difference between the two uses, since *banausoi* were thought to reflect their menial trades in their characters and bodies. Fittingly, the word even sounds ugly and grating, much like *graus* discussed in the previous chapter. In Plato's *Epistles*, 'vile friendship' (*banausos philotês*) is contrasted with 'liberal education' (*eleuthera paideia*) (334b). On several occasions, moreover, Aristotle makes it clear that the *banausoi* were among the basest portion of Greek society and even denies them political rights in his utopian city (see Chapter 4.2). The contrast between the *kaloi kagathoi* and the *banausoi* is also found in comedy. The Sausage-Seller in Aristophanes' *Knights* explicitly contrasts lamp-sellers, cobblers, tanners, and leather-sellers with the *kaloi kagathoi* (735-8). While these lines are almost surely a jibe at Hyperbolos, who owned a lamp-making business, and Aristophanes' arch-rival Cleon, who was allegedly a tanner, it nevertheless implies that an association with industry and retail, even as the owner of a workshop, was considered incompatible with being a *kaloskagathos*.

The ideological connection between labour and an inferior or damaged body existed at least as far back as Homer and is notably expressed by his depiction of Hephaistos, the lame 'god of the forge'.[51] Even from this early date, there is a disconnect between the often wondrous items a craftsman produces and the craftsman himself, whose body reflects the toll of his work.[52] Even though Hephaistos' body is not actually damaged by labour (he is maimed when Zeus hurls him from Mount Olympos), the ideological connection between labour and physical deformity is clear; after all, Hephaistos is the only permanently physically imperfect Olympian and the only one directly associated with forging, which was one of the most dangerous types of manual labour. As Burford writes: 'The muscular development of the smith could be and was considered a deformity in itself.'[53] This is perhaps what Homer had in mind when he illustrated Hephaistos as a panting, limping, monstrous bulk (*pelôr*) with slender, nimble legs (*Il.* 18.410-11). Certainly, to his fellow gods Hephaistos was an object of derision, which is notably expressed when they laugh insatiably (*asbestos*) as he moves his bustling, sweating, ungainly body while he fills their cups (*Il.* 1.599-600). Comparisons have been drawn between Homer's depictions of Hephaistos and Thersites, both of whom have imperfect bodies and are similarly mocked by their physical betters.[54]

The negative impression of craftsmen expressed in many Greek sources continued well into the Classical period and is a feature of Athenian literature. In Plato's *Statesman*, the Stranger associates labour with the fall of man from a former existence in a world which had voluntarily produced for him his every need (274b-d). Certainly, the environment in which artisans spent much of their time would have been rather different from the easy stillness of workshops pictured in pot-paintings. Many crafts required long hours of repetitive work indoors, in dark, hot, noisy, noxious, dusty workshops. The connection between the workshop and an unhealthy body and mind is made explicit in Xenophon's *Oeconomicus* when Socrates states that craftsmen, because of their sedentary, indoor work, have bodies that become 'soft ... and this is accompanied by a considerable weakening of the mind' (4.2). Not surprisingly, the workshop environment was not considered conducive to the elite ideal of body-enhancing physical activity out of doors, such as wrestling and racing, or the mind-enhancing activities of politics and philosophy.

Wealthy Greeks and poor labourers were even associated with different types of movement. Today we tend to see most types of physical activity as beneficial to one's health. The Greeks, however, differentiated between two primary types of physical activity, namely that which was undertaken through necessity, such as menial labour, and that which was undertaken at one's leisure, such as athletics. While the former was deemed slavish, the latter was deemed more appropriate for members of the leisured classes. This is made explicit by Aristotle when he specifies that bodily excellence is being 'fit for athletic contests' (*Rhet.* 1360b39). A similar idea is expressed by Isocrates, when he urges the young Demonicos to undertake only 'suitable exercises' (*summetrois ponois*) (1.12). The exercises he had in mind were doubtless those carried out by athletes, which is implied by his instruction to Demonicos to vie with his father's accomplishments as an athlete would against his competitors and, more explicitly, when he urges Demonicos to train his body with exercises (*gumnasiôn*) which are conducive to health, not brute strength (*rhômên*), so that he can preserve energy to exert himself in other ways (namely exertions appropriate for elites, such as politics and higher learning) (1.14). The walk of the wealthy is even parodied in Aristophanes' *Wasps* when a son tries to teach his father to walk with the luxurious swagger of the rich (1169). One can imagine that the walk the actor performed was a slow, lazy, effeminate stride, which was perhaps a distant relative of the long stride of the aristocratic warrior of pre-classical Greece; on several occasions, Homer describes the great heroes stepping out from the throng with a long stride (*makra bibasthôn*) (*Il.* 3.22, 13.809, 15.676, 16.534).[55]

In the less ostentatious times of the democracy, however, the wealthy were characterized by a slow, quiet, walk. Demosthenes notably defines *kalokagathia* as 'peaceable, hesitant, and slow' (25.24) and the fourth-century comic writer Alexis associates a graceful gait with being a *kalos kagathos* (Fr. 263 Kock tr. C.B. Gulick). Slow movement is similarly connected with other elite ideals, such as *sôphrosunê* and *kosmiotes*. In Plato's *Charmides* when Socrates asks what *sôphrosunê* means, Charmides responds that it is doing everything quietly, including talking quietly and walking quietly in the streets (159b). Similarly, in the *Physiognomonica* the author associates men who are *kosmios* ('moderate', 'well-behaved', 'orderly') with slow but deliberate movement. Later on, Plutarch claims that Pericles walked with a 'gentle gait' and always remained *kosmiôs* (*Per.* 5.1-2).[56] No doubt some men who

57

were overly concerned with being associated with the upper classes even exaggerated this walk by walking too slowly. In doing so, they risked becoming fodder for comedy, where an excessively leisurely and swaggering gait might lead to the accusation that such a man was a passive homosexual, or an *erômenos*.[57]

The association between the elite and a certain type of movement was important because a leisurely stride suggested a leisurely life. By adopting a slow, measured walk, a man could convey that he had mastery over his own body and time. He also demonstrated that he had *sôphrosunê*. More importantly, perhaps, he created a visual separation between himself and the labourer. Images of workshops often contrast the labourer with the leisured elite, who lean on their staffs, gazing with seemingly half-hearted interest at the craftsmen who are busy at their work.[58] The comparatively frenetic movement of the labourer is perhaps why literary sources sometimes associate labourers with a lack of physical and moral control. Put quite simply, if a man (or woman) was dependent upon an employer or a customer for a livelihood, he was subject to being viewed as little better than a slave and might even have his citizenship called into question.[59] Quick movement, particularly running, was considered slavish as it signalled a person who was at the beck and call of an employer, master, customer, or even a magistrate. In the *Constitution of the Lacedaimonians*, Xenophon suggests that the Greeks, with the notable exception of the Spartans, view running as a sign of slavery. While in most city-states powerful men think that being afraid of the leaders (*tas archas*) signifies slavery (*aneleutheron*), the Spartans, Xenophon claims, think that they should run rather than walk to answer any call (8.2).

In Attic comedy, it is the slaves who usually run to keep up with the relentless (and sometimes impossible) requests of their masters. This, in turn, provided the comic poet with the opportunity to mock the harried slave, whose physical comedy often made up a significant part of the action. By the Roman period, the running slave even became a character type (*servus currens*).[60] Commands to slaves are frequently prefaced with imperatives such as 'Quick!' (e.g. Ar. *Ach*. 1003). In Menander's *Dyscolos*, the slave Pyrrhias enters the play at such break-neck speed that Sostratos asks: 'Where are you going, you wretch (*kakodaimon*)?' (84). The slave's frenetic physical movement is further implied by his fragmented and frightened words, verbal repetition, and Sostratos' request for clarification. This might be compared with Smicrines' words to the slave Daos: 'Daos, you wretch (*kakodaimon*), where are you running to?' (Men. *Aspis* 410). These kinds of depictions recall the frantic and fearful slaves of tragedy, such as the Phrygian slave in Euripides' *Orestes*, discussed in Chapter 1. Of course, such behaviour

58

might also be applied to slavish free persons, such as the Sausage Seller in Aristophanes' *Knights*, who is riled by the slaves because he is running in fright from the slave Paphlagon: 'Hey, why are running? Why don't you wait? Noble (*gennada*) Sausage-Seller, don't betray our cause!' (240). Even though the Sausage Seller's reaction is almost surely a play on the fear that the real Cleon must have induced in some of Athens' citizens, the slavish behaviour of this character expresses the idea that the lower, working classes were subject to the same type of behaviour as slaves.

Drunkenness was also considered to be a sign of a lack of self-mastery, or *sôphrosunê*, and was associated with slavishness. Although wine was an integral component of the 'highly ritualized' symposion, which was associated with the wealthier members of Greek society, inebriation tended to be looked upon with disdain.[61] In Plato's *Laws*, drunkenness is associated with degradation, ignorance, cowardice, childish lack of self-control, and even physical ugliness (*aischos*), all characteristics we have seen connected with slaves (646b).[62] Drunkenness was also associated with barbarianism, violence and danger. In Aristophanes' *Wasps*, Philocleon states that drinking is *kakos* because it leads to physical violence and property damage (1252-5). This connection is also expressed by the myth of the wedding of Pirithous, in which the centaurs become so inebriated that they seize the bride and the other female guests and the whole gathering degrades into a violent battle. The importance and popularity of this myth is demonstrated by the fact that it was illustrated on prominent monuments, including the west pediment of the Temple of Zeus at Olympia and the metopes of Athens' Parthenon. Due to the fact that alcohol is the primary impetus of the events, it is tempting to view the myth's importance as a warning against excessive drinking. The fact that it was the centaurs, who were connected with animalism and barbarianism, is further representative of Greek ideology.

Primarily to guard against such impropriety and barbaric behaviour, the Greeks had a peculiar practice of diluting their wine with water in large craters (mixing-bowls) or in the cups themselves – drinking undiluted wine, on the other hand, was associated with the 'Other', and with the Scythians in particular.[63] Moreover, every symposion had a symposiarch ('leader of the symposion'), who was responsible for restricting consumption to three kraters or less of mixed wine depending upon the size of the gathering (Pl. *Laws* 640d).[64] The presence of such safeguards, however, does not mean that in practice the guests always observed acceptable behaviour. As Davidson contends, 'the picture of the classic moderate drinking-party ... is a symptom of anxiety about how to drink properly' rather than a mirror of the real situation.[65] Much like the myth of the centauromachy, above, such depictions might be didactic in that they were intended to teach appropriate behaviour, which *de facto* implies that there was a need for such instruction. Indeed, there is plenty of evidence to indicate that symposiasts often did not moderate their drinking or their behaviour and that such situations could become violent. This behaviour was most likely to occur during the *kômos*, which in this context refers to the drunken revel through the streets following a symposion.[66] In Bdelycleon's response to his father's observation of the effects of drinking, quoted above, he admits that *kaloi kagathoi* do sometimes get drunk and damage property, but adds that they can always avoid trouble by bribery and sweet-talking (Ar. *Wasps* 1256-61). Moreover, although the guests in Plato's *Symposion* decide amongst themselves to restrict their drinking, this is because they are suffering from hangovers from the previous night's commensality (176b-e). Although they manage to conduct themselves moderately for much of the party, it is eventually crashed by the handsome and impetuous aristocrat Alcibiades, who is described as fully inebriated and 'bawling' (212d); a little later, the party is crashed once again by more revellers, who finally bring any semblance of order to an end (223b-d).

Although vulgar and violent activity is therefore sometimes associated with elite revellers, it was nevertheless the common tavern (*kapêlion*) which was considered to be a place of ill-repute, doubtless because *kapêlia* were open to almost anyone, free or slave, Greek or barbarian, and in some cases even women.[67] This inclusive, democratic, setting drew a stark contrast with the more 'private and selective *andrôn*' ('men's room') where symposia took place.[68] Isocrates expresses a particularly negative view of these establishments when, in the context of a complaint about the waning morals of the youth of his day, he states that *kapêleia* are places of such depravation that they are even unworthy of the better sort of slave (*epieikês oiketês*) (*Areopagitikos* 7.49). Like their customers, the proprietors of *kapêlia* were likewise associated with poor behaviour, such as cheating their customers (cf. Ar. *Wealth* 435-6, *Thesm.* 347-8). This helps to explain why proprietors of *kapêlia* sometimes appear as the objects of curses, or *defixiones*; not surprisingly, tavern-work tended to be associated with metics and slaves. A late fourth-century *defixio* names a metic from Melite who was a tavern-keeper, as well as two women who are described as *graus kapêlis* ('the old-woman taverner').[69] Several former slaves are also described as *kapêloi/-eis* in the late fourth-century Attic manumission inscriptions.[70] At the same time, however, Isocrates also indicates that *kapêlia* were not the preserve of the low-born but were also frequented by wealthy citizens or, to be more precise, the sons of

60

wealthy citizens (*Are.* 7.49). Once again, the distinction between the *kaloi kagathoi* and the rest of the population weighs more heavily on the side of an ideological division which is not always played out in practice.

A distinction might also be made between the drinking which took place at the rule-bound, exclusive, and elite symposion and that which occurred freely at the common tavern. Alcohol-consumption was an integral part of the symposion and while such commensality helped foster ties between members of the upper class, drunken violence was also 'a recognized characteristic of its proceedings'.[71] As mentioned earlier, symposia appear not infrequently to have ended with drunken revelry in the streets, which sometimes led to violent attacks upon people unlucky enough to be at the wrong place at the wrong time. It is probably going too far to say that this behaviour was encouraged amongst the upper classes, particularly in democratic Athens, where in fact there were laws against such sumptuary displays of wealth and power. Komastic revelry, however, was likely a relic from the past and had a specific purpose, namely reiterating the supremacy of the aristocracy by deliberately dishonouring those who were considered inferior. In this respect, it may therefore have been deemed more acceptable (or at least forgivable) than the comparatively disorganized, random, and purposeless revelry which took place at the common tavern amongst slavish men (this will be discussed in more detail below).

It is noteworthy that images of sympotic revelry, while admitting the sometimes vulgar behaviour of the symposiasts, also sanitize it to some degree (if the revellers are free Greeks – the same cannot always be said of the attendant prostitutes or barbarian revellers, who were thought much less able to control their drunken behaviour). A case in point is an image from an early fifth-century Attic red-figure kylix by the Dokimasia Painter (frontispiece). Even though the bearded reveller is shown vomiting rather unceremoniously into a large vessel on the floor, he appears composed. Leaning just enough to position his head above the vessel, he props himself up with a staff, of the type commonly associated with elite men on Attic pottery (cf. Fig. 7), and is assisted by a slave who helps him hold up his head, seemingly both to stop him from toppling over and to avoid his wreath falling into the pool of vomit (there are other sympotic images on the tondos of kylikes with a similar composition, such as one showing a bearded man leaning on his staff while he vomits onto the ground, and another showing a female slave holding up the head of a youthful reveller, also leaning on a staff).[72] A similarly vulgar yet sanitized image is depicted on another Attic red-figure sympotic vessel, which shows a man urinating into a pot held by

Fig. 1. Attic red-figure chous by the Oinokles Painter,
c. 470 BC.

a slave (Fig. 1). As Sutton notes, the man is so composed that he 'barely miss(es) a beat', gesturing to his companions as though he is singing or reciting poetry – in this context, the act of urinating or vomiting in public appears to be 'a relatively inoffensive consequence of heavy drinking'.[73] Further examples of the drunken behaviour of elites and the problems which could arise from it (such as being indicted on charges) will be examined in the discussion of *hubris*, below.

To sum up, it should come as no surprise that all labourers, slave or free, were subject to the same sort of stigma. It is conceivable, however, that the conflation of slave and free labourers found in the literature and, as we shall see shortly, the imagery, was not merely a product of elite ideology but might also reflect, to some extent at least, the possibility that it was not always easy to differentiate visually between the two. This is expressed in Euripides' *Electra* when Orestes mistakes his sister for a servant because she performs the same type of work (i.e. carries a jug of water on her head) and her hair is cropped short (*kekarmenôi*) like a slave's (107-8; see Chapter 3.1 for the association between slave women and cropped hair). The word Orestes uses to describe Electra, *prospolos*, is further ambiguous in that it can mean either a free or slave labourer. The so-called Old Oligarch sardonically expresses a similar idea when he claims that it is often difficult to tell the difference between a slave and the common Athenian, since both have the same general appearance (Ps.-Xen. *Ath. Pol.* 1.10). It is difficult to tell, however, whether this was meant to imply that the slaves were generally well-dressed or that the average citizen was poorly dressed. In favour of the second meaning, there were few, if any, occupations exclusive to slaves and slave and free labourers probably wore the same type of clothing (e.g. the *exômis*, a short belted chiton associated with labourers).[74] More importantly, perhaps, even if the greater number of slaves were non-Greek in origin, many came from regions not far from Greece and would have looked little if at all different from citizens.

While slaves and free members of the lower classes might have looked similar, however, in practice there were stark differences between the two. The next section will examine these differences as expressed in the law and in the treatment of slaves, whose bodies were seen as 'fit for abuse'.

2. The slave body: fit for abuse

Slaves and the law

In the second century BC, the Macedonian city of Beroia passed a law barring certain people from exercising in the gymnasion and anointing themselves with oil, namely slaves, freedmen and their sons, drunks, market-place types (e.g. craftsmen and merchants), male prostitutes and madmen.[75] What makes this law noteworthy is not so much that it excluded slaves, but that it also excluded free persons who were considered in some way similarly undesirable (slavish). With the exception of male prostitution, for which an Athenian citizen might be charged with a *graphê hetairêseôs*, there is no evidence from the Classical period of legalized exclusion of free men from certain places or activities based upon a particular type of occupation or character.[76] Slaves, on the other hand, had long been subject to such restrictions. In the fourth century, Aeschines quotes an Athenian law forbidding 'slaves from exercising (*gymnazesthai*) and anointing themselves with oil in the palaistrai'

(1.138), Plutarch relates that Solon forbade slaves to have a rubdown by free boys or to practice gymnastic exercise (*Moralia* 751b; *Solon* 1.3), and there were similar laws in other parts of the Greek world, including Sparta and Crete. Although the verb *gumnazesthai* is ambiguous since it can refer to exercising in the gymnasion, to undertaking gymnastic exercises (inter- or extramural), or even just to exercising naked, it is clear that slaves were not to be associated with the pursuits of the gymnasion. After quoting this law, Aeschines further explains that because 'beauty' (*to kalon*) results from gymnastic exercise, the laws permit only free men to have a share in this. His word-choice here is significant, since it illustrates that physical and moral beauty, both of which are accommodated by the word *kalon*, are not only the preserve of free persons, but also that slaves were actively excluded from activities which might allow them to develop *kalon*. In this way, the law, as 'a conjoint expression of power and ideology', enforced the ideological separation between slaves and free persons.[77] Indeed, Socrates in Xenophon's *Symposion* claims that free men exercising in the gymasion even produce a distinctively sweet smell (sweat mixed with olive oil) which signifies freedom (2.4). Although the Hellenistic period furnishes a few exceptions, as a rule in both the Classical and Hellenistic periods, slaves were permitted in athletic complexes only in the capacity of servants, specifically as *paidagôgoi* ('attendants of children') and *palaistrophulakes* ('keepers of the palaistra').[78]

Yet, although some laws reflect the stigma of slavery and low social position of slaves, the legal status of slaves was in no way straightforward. This is because, quite simply, a slave is 'both a chattel and something more than a mere chattel'.[79] We have seen that the treatment and perceptions of slaves were sometimes conflated with beasts of burden, yet there was also the unavoidable recognition that slaves were human beings. While it may have been easier to consider a barbarian as subhuman, more beast than human, more slave than free, the Greeks also had experience of being reduced to slavery themselves, primarily through kidnapping and warfare. As a result, they knew that slavery and freedom were fluid conditions, that slavery was not a preserve of non-Greeks, and that their own freedom should never be taken for granted (for a discussion of the complex representation of the war captive, see Chapter 4.1). The law, therefore, is another area of slave representation in which, similar to ideas about lower class citizens and labourers, the boundaries between slave and free are rather indistinct.

One of the areas where this is apparent is in religious matters. In addition to being barred from making use of gymnastic facilities and taking part in gymnastic exercise, slaves were also excluded from certain temples and religious festivals, such as those honouring Demeter and Persephone. This is indicated by Isaios in his speech on the estate of Philoctemon (6.48-50). The reference here is likely to the Thesmophoria, from which women of poor reputation (i.e. adulteresses) were also excluded. Slaves were not, however, barred from all religious activities. Demosthenes, in his speech against Neaira, states that a slave prostitute named Metaneira was initiated into the Eleusinian Mysteries (59.21-3), and there is evidence that the mining slaves of Laureion established cults to various gods, including Artemis, Athena and Bendis.[80] Conversely, in the fifth century, the Athenians adopted the cult of Bendis, which was perhaps introduced to them via Thracian slaves.[81] Therefore, while there were restrictions placed upon slaves' involvement in religion, they were permitted a measure of inclusion, which points to a recognition of their humanity.

Most illuminating, however, is how the law treated the body of the slave. As a rule, slaves were chattel and as such had no rights over the use of their own bodies. With the possible exception of *dêmosioi* and slaves who were *chôris oikountes* ('living apart' from their masters), slaves could not initiate judicial proceedings or even provide evidence unless under torture (see below).[82] Demosthenes in two different speeches notably contends that one of the most distinct differences between slaves and free men is that slaves must answer for all of their wrongdoings with their bodies (22.55; 24.167). This, however, is somewhat misleading since a man could not treat his slave any way he wanted with legal impunity. In Plato's *Euthyphro*, Euthyphro brings an indictment against his own father for killing a hired-labourer who was probably a slave (4c-d, 9a). Although this is clearly an exceptional and perhaps only theoretical case, it does suggest that such an indictment was possible. The issue for Euthyphro, however, is not concern for the murdered man but rather for the pollution that his father brought upon himself, and on his family by association with the blood-guilt.

The law of *hubris*, on the other hand, provides compelling evidence that penalties were possible for the killing or maiming of slaves. Athenian law stated that anyone who commits *hubris* against someone, whether free or slave, was liable to punishment (Dem. 21.47-9; cf. Aesch. 1.15-6). Demosthenes claims further that men have not only been indicted on similar charges but that many have even been found guilty and put to death (Dem. 21.178-81). Yet both Aeschines and Demosthenes do express a degree of confusion that the law gives slaves any protection at all. Aeschines in his speech against Timarchos states that when a person first hears about the law of *hubris* they might wonder for what possible reason the word 'slave' was included (1.17). Demosthenes similarly stresses that this law protects *even* slaves (21.48). The reason for this reaction was perhaps because of the connection between *hubris* and *timê* ('honour'). To commit *hubris* against someone was to bring them *atimia* ('dishonour'). It is unclear how a slave can be dishonoured if by design slaves are not supposed to have honour. Under Athenian law, moreover, the concepts of *timê* and *atimia* were bound up with the legal status of the citizen – *atimia* could refer to the loss of citizenship rights, which of course has nothing to do with slaves.[83]

After referring to the law of *hubris*, both orators considered it necessary to provide explanations for the inclusion of slaves. Demosthenes argues that the law demonstrates the magnanimity of the Athenians, who he describes as such philanthropists (*philanthrôpoi*) that their laws even protect slaves (Dem. 21.49). Aeschines, on the other hand, reasons that the law was not really intended to protect slaves so much as to prevent citizens from committing outrage against anyone, slave or free (1.17). Neither of these explanations is quite satisfactory, although Aeschines seems closer to the truth. A clue may lie in the law's form as a *graphê*, which suggests that the original lawmaker, purportedly Solon, considered it to be in the public interest, as opposed to a *dikê idia* ('private indictment'), which only affected the individuals involved in the case.[84] But why would it be in the public interest to protect slaves? There is some indication that the original law was intended to protect aristocratic rights, since at this time it was the aristocracy who identified primarily with the right of *timê*. Murray argues that in this context 'to dishonor a slave may in fact be to dishonour the master, and at least it is likely to lead to wider consequences'.[85] If a man wounded or killed another man's slave, the master could view this as an assault upon his own honour and this could lead to retaliatory action, which was a particular threat during the seventh and sixth centuries when the law was probably introduced.

Hubristic behaviour continued to be associated with the upper levels of society in the democratic period, which is perhaps why the law was still in place.[86] In one of two forensic examples of cases of *hubris*, the plaintiff Ariston accuses the sons of Conon and his drinking companions of regularly taking drunken pleasure in assaulting men they deemed inferior to themselves (Dem. 54.4-5).[87] He also describes how the sons of Conon and their companions used to commit *hubris* against other people's slaves by beating them, emptying chamber pots over them, and urinating on them (54.4). As Fisher states, such *hubris* committed under the influence of alcohol 'would seem a natural and normal type, characteristic of the upper class, and hence was especially what the law was designed to stop'.[88] The other case, which concerns a physical assault Demosthenes claims to have suffered at the hands of his rival Meidias, does not associate alcohol with Meidias' hubristic behaviour (Dem. 21). The assault, however, occurred in a public place and, as Demosthenes argues, was intended to shame him before the all-important citizen gaze at the City Dionysia. At one point in his speech, Demosthenes draws a parallel between Meidias' behaviour and that of a drunken festival-goer named Ctesicles who committed a similarly violent and demeaning assault upon an enemy and was condemned to death 'for treating a free man like a slave', namely for whipping the plaintiff with a leather strap (180). Demosthenes claims further that many less powerful men had been intimidated into keeping silent about Meidias' violent behaviour due to his wealth, self-confidence, and gang of henchmen (20, 139-41). In both the Archaic and the Classical periods, therefore, the law of *hubris* may be seen as a guard against aristocratic antisocial behaviour, which if left unchecked might lead to wider social unrest.

In short, as we shall see frequently throughout the course of this study, what might at first suggest philanthropic motives towards slaves can usually be explained by the interests of the citizens, particularly the elite members of Greek society who composed the slave-owning class. Any benefit the slave might have gained as a result of such laws was a by-product. Moreover, although it is untrue that slaves had no protection under the law, in a society in which it was up to citizens to bring charges against each other, it is questionable to what extent the law actually protected slaves.[89]

Another illuminating feature of Athenian law *vis-à-vis* slaves is that the evidence of slaves in judicial proceedings was only permitted if provided under physical torture (*basanos*). Any evidence given freely (i.e. without torture) was inadmissible. It is important to stress this point because it reveals how in this context the law sought to distinguish between free and slave bodies by not only permitting but enforcing brutal treatment upon the body of the slave.[90] In this respect, the law, as 'an instrument of domination', played an important part 'in shaping ... class relations' and, more specifically, forming distinctions between slave and free.[91] Yet, the concept of *basanos* seems at odds with the inclusion of slaves in the law of *hubris* unless, as argued above, the law was really intended to protect free persons.

One of the primary questions regarding *basanos* is why slaves were permitted to provide evidence only under torture. A reason given by orators is that testimony provided under torture is more trustworthy. The speaker of Isocrates' *Trapezitikos* argues that 'nothing is more trustworthy, or is truer, than testimony given under torture' (17.54). Demosthenes likewise reasons that when given the choice between free and slave testimony, slave testimony is preferable because it is provided under torture (30.37).[92] As has often been noted, the veracity of this claim is dubious, since most people will say anything under the compulsion of pain. Although this weakness was also recognized by the Greeks (Arist. *Rhet.* 1.15.26, 1377a; Ant. 5.32), the view that testimony provided under torture is more trustworthy nevertheless permeates the speeches of orators, who must have assumed that this perception was part of the 'collective ideology' of the jurists.[93] The surviving forensic speeches provide forty-two challenges of *basanos*, although there is no direct evidence that any were carried through, an issue which has added further to the complexity.[94]

Various theories have been proposed to explain this, ranging from Headlam's view that torture was a 'dispute-ending procedure' and thus successful cases would never have been brought to court, to Gagarin's view that *basanos* was a 'legal fiction' which allowed slave evidence to be permitted in judicial proceedings.[95] As Mirhady points out, 'The great number of speeches that mention the possibility of slave torture suggests that its employment continued to be an actual possibility in many disputes.'[96] Even if the challenge was rarely successful, it is difficult to imagine that a litigant would take the risk of not only proposing but also praising something that was seriously in conflict with the beliefs of his audience. A primary reason why such challenges were rarely if ever taken up might simply have been that slave-owners did not want to risk their slaves being maimed or mortally wounded, and conversely that litigants did not want to have to pay indemnities to the owners for damaged property. There might even have been a fear that a *graphê hubreos* would be brought against the torturer. Alternatively, if a man were guilty and his or his opponents' slave(s) knew the truth, then it is reasonable to assume that he would not want to allow the slave to be tortured. Moreover, many slaves would no doubt have been loathe to testify against their masters for fear of later reprisal.[97] In short, there is probably no single reason why such challenges appear to have been rarely successful.

Scholars have also expressed surprise at such praise for a practice which appears pointlessly barbaric. Although there has been a significant amount of consideration of the possible legal and rhetorical factors that might have contributed to the challenge of *basanos*, Mirhady states that 'no one has yet offered a sufficient explanation as to why the Athenians tortured slaves in this context'.[98] An answer may lie in the meaning and evolution of the word *basanos*. In her book *Torture and Truth*, Dubois argues that 'the literal meaning [of *basanos*], "touchstone", gives way to a figurative meaning, "test", then over time changes to "torture", as the analogy is extended to the testing of human bodies in juridical procedures'.[99] There is evidence that from the Archaic period the word *basanos* was used to denote a metaphorical test one might undergo to determine one's own worth. Theognis notably describes *basanos* as a test to determine whether someone is a 'loyal comrade' (415-18). In the democratic period, the term retained its general meaning of a 'test', however, when used with reference to a person *basanos* was almost always restricted to the evidential torture of slaves.[100] The term *basanos*, therefore, came to imply a status distinction, namely between free and slave, or at least between a person with certain rights and a person lacking these rights. There is clearly an implied relationship between the literal meaning of the word and its use in the context of torture. In both cases, a physical test is denoted, one involving rubbing a touchstone and a piece of metal together to assess the purity, or 'truth', of the metal, and the other involving the application of a pain-inducing device to the human body to assess whether the person is honest or 'true'.

Yet this still does not address why torture was restricted to slaves. The simple answer is that it was because slaves *could* be tortured, whereas it was illegal to torture citizens. But there is more to the issue than this.[101] The sources suggest that slaves were considered to be untrustworthy – any possibility of the intellectual capacity of slaves was consistently suppressed. This is perhaps because the idea that slaves could be truthful might undermine the institution, which relied principally upon the perceived inferiority of the slave. On the other hand, lying except under exceptional circumstances was considered inappropriate for citizens. As Hesk argues, in democratic Athens 'trickery and deceit' occupy 'the realm of the "other"', which includes both non-Athenians (e.g. the Spartans) and barbarians.[102] In Sophocles' *Trachiniae*, Deianeira associates the truth with free-born men when she states that 'it is an ugly bane for a free man to be called a "Liar"' (453-4).[103] Because the slave is ideologically the polar opposite to the citizen, it makes sense that lying was considered perfectly natural for slaves, even expected. This is perhaps what Aristotle had in mind when he claimed that slaves can apprehend reason but do not possess it (*Pol.* 1254b21-4), although he was certainly not the first philosopher to doubt the capacity of slaves to think (Pl. *Laws* 4.720c-d, 12.966b; Xen. *Oec.* 13.9, *Cyr.* 8.2.4). Moreover, the ideology which associated slaves with animals and children perhaps further contributed to the perception that slaves were innately unable to reason and so must be physically forced into telling the truth.

Using physical force on one's own children and slaves was widely acceptable in Greek society (although not without restrictions, as noted above), as it was in many parts of the world, even up to today in some cultures.[104] This provides another overlap between slaves and children, similar to the use of the word *pais* for both. In Aristophanes' *Peace*, Trygaeus light-heartedly (in a song) threatens to punch his daughters

69

in the face (123) and Protagoras similarly claims that poorly behaved children should be 'straightened' with physical punishment (Pl. *Prot.* 325d; cf. *Lys.* 208d-e). There is no doubt that physical force was seen as an integral component of relationships of domination, whether between parents and children, Greeks and barbarians (via warfare), teachers and students, husbands and wives, or masters and slaves. This is especially true, however, for the master-slave relationship. Patterson, in his discussion of the 'peculiar role of violence in creating and maintaining' the domination of master over slave, cites several important studies on the role of violence in various slave-holding societies throughout history.[105] In the context of slavery, violence is 'necessary continually to repeat the original, violent act of transforming free man into slave'.[106] This is expressed in Plato's *Laws*, when the Athenian repeatedly stresses how difficult it is to reduce people to slavery, which is why, he reasons, some masters resort to violence (777a-d). Torture would seem to be a corollary of the master-slave relationship, which likewise compels slaves to a required action (i.e. telling the truth) through physical violence.

Both general violence against the body of the slave and judiciary torture therefore reinforce the slave's subservient position. Aside from judicial torture, whipping was particularly connected with slavery and was similarly considered inappropriate for citizens.[107] As seen above, a man who whipped a free man risked being indicted on a charge of *hubris* for 'treating a free man like a slave' (Dem. 21.180). Since horses and cattle are driven by whips, the whip signified the animal-like subjection of the slave and reinforced his position at the bottom of the human hierarchy. As Rawick argues, 'Whipping was not only a method of punishment. It was a conscious device to impress upon the slaves that they were slaves.'[108] Although the Athenian in Plato's *Laws* criticizes the use of extreme violence on slaves, he states that some masters whip their slaves like animals to reduce their souls to subjection (777a). Comedy is a particularly rich source for the whipping of slaves. The Chorus of Aristophanes' *Peace* describes a slave being lashed by a bristle-whip (46-8) and one of the main complaints of the slaves in *Knights* is that they are being regularly whipped (1-11, 65). The connection between slaves and the whip was so strong that slaves were even sometimes called *mastigai* ('whip-fodders') (e.g. Ar. *Lys.* 1240, *Frogs* 501, *Knights* 1228).[109]

In line with the popular Greek perception of barbarians as slavish, whipping was also associated with non-Greeks, particularly the Persians following the Persian Wars. Herodotos writes that the Persian soldiers were driven into battle with whips (7.223). This metaphor is also found in Plato's *Gorgias,* where the Persian king's soul is said to have been 'striped all over by the whip' (524e).

2. The Body of the Slave

In sum, the association between demeaning physical violence and slaves brings into focus, once again, a primary difference between citizens and slaves. Dubois neatly sums it up when she states that 'slaves are bodies; citizens possess *logos*, reason'.[110] While citizens could be reasoned with and expected to tell the truth, slaves were not expected to be honest and so had to be compelled to be truthful by physical force. In other words, while citizens were expected to be 'good' (physically and mentally), slaves were expected to be 'bad', because, in ideological terms, this was their nature. The way in which the body of the slave was treated served to reinforce this.

Slaves and sex

One of the most dehumanizing features of slavery throughout the ages, and one which is also connected with physical violation and violence, is the expectation that slaves perform sexual services for their masters. This not only underlines the slave's status as an object, it also reinforces the power relationship intrinsic to slavery. The most useful literary resource is Attic comedy, which provides a number of references to the sexual objectification and abuse of slaves. Tragedy also furnishes some interesting examples, but due to the special nature of representations of tragic female war captives, this topic will be examined in Chapter 4.1.[111] There are more references to the sexual use of female than male slaves, and many of these are furnished by Aristophanes' plays. For example, the Chorus of *Peace* includes in a list of life's joys kissing the female Thracian slave while the wife is in the bath (1138-9). This reflects an earlier list of joys given by Trygaios, in which 'a drunken female slave' is included, along with wine-strainers, women's bosoms, sheep and overturned jugs (*Peace* 537).[112] A similar reference appears in *Acharnians*, when Dicaiopolis in a hymn to Phales (the god of the phallos) sings of grabbing Thratta (a Thracian slave) and raping her (literally 'taking out her kernel') (270-4).[113] In this case, the slave woman is raped as a punishment for stealing wood. This kind of rough treatment of female slaves is also reflected in Attic iconography, particularly sympotic imagery. In a particularly memorable example, an Attic red-figure cup depicts a woman with cropped hair, surely a slave prostitute (see below), being penetrated by two men, frontally and anally, while one of the men simultaneously slaps her with a sandal.[114] It is noteworthy that while the subject of sex is not uncommon in Greek literature and iconography, the sources suggest that anal and oral penetration, which were considered particularly demeaning, were reserved primarily for slaves and prostitutes, who would likely have also been slaves.[115]

Such references to the sexual objectification and abuse of female

71

slaves are not surprising in the context of the patriarchal society of ancient Greece, where women in general were more vulnerable to sexual violence. As Omitowoju argues in her study of rape in Classical Greece, female consent to sex was neither asked for, nor expected: 'In ancient Greece ... we must acknowledge the dominant structure of sexual power, which, through a patriarchy which informs both modern and ancient myths of rape, prioritizes a reading of sex which admits antagonism and control as standard ingredients of inter-gender and even intra-gender relations.'[116] What is less commonly recognized, however, is that male slaves were also subject to sexual use by their masters and perhaps even their mistresses (cf. Ar. *Thesm.* 491-2).[117] Considering the characteristically Greek admiration of the youthful male body, indications of erotic interest in male slaves should perhaps come as no surprise. What is particularly noteworthy is that slaves could be admired and desired for their beauty, which seems incongruous with the strong connection the Greeks made between slaves and inner and outer ugliness. While such representations might merely be reflections of a reality that some slaves were attractive, we must keep in mind that slaves were required in a variety of capacities, including sexual use, whether for personal reasons, for profit (e.g. brothel work), or for entertainment, and this must also factor into our understanding of images of slaves. Just as the concept of ugliness can be useful in the context of slavery, so can beauty. This point will be revisited shortly.

Aristophanes' *Knights* provides an example of the sexual objectification of male slaves when Demos receives a 'split-bottom chair and a big-balled *pais* ("male slave")' as his prize. For further emphasis, the Sausage-Seller adds that Demos can use the slave himself as a 'split-bottom' (1385-6). Although more rarely, male slaves are also depicted suffering similar humiliations to the female slaves at symposia.[118] Athenaios tells a story of how the tragedian Sophocles, who as a guest at a Chian symposion, flirted with a blushing male slave (*pais*) and then stole a kiss from him as he bent down to blow a speck from Sophocles' cup (*Deip.* 13.604c). This rather saccharine description of an encounter between a reveller and a male slave contrasts with the iconography, which illustrates quite a different picture of the treatment slaves might be forced to endure at symposia. An image on an Attic red-figure drinking cup (kylix) shows a small male figure who is probably a slave placing a wreath on a reveller's head, while the reveller takes the opportunity to the fondle his genitals (see below and Chapter 3.1 for artistic connection between size and servility).[119]

The sexual vulnerability of male slaves signifies their connection with an emasculating powerlessness more typically associated with females. Indeed, unlike intercourse between free boys and slaves, Plutarch claims that Solon did not forbid slaves and women from having sexual intercourse because both are similarly base (*Moralia* 751b; see below). That said, there is some comparison between free male youths and slaves to the extent that each might find himself in a subordinate homosexual relationship with an older male citizen.[120] In both cases, a hierarchy is established, with the citizen/master at the top and the subordinate male at the bottom. While the youth would eventually make the transition to a position of power himself, however, the slave, like a child, remained forever sexually subordinate. Moreover, sexual liberties could be taken with a slave which would be unacceptable with a free youth. Not only must the youth agree to grant the desired sexual favours (the Greek verb is *charizesthai*, 'to favour'), the evidence for *erastês-erômenos* relationships points to the *erômenos* ('the beloved'; the younger partner) being more in control than his older lover, the erastês.[121]

One is hard-pressed, however, to find literary references to free men having sex with male slaves. Perhaps this should not cause too much pause since Greek literary sources provide little direct discussion of homosexual intercourse, regardless of whether it was between free men or slaves.[122] It might also have been the case that sex with male slaves was not something to boast about. Although there is no comparable comment from the Classical period, Plutarch suggests that sex between free men and male slaves was considered 'base and unworthy of free men' (*Moralia* 751b). A possible example of a sexual relationship between a male slave and a free man is found in Lysias' third speech, *Against Simon*, which centres upon a dispute regarding a youth named Theodotos, who was the love interest of both the defendant and the prosecutor. Although Theodotos' status is unclear, there is compelling evidence to indicate that he was a slave. Theodotos was in a contractual sexual agreement with Simon and was therefore a prostitute, a trade not typically associated with free men. Moreover, the litigants are also clearly not ashamed of admitting publicly their involvement in a sexual relationship with a young male prostitute. This makes it unlikely that Theodotos was a citizen, since citizens who engaged in prostitution and those who purchased their services were at risk of disenfranchisement or even of being condemned to death.[123] At no point is Theodotos referred to as a citizen, although in one instance he is identified as a Plataian, which makes it possible that he was an Athenian *politês* (3.5).[124] It is more likely, however, that he was a Plataian slave.[125] He is also said to have been capable of providing evidence under torture which, as we have seen, was restricted to slaves under Greek law (3.33).

While free persons might be represented as erotically interested in male slaves, male slaves are typically represented as sexually stymied, which further reflects their powerlessness. This is expressed in part by the association between slaves and masturbation, which was only rarely associated with free persons. A singular literary example is the citizen Strepsiades of Aristophanes' *Clouds* (734), who is likewise associated with barbarianism and whipping (492-4).[126] In a communal society such as ancient Greece, the solitary sexual act of masturbation represents the slave's 'Otherness', namely his transgression of socially acceptable behaviour, his lack of self-control and dignity, and not least his barbarianism. Aristophanes treats masturbation as a virtual preoccupation of male slaves. Two slaves in *Knights* speak as if they are well-versed in it (24-9) and in *Peace* masturbation is associated with slaves and barbarians (289-91). *Frogs* parodies this connection when Dionysos imagines himself switching places with his slave Xanthias so that Xanthias is the one kissing the dancing girl (who is presumably also a slave), while he stands alone watching and masturbating (541-7).

The idea that slaves are oversexed and unable to control their erotic desires is part of a broader association the Greeks made between slaves, barbarians, and uncivilized, animalistic behaviour. Herodotos draws a clear parallel between public sexual intercourse, barbarians and domesticated animals when he claims to have heard that some Caucasans have open intercourse like sheep (1.203), and that Indians have sex openly like cattle (3.101). He further claims that the Babylonians have a 'most shameful custom' in which every woman must have intercourse once with a stranger outside the temple of Aphrodite (1.199). Xenophon similarly describes the Greek soldiers' disgust at the Mossynoecians, who are 'most barbaric and 'do in public things that others would only do in private' (*Anab.* 5.4.33-41).[127] This perceived relationship between barbarians and antisocial sexual behaviour is expressed pictorially by a mid-sixth century black-figure skyphos depicting men in turbans (Lydians?) lying on the floor fondling their abnormally large penises alongside a defecating dog.[128]

The Greeks' apparent disdain for exhibitionist sex seems incongruous with the number of sexually explicit images found in Greek pot-painting, particularly of the Archaic period. In response to this, Sutton argues that such images as scenes of open sex 'cannot be used to assert that it was an acceptable, normative practice'.[129] It is disputable to what extent iconography can reveal the real-life experience of the Greeks. On the other hand, iconography was highly motivated by ideology and, with the aid of other source material, can reveal a great deal about Greek views and attitudes. The next section will examine how slaves are depicted in Greek art, which was another important medium through which ideas about slaves were communicated.

3. The image of the slave in Greek art

It has been said that the Greeks had a 'representational habit', much as the Romans had an 'epigraphical habit'.[130] Yet iconography does not reveal everything about Greek society and consequently 'both reality and ideology are always radically *underdetermined* by images'.[131] Greek pots tend to admit only generic scenes, such as religious and cultural subjects (e.g. myths, festivals, funerals, weddings and sacrifices), women at common tasks (e.g. weaving and fetching water), sympotic revelry and, more rarely, scenes of educational training and workshops. On the other hand, scenes of historical events, such as specific battles or events involving specific people, are exceedingly rare.[132] This does not pose a problem for the present study, however, since the focus is upon how the slave was represented, not what specific historical slaves actually looked like. What is of interest here is how slaves can be identified in the imagery and, more broadly, to what extent physiognomic and environmental explanations of a person's character and body influenced artistic images of slaves.

Before addressing these questions by means of iconographic examples, it is worthwhile to consider briefly the context of the evidence itself, which due to limited space will largely be restricted to pot-painting. If we are to attempt to 'read' successfully an image on a pot, it is necessary to consider the audience, the geographical and historical contexts in which the pots were produced and found, which relates back to the question of intended audience, and the relationship between vessel-type and image.

One of the most contentious issues in recent scholarship is the relationship between the find-spot of a pot and its provenance, or place of production. This is because the vast majority of images used in studies of ancient Greece come from pots found outside mainland Greece, primarily in Etruria and Greek settlements in Southern Italy and Sicily. Additionally, most surviving pots have been found in sepulchral contexts. This latter issue does not pose a serious problem of interpretation, however, since there need not be a direct or discernible relationship between the subject of death and the image shown on the pot. More important than the image was the status of the pot as an item of value. When the cost of manufacture and transport is taken into account, decorated pots, although not excessively expensive, were not cheap, and so made suitable grave offerings for those who could afford them.[133] The former issue of provenance, however, raises a number of complex questions. One question important to the present study is how one can justify the use of an image on a pot intended for the foreign export market. In other words, to what extent should the find-spot have any bearing upon how the image is interpreted?

In her study of women in Attic pot painting, Lewis notes that 'only about half of recovered pots have a provenance recorded today'.[134] Of those whose provenance is known, almost all Greek-made pots have been found outside Greece. Some pots appear to have been made exclusively for the foreign export market. For example, the range of 'married couples in chariots, and [the] many scenes of Dionysos and his followers, as well as mythic and real warriors' on Greek pots exported to Etruria are all 'assimilable to funerary themes in Etruscan culture' and therefore might speak specifically to the Etruscan market.[135] There is also evidence that some pots were 'tailor-made to order', such as those with religious dedications naming both the dedicator and the deity. One such pot even has 'a good imitation of the cartouche of the Pharaoh Apries' on it.[136]

Yet pots with unambiguously non-Greek subjects are rare, leading Boardman and others to conclude that 'it was the vases that were exported, not the images'.[137] While a number of exported pots have non-Greek shapes, the images are almost always 'demonstrably the work of Greek craftsmen' and have a Greek, usually Athenian, character.[138] For instance, the *kalos*-inscriptions found on a number of pots are distinctly Athenian, as are the Panathenaic prize amphorae. The latter are particularly puzzling when found in the Etruscan context since non-Greeks were expressly barred from taking part in the Panathenaic Games.[139] Pottery speaks, but how it is interpreted depends upon the viewer. Although Etruscans must have applied their own meanings to the images (e.g. they too staged athletic competitions), the types of scenes depicted are almost always reflective of Greek culture and attitudes and, as we shall see, repeat and reflect themes familiar to those found in other genres. This 'apparent indifference to any but Athenian subjects in choice of decoration' has led Boardman to posit that there was a second-hand trade in exported pots.[140] As for the question of intended audience, since the majority of themes addressed on Greek pottery are Greek, it can be assumed that the artist usually had in mind a Greek audience. How a non-Greek purchaser might have interpreted the image is a different sort of question and is not relevant here.

There does, however, appear to have been a relationship between vessel-shape and the type of image depicted on it. The most common type of decorated shape, which is also one of the most useful for the present study, is the long-stemmed, two-handled drinking cup, typically called a kylix, which is actually just a generic word for 'cup'.[141] These were used in the sympotic setting for wine-drinking and, not surprisingly, tend to depict scenes associated with the symposion, such as drinking, entertainment, and komastic revelry. The presence of slaves at such gatherings, where they worked as servants and entertainers, is reflected in the imagery, which makes sympotic vessels a good resource for visual representations of slaves. Moreover, since Greek women were not permitted to take part in symposia, we can assume that the images shown on these cups were intended for the male gaze. This might also explain the fact that explicit sexual imagery tends to be restricted to the types of vessels used at symposia (e.g. kylikes, krateres, oinochoai and choes).

Other types of pots on which illustrations of slaves appear relatively frequently are the lekythos and the loutrophoros. Unlike sympotic pottery, these were not intended for an exclusively male gaze. These types of pots correspondingly tend to have much tamer, more generic imagery, suitable for a general audience. While it may be said that both shapes had predominantly female audiences, the loutrophoros was more often associated with women, since it was used to carry water for bridal bathing rituals and, conversely, the deceased.[142] As such, loutrophoroi often depict women being assisted by slaves at their baths, on their death beds, and at the tombs of their ancestors. Although the character of the images on these types of pots is more conservative than that of the sympotic vessels, we shall see that both are representative of ideas about slaves found in other contexts. That is, while the images tend to be suited to the vessels' intended use, they also conform to an ideology of slavery.

Identifying the slave

One of the principal issues encountered when using images in an examination of Greek slavery is how to identify which figures were meant to represent slaves (this will be examined further in Chapter 3, which examines slaves on tombstones). Greek artists seldom provided labels, so it is often challenging for the modern viewer to identify any figure definitively, let alone such peripheral figures as slaves. Allowing for the inevitable possibility that some artists were illiterate and thus could not provide labels even if they had wanted, judging by inscriptions on pots there is good evidence that some artists could write but chose not to identify the figures they painted, perhaps because labels detract from the artistic value of the scenes. More importantly, artists conceivably expected the viewer to be able to identify the figures for themselves, which contemporaneous viewers could of course do with significantly more ease than a modern audience. Over two thousand years later the modern viewer must often utilize other source material in order to understand the scenes depicted on Greek pots. Yet, even then a definitive reading is frequently impossible. With the exception of the first example, the following examination will not claim that the

Fig. 2. Apulian volute krater by the Varrese Painter, *c.* 340 BC.
Detail of a slave

figures discussed are indisputably slaves but will rather highlight ways in which certain figures might be interpreted as slaves.

The only indisputable representation of a slave on a Greek pot is a figure labelled as a 'slave' in a scene on a late fourth-century red-figure Apulian volute krater attributed to the Varrese Painter (Fig. 2).[143] The pot shows the slaying of Thersites and depicts an alternate version to the Thersites episode in the *Iliad*, in which Thersites is decapitated, rather than merely struck by Agamemnon's sceptre. All of the figures are labelled and the artist evidently thought it suitable also to identify the slave, even though he is unnamed (he is simply called 'slave'). There are several points of interest concerning the slave, not least the word chosen for him, *dmôs*. As discussed in Chapter 1, this is an archaizing word for 'slave' and, with the exception of tragedy, was rarely used in the Classical period. This late Classical pot therefore recalls the austere language of fifth-century tragedy and, by doing so, literally sets the stage for its mythological scene.

Also of interest are the slave's body and behaviour. Although his unclothed body is in no way unattractive, and in fact is just as idealized as those of the other youthful male figures, there are a few details which set him apart. For instance, he looks more vulnerable than the other figures due largely to his complete lack of clothing. The meaning of and distinction between nudity and nakedness in Greek art is a complex topic and has duly received a great deal of scholarly attention.[144] While an unclothed mortal male body might be seen as a celebration of the youthful, athletic *kaloskagathos*, as it is in much of Greek statuary, particularly the *kouroi* statues, it could also signify 'weakness and powerlessness', characteristics which tended to be associated with women and other 'Others', such as slaves.[145] In the image on the pot, several of the figures are shown with little or no clothing and their genitals are exposed, yet they do hold weapons or staffs. The slave, on the other hand, is completely naked and holds nothing save a garment. In this image, therefore, the slave's nakedness stands in contrast to that of the other figures and only seems to be further stressed by the garment hanging over his arm. He is also the only figure who looks directly at the disembodied head of Thersites while he runs in horror in the opposite direction. By contrast, the other figures appear calm, controlled, and preoccupied with other things. Even Diomedes, wearing a *pilos* (a conical hat), appears calm while he is being restrained by Menelaos, who appears to be trying to stop Diomedes from taking vengeance for Thersites' murder.

In short, while the slave would have been difficult to identify if it were not for his label, there are other details which contribute to his identification as a slave. His vulnerability is expressed by his nakedness and lack of weapon and his deportment expresses a 'fright and flight' reaction, both of which are characteristics associated with slaves in Greek drama. On the other hand, the reason why he is the only figure who appears frightened by the murder of Thersites is more difficult to determine. If this slave is the servant of Thersites, he would have been directly affected by his death, since he would then be a slave without a master. As we shall see in Chapters 3 and 4, slaves in Greek tragedy frequently lament the misfortunes of their households because the slaves' fortunes are linked with those of their masters and mistresses. Even if the slave were not the servant of Thersites, however, as discussed in Chapter 1, domestic slaves are often represented as deeply frightened by tragic events in the household. Moreover, as we have also seen, above, fear is a characteristic associated with barbarians. In Greek imagery, Persians are sometimes shown running in fear from their Greek foes and might even take on much the same posture as the slave in this image (i.e. looking at the source of fear while running in the opposite direction).[146] While it is probably going too far to state that this slave is meant to be a barbarian, at the very least his posture illustrates the type of fear typically associated with slaves in Greek drama.

Further examination of Greek art indicates that there were various other ways in which the low status and the correspondingly base character of slaves could be illustrated. One of these is by depicting slaves as smaller than free persons, which sometimes results in slaves being mistaken for children. Although size could, of course, indicate age, it was also used to signify status, in much the same way that Greek iconography and statuary often depict gods as taller than mortals. This is in line with the literature, where size can be equated to status. For instance, in their natural form, the gods in Homer are much larger than human beings, while heroes are generally conceived of as being larger than regular mortals. Small size could also be used to show vulnerability and weakness, as it is, for example, on a plate by Paseas, which shows the tiny figure of the naked, pitiful war-captive Cassandra flanked by Ajax and a statue of Athena towering over her.[147]

The use of size to illustrate status (or lack of it) is also found outside of the mythic context. One late fourth-century sepulchral relief depicts a deceased girl named Demainete, and a female who probably represents a family slave (Fig. 3). As will be discussed in much more detail in the next chapter, slaves sometimes appear on grave reliefs to illustrate family wealth and, as in this image, are usually shown carrying something for their masters or mistresses. Unlike family members, moreover, slaves also do not make eye contact with their owners. Here the girl towers almost comically over the slave who is looking up at her, while she looks at the bird in her hand. This stone might be compared to a similar relief that shows a boy, Deinias of Oê, standing with his hand resting on the head of what appears to be a miniature *paidagôgos* – the adult male figure is fully formed but unnaturally small.[148] These images clearly do not represent a physical reality but rather the low status and vulnerability of slaves, even in respect to free children. They also recall the use of the word *pais* for slaves, discussed in Chapter 1.

Another way of expressing the inferiority of slaves was to illustrate them with barbarian characteristics. This is in line with the literature, where parallels are often drawn between slaves and barbarians. Although it cannot be doubted that depictions of barbarian slaves to a

Fig. 3. Attic grave naiskos, c. 310 BC.

certain extent reflect a historical reality, more importantly, as we have seen, foreignness also functioned ideologically to create an even greater gulf between slave and free.[149] Artists sometimes contrasted slaves and masters by depicting slaves with physical characteristics associated with non-Greeks, such as light-coloured or reddish hair, non-Greek ethnic facial features, dark skin, and/or tattoos. A mid fifth-century

81

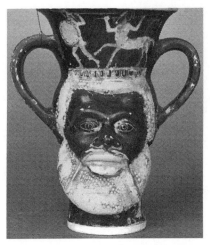

Fig. 4ab. Attic red-figure kantharos, *c.* 450 BC.

Attic red-figure head-kantharos depicting a white woman on one side and a black man on the other is often thought to represent a Greek woman and her black slave (Fig. 4ab). As Claude Bérard argues, however, it is unclear whether the man was meant to represent a slave or whether the pot was intended simply to 'exploit the contrast of racial differences'.[150] It is true that there does not appear to be anything disparaging about the way in which the black man is depicted; both faces are beautifully sculpted and equally attractive. Yet, the scenes above each of the two heads might provide some indication for how this pot should be interpreted. The scene painted above the white woman's head depicts three figures fully dressed in conventional Greek clothing associated with members of the elite; each is wrapped in a long himation and the bearded figure also wears a wreath around his head. The two male figures, moreover, stand in characteristically composed postures while the female figure elegantly gestures towards them. The scene above the head of the black man, on the other hand, depicts figures who can be classified as 'Others': a centaur and a warrior dressed in barbarian, possibly Thracian, garb. The pair's animated pose and the warrior's non-Greek clothing draw a striking contrast with the comparatively calm Greeks on the other side of the pot. This is further stressed by the fact that the barbarian warrior is running from his attacker in a decidedly cowardly and thoroughly non-Greek way. While it remains unclear whether this pot was meant to contrast a free Greek woman with a black slave, it does at the very least illustrate a contrast between civilized Greeks and wild and exotic 'Others'.

An iconographic example of what can more decisively be identified as a black slave is found on a mid-fifth century Attic white-ground

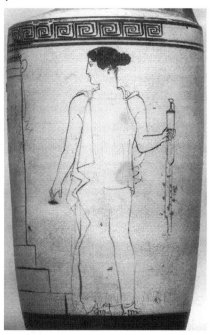

Fig. 5ab. Attic white-ground lekythos, *c.* 440 BC.

lekythos attributed to the Bosanquet Painter (Fig. 5ab).[151] Although the woman carrying the stool on her head does not have dark skin, her facial features indicate that she is African. Her snub-nose and thick lips draw a strong contrast with the idealized profile of the woman, probably her mistress, on the other side of the pot.[152] As we have seen, race alone is insufficient to identify a figure as a slave, yet when the woman's foreign ethnicity and activity vis-à-vis the other woman are combined, this image appears to depict a black slave serving her mistress at a tomb.

A similar example is a red-figure loutrophoros depicting what appears to represent a barbarian domestic slave (perhaps a Thracian nurse) with light-coloured, cropped hair, suitable for slaves (see Chapter 3) and tattoos on her face (Fig. 6).[153] Similar to the lekythos, above, this figure draws a striking contrast with the other two women, who have the more typical, long black hair shown on Greek women in pot-painting; the deceased woman's hair is in a proper up-do while the other woman's hair is hanging loose, as was suitable for a woman in mourning. The other women also do not have tattoos. Although tattooing was not a popular practice in Greek culture, it was widely practised by some other ethnic groups, such as the Mossynoecians (Xen. *Anab.* 5.4.31-2) and the Thracians, for whom tattoos were decorative and

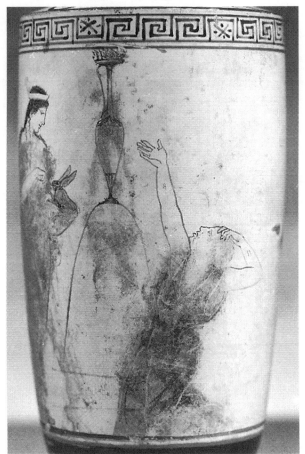

Fig. 6. Attic red-figure loutrophoros, *c.* 460 BC.

signified religious as well as other cultural practices. Herodotos comments that for Thracians 'to be tattooed is a sign of the well-born; to not be tattooed is a sign of the baser-born' (5.6.2). The Greeks, on the other hand, associated tattoos with barbarians and runaway slaves, who were sometimes punished with penal stigmata. As a result, the Greeks considered tattoos signs of degradation and 'Otherness' and were used to signify slaves and barbarians in Greek pot-painting.[154]

Another example of what is likely a slave, complete with barbarian tattoos, is found on a mid fifth-century Attic red-figure skyphos depicting Heracles and his slave nurse Geropso, who follows behind him carrying his lyre (Fig. 7). While Geropso's skin is lined with what appear to be tattoos on her face, arms, and feet, Heracles' skin is comparatively free from any such blemishes. This image also draws a

Fig. 7. Attic red-figure skyphos by the Pistoxenos Painter, *c.* 460 BC.

strong contrast between youth and old age, the latter of which is also made apparent by the nurse's name, Geropso ('Old Face'). Heracles' upright body is accented by the straight staff he holds in his right hand while Geropso's bent back is accented by her crooked walking stick. In this image, Geropso is an 'Other' in several ways: she is a slave, a barbarian, and an old woman.

In short, when foreignness was represented in the fifth and fourth centuries, it does not appear to have been something that was usually incidental or extolled but was more often used as an expression of degradation and 'Otherness'. While there were political purposes for propagating the fiction of the intellectually and physically inferior barbarian, particularly subsequent to the Persian Wars, this idea was also useful, for obvious reasons, in the context of slavery. It must also be remembered that while many Greeks, such as soldiers and merchants, had actual experience of foreigners and were perhaps less likely to 'buy into' the typification, many more Greeks experienced foreigners primarily as slaves.

Finally, although the majority of extant theatral art postdates the Classical period, it nevertheless yields further evidence of how the same types of ideas about slaves continued to be transferred to the visual imagery. This is particularly evident in the slave mask, which the art suggests typically had a wide, gaping mouth, twisted eyebrows and red-hair. These are the types of features Pollux attributes to the Slave Mask, although they are shared by some other non-ideal charac-

Fig. 8. Attic terracotta, second century BC.

ters, such as the Old Man and the Scoundrel (*Onomasticon* 4.143-54). A number of terracotta models of theatral masks fitting this description have been found, and they are also represented in pot paintings, several of which seem to depict the ever-popular slave characters (Fig. 8). The gaping mouth, distorted expression, and red hair are non-ideal and express several of the characteristics already discussed, such as barbarianism and ugliness, both of which are illustrative of slave representation. Moreover, the distorted, expressive eyebrows of the slave mask are further suggestive of the various qualities attributed to comic slaves, such as mischievousness, impudence and roguishness.[155]

The ideal slave in Greek imagery

It is noteworthy, however, that some images illustrate not only characteristics associated with barbarianism and 'Otherness', such as tattoos and light-coloured hair, but also qualities which were deemed useful in slaves. The lekythos discussed above (Fig. 5) shows a barbarian slave obediently serving her mistress during a visit to a tomb, while the loutrophoros (Fig. 6) depicts a barbarian slave mourning her mistress

86

in an expression of grief, care and loyalty. Since these are precisely the types of characteristics one can imagine owners would want in their slaves, this kind of imagery illustrates what scholars sometimes call the 'noble slave', who, as we shall see in the next chapter, justifies and perpetuates the institution of slavery just as much as the more common derogatory representations. These types of images might also reflect representations of domestic slaves in Greek tragedy, where they are often depicted as deeply loyal and caring.

Although the artists of the scenes on these pots seem to have wanted to express slaves as physically different from their owners, in other images the bodies of slaves do not appear any less idealized than those of free persons. One example is the fifth-century Attic red-figured chous already mentioned above, depicting a bearded reveller urinating into a pot held by a male figure who is almost surely a slave (Fig. 1). The figure's servile status is suggested by the fact that he is carrying the reveller's belongings, and, not least, by his assistance with the pot (this image, complete with a small, yet attractive male servant, might be compared to the scene by the Dokimasia Painter on the frontispiece of this book). Yet the slave's body in isolation is virtually indistinguishable from images of young free Greek males. His servility is only apparent by his assistance and perhaps also by his short stature and nakedness, both of which, as mentioned earlier, could be used to signify low status and vulnerability. Although it is difficult to determine what exactly the artist had in mind (outside of the joke that this vessel might have an alternative, less palatable, use), the purpose of depicting the slave with a lithe, unclothed body might be explained by the context of the image. In addition to their many duties at symposia, slaves were required to be part of the entertainment, which could involve anything from dancing and singing, to sexual activity. A possible erotic overtone is further emphasized by the partially ithyphallic reveller. Attractive slaves would be very useful in the sex-trade. Slave courtesans, for instance, are often represented as beautiful, a quality that would doubtless make them more lucrative and thus more valuable to their owners.[156]

Another possible reason for depicting slaves as physically attractive is that beautiful slaves, like other beautiful belongings, were a striking advertisement of the wealth and good taste of their masters. It was certainly no accident that the noblest and most famous of heroes in the Homeric epics were rewarded with the most beautiful 'well-girdled' war captives; this is later reflected in Athenian tragedy. One can imagine that beauty would have been particularly important for domestic slaves, who would be the most likely to come into contact with guests. Similarly, slave narratives from the American South comment upon domestic slaves, who were often chosen primarily for their beauty, which was sometimes defined in terms of their looking more European and therefore less different from their owners.[157] Although such examples might suggest the reality that some slaves were, indeed, attractive (as some must have been), their beauty can be seen primarily in terms of an advantage to the slave-owners and is therefore something that slave-owners might have wanted to see portrayed in the imagery.

While it is not difficult to understand why slaves were sometimes depicted as beautiful, it is less often considered that non-ideal physical characteristics might also have been sought after by slave-owners. Greek terracottas, which are typically thought to depict slave nurses, show strong matronly females with large breasts and hips and rather aged and pronounced facial features (e.g. Figs 16 and 17).[158] Although such exaggerated features might be representative of comic costume (and so, represent comic nurses), their bodies have more realism than obviously comic figurines; they do not appear to be wearing costumes or masks. These figures perhaps represent characteristics that owners would desire in their slaves, although which characteristics were desired, of course, depended upon the context in which the slaves were to be used. Slaves best suited for the role of a nurse, whose primary responsibility was to care for young children, would probably be chosen primarily for their matronliness, loyalty, and perhaps also for their mature age. Beauty, on the other hand, would probably not head the list of desired characteristics and might even be considered a distraction (at least, to the masters and perhaps also to the other household slaves). Ischomachos in Xenophon's *Oeconomicus* provides some evidence for this in his list of desired attributes for the head female domestic slave. Although she should be temperate in eating, drinking, and sleeping, as well as modest, loyal and caring, he does not mention that she should be beautiful (9.11) (the topic of the slave nurse will be revisited in the next chapter).

Weiler provides some evidence that in antiquity there was even a demand for deformed or handicapped slaves and that these were sold in 'monster markets'. Some slaves might even have been intentionally maimed by their owners in order to increase their value.[159] Although considered relatively useless for hard labour,[160] 'monstrous' or handicapped slaves would be desired largely for their capacity to entertain, for instance, as dancers, musicians, and jesters. Ps. Aristotle claims that some deformities could be induced in animals and humans, such as stunted growth through lack of nutrition or narrowly confined spaces (*Problemata* 10, 12, 892a). There was apparently a market for thieves and other villainous people in Athens, the *Kerkopon agora* (named after the Kerkopes, the two monkey-like or gnomish thieves in the Heracles myth). It is conceivable that this would also be the market for mal-formed slaves.[161] By the Roman period, extraordinary and exotic-looking slaves were sought after by wealthy households, 'whose principal duty', Garland writes, 'appears to have been to undergo degrading and painful humiliation in order to provide amusement at dinner parties.'[162] In short, what might ostensibly be considered non-ideal physical features could in fact be viewed as ideal in the context of slavery.

3

The Good Slave

Introduction

So far the primary focus of this book has been upon the derogatory physical and moral characteristics associated with slaves in Greek language, literature and art. But what can be said of the faithful *paidagôgos*, who led his young male charge to and from school and sometimes remained his companion even after both were advanced in age? Or the devoted wet-nurse (*titthê*), whose praise in the literature is reflected on sepulchral stones? To what extent do these representations, so ostensibly contradictory to the vulgar slaves of Aristophanes and to the broader idea of the innate inferiority of the slave, correspond with the ideology examined in the previous chapters?

When the Athenian in Plato's *Laws* observes that the slave is 'a difficult chattel indeed' (777b) he is referring to the question of control, but this sentiment has broader applications. We have already seen that the word 'slave' is exceedingly difficult to define, since conceptually slaves existed somewhere between man and beast, human being and animate object. Yet any detailed examination of Greek ideas about slaves also leads one to the inevitable conclusion that the Greek conception of the slave does not fit neatly into a category of complete, natural and irreversible inferiority. While the Greeks sought to justify and reinforce slavery through a rationalizing ideology which expressed the slave as innately inferior, the requirement that slaves also have positive characteristics, such as loyalty and industriousness, would seem to challenge the idea that slaves must always lack good qualities.[1] After all, while a person who is truly vile and lacking in reason might be seen as deserving of subjugation, this sort of person would not make a very desirable slave. Yet, while there must surely have been good slaves in practice, it is no accident of survival that the positive qualities most often attributed to slaves are precisely those which were most useful in the context of slavery. It must also be kept in mind that good slaves reflect positively upon their masters in much the same way that well-behaved children reflect positively upon their parents. One of the primary purposes of this chapter will therefore be to demonstrate that representations of good slaves are as much a part of the rationalizing ideology of slavery as bad slaves, as both help to justify and reinforce the institution.

3. The Good Slave

This chapter will examine what Finley terms the 'nursemaid-governess-*paidagôgos* class'.[2] Although domestic slaves as a group will be considered, the primary focus will be upon the figure of the slave nurse as depicted on Athenian tombstones, in tragedy, and in terracotta art. Considering that there are only a handful of memorials commemorating deceased slaves, it can be assumed that it was not particularly common for slave-masters to erect such monuments for their slaves. Of those which can be identified for slaves, all are for domestic slaves and the majority are for nurses. The first section of this chapter will examine these stones and will consider how the inscriptions and the relief imagery construct a positive identity for nurses by emphasizing, above all, their usefulness. Through the use of key examples from the tragedies of Aeschylus, Sophocles and Euripides, the next section will consider how the slave nurse was represented in Athenian tragedy. Although the nurse might be considered the principal example of a good slave, tragedy also illustrates that positive qualities are subject to subversion. For instance, a slave who is exceedingly loyal to her mistress might also misbehave, usually in the form of gossip and lying, and thus conform to ideas about slaves discussed in earlier chapters. Indeed, since this type of misbehaviour could lead to dangerous consequences affecting the entire household, it is tempting to consider such representations as an implicit warning against becoming too intimate with one's slave. The final section of this chapter will examine terracotta figurines of nurses with a specific focus upon how the figurines emphasize visually precisely the characteristics slave-owners associated with domestic slaves.

1. Domestic slaves on Attic tombstones

In ancient Greece, slaves served in a number of capacities with varying degrees of subjugation. Public, or state-owned, slaves (*dêmosioi*) were employed as coin-testers (*dokimastês*), administrative assistants (*grammateis*), crowd control, public sanitation, and at other jobs considered unsuitable for citizens.[3] These slaves enjoyed comparatively more freedom than the majority of privately owned (chattel) slaves, who lived closely with their masters and were consequently subject to more scrutiny and control. Yet, some chattel slaves were also permitted to live and work separately from their owners (the so-called *chôris oikountes*, or 'living-apart' slaves), maintaining their own households, and even their own families.[4] Although manumission appears to have been relatively uncommon in Classical Athens, some chattel slaves, such as those involved in banking and prostitution, could earn enough money to purchase their own freedom and even that of their children and 'spouses' (in quotes because slaves could not legally marry).[5]

Yet, while Greek slavery in practice encompassed a range of occupations and contexts, the vast majority of representations nevertheless focus upon chattel slaves who worked in their masters' households. These slaves, moreover, are usually given a stock range of good and/or bad qualities, each of which, as stated above, conforms in some way or another to the ideology of slavery. The most obvious reason for the broad presence of domestic slaves in Greek sources is at least partially due to the nature of the evidence. From oratory to drama to philosophical treatises and dialectics, slaves appear not in their own right but as part of the overall setting of the elite *oikos* ('household'), which was central to Greek literature. This, in turn, reflects its central importance within Greek society, where the *oikos* was seen as a building block for many other institutions, most notably the *polis* (cf. Thuc. 2.15.2).[6] The domestic slave's close proximity to the family ensured that he, or more often she, would be the most common type of slave represented, whether as part of the background or in a more important capacity as the close personal servant of one or more members of the household.

Because of the domestic slave's proximity to the master or mistress, there was the possibility that a close relationship might develop between them. A female slave might become the confidante and companion of her mistress, while a *paidagôgos* might remain the companion of his charge long after his charge had grown into a man. Moreover, female slaves and their mistresses often worked alongside each other, carding wool or preparing meals, and many children spent a good part of their youngest years under the care of slave wet-nurses (*titthai*). It is therefore no surprise that it is this type of close, personal servant who is most often subject to a more multifaceted and some might say humane representation.

Part I. Tombstones commemorating slaves

For centuries, Attic tombstones have provided a fascinating source of study and comprise some of our most abundant evidence for the social history of ancient Greece. Yet 'reading' the relief imagery on tombstones often raises more questions than answers, not least the issue of how to identify which figures are slaves. Since sepulchral imagery is often thought to reproduce 'standard and recognizable iconographic types', a consideration of how the figure of the slave was represented can reveal a great deal about how the Greek community viewed slaves, as well as the slave's role in Greek society.[7] The first part of this examination will consider stone memorials commemorating deceased

3. The Good Slave

slaves and the second will consider the appearance of slaves on monuments for their masters or mistresses.

Although much has been made of them in studies of Greek slavery, it should be stated outright that tombstones commemorating slaves are relatively rare. Of those extant, the majority are for wet-nurses (usually identified as *titthê*), which is not surprising since wet-nurses were in the most likely position to gain the affection of the families they served.[8] The tombstones in question date to the late Classical period (mid to late fourth century); however, the importance of wet-nurses in childrearing is reflected throughout Greek literature, where from Homer to the Classical period and beyond 'heroes and kings, poets and philosophers were entrusted in childhood' to female household slaves.[9] This is particularly evident in tragedy, which produced several memorable and important nurse characters (see below). The close bond which could develop and endure between a wet-nurse and her charge is also reflected in oratory. The speaker of a forensic oration attributed to Demosthenes claims that he took back into his home an elderly widow who had been his wet-nurse, even though she had long ago been freed by his father (Dem. 47.55). Although the speaker is clearly trying to reinforce his reputation by providing examples of his beneficence, there are plenty of other expressions of this kind of reciprocated love on the parts of wet-nurses and their charges in Greek art and literature. Thalmann refers to this type of representation as the 'persuasive model', which 'depicts slavery as a mutual exchange of benefits and disguises an exploitative relation as reciprocal, often invoking the model of kinship'.[10]

Yet wet-nursing was not confined to slaves, so an examination of tombstones for wet-nurses raises the question of status. In another Demosthenic speech, Euxitheos, defending himself against a charge of spurious citizenship, admits that his mother had to take work as a wet-nurse while his father was away on campaign, and claims further that many other Athenian women served as wet-nurses during desperate times (Dem. 57.35). The fact that his accuser, Euboulides, used Euxitheos' mother's former occupation as evidence against Euxitheos' claim to Athenian citizenship, however, illustrates both that there was a stigma against such work and that the occupation was viewed as atypical for Athenian women, to the extent that even many years later those who had worked as wet-nurses were at risk of having their own and even their children's freedom questioned. Plato reflects the perceived servile nature of this occupation when in the *Laws* wet-nurses are said to have 'slavish characters' (*douleia êthê*) (790a). Moreover, images of tattooed and light-haired women in Thracian garb accompanying Greeks suggest that Thracian wet-nurses were particularly popular, to the extent that the Thracian nurse became a stereotype in Athenian art.[11]

In view of the negative attitude towards such work, as towards menial labour in general, even if a woman had taken employment as a wet-nurse it is unlikely that her family would publicize it on her tombstone. On the contrary, the sepulchral evidence strongly suggests that it was rare to record one's occupation so publicly, leading to the assumption that in ancient Greece, 'one's profession was not an important means of self-identification'.[12] Athenian men are more commonly associated with symbols connecting them with wealth, citizenship, and bravery, such as horses, strigils (connected with athleticism), family and armour, while Athenian women are regularly associated with marriage, child-rearing, wealth, and wool-working, the latter of which in the sepulchral context is symbolic of feminine virtue rather than employment.[13] On the other hand, slaves are typically identified by their occupations, which once again emphasizes one of the major differences between free persons, who generally avoided public association with slavish employment, and slaves, who were identified by it.[14] It is therefore the likelier scenario that the majority of women identified as wet-nurses on tombstones were slaves and that these stones were erected by the families which they had served.[15]

According to Kosmopoulou, one of the most fascinating features of tombstones for wet-nurses is that, unlike depictions of slaves in other genres, the wet-nurses are not depicted at work. Instead, they are shown sitting on chairs, which are sometimes decorated with elaborate textiles. In this regard, Kosmopoulou notes that 'such monuments reproduce the stereotypical imagery of a large number of contemporary Attic memorials representing Athenian *astai*' ('citizen' women).[16] Rossi goes a step further and interprets the similarity between the funerary iconography of the nurse and the Athenian woman as an indication of the increasing importance of the wet-nurse within the Greek household: 'She is no longer represented as the old white-haired foreign slave of the Archaic and Classical periods, but as an Attic citizen through and through, identifiable as a wet nurse only by the inscription.'[17] Notwithstanding the fact that the majority of the tombstones in question actually date to the Classical period, it seems to be stretching the evidence to claim that such iconography was intended to raise nurses above their servile status. There is no question that in the absence of accompanying inscriptions it is difficult to differentiate between tombstones for wet-nurses and those for Athenian *astai*. Both categories of women are usually shown seated and are sometimes in *dexiôsis* (clasping hands in a gesture of farewell and/or familial unity) with children and adults.[18] Yet, just because the iconography is similar, the images

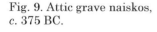

Fig. 9. Attic grave naiskos,
c. 375 BC.

need not be interpreted in exactly the same way. In the case of Athenian women, the presence of children on tombstones suggests marriage and motherhood, whereas for wet-nurses, it suggests their work. Moreover, while other adults in reliefs commemorating Athenian women surely illustrate family members, in reliefs for wet-nurses the adults conceivably represent their charges now grown or other family members who had also benefited from their services.

Further aiding in their identification, wet-nurses are sometimes shown on tombstones wearing the *chitôn cheiridôtos* ('long-sleeved chiton'). This garment was primarily associated with women (slave and free), children, and even foreigners, and was perhaps connected with the concept of *aidôs* ('shame' or 'modesty').[19] As Dué and Ferrari contend, such enveloping garments are symbolic of the constraint and protection of 'those who are incapable of exercising agency, such as women, children, and slaves'.[20] This type of garment is evident, for instance, in an early fourth-century relief of a woman named Pyraichme, whom the inscription identifies as a *titthê* (Fig. 9). Pyraichme is also sometimes described as having cropped hair, which might further indicate servile status (see below).[21] It is unclear, however, whether the woman in the image has cropped hair or whether her hair is simply tied up in a bun, which was a common hairstyle for women in Athenian iconography. There has also been some discussion about the skyphos in Pyraichme's hands and the chous at her feet. While scholars agree that the portrayal of these vessels is important because they only rarely appear on tombstones, there is disagreement about what exactly they are meant to represent. It is possible that the vessels were intended to associate the wet-nurse with infant care, since milk could have been carried in them. Since the skyphos and the chous are more commonly associated with wine, however, it has been suggested that they were intended to represent the woman's participation in the Anthesteria, an Attic festival in which slaves were permitted to take part.[22] While both possibilities are compelling, the vessels might simply reflect the service Pyraichme rendered to her owners, whether she was administering milk or some other beverage. Although she is not shown actively working, as with images of wet-nurses with children, the image associates her with the type of service she doubtless performed in her daily life.

What is truly remarkable about such images, in stark contrast to representations of slaves discussed in previous chapters, is the unmistakable affection for these women. Not only are they the recipients of elaborate memorials, they are also shown making hand and eye contact with other figures in precisely the same way as Athenians, which suggests that they were (almost) considered members of the families they had served (slaves are not always shown this way on tombstones; see below). It is particularly striking that they appear just as idealized as any free woman depicted on an Attic tombstone. As we shall see, wet-nurses were also subject to derogatory representations, notably in terracotta sculpture, so memorials for wet-nurses seem to form a special and separate sort of evidence. That said, the similarity between sepulchral relief imagery for wet-nurses and other women should perhaps not cause too much pause. Judging by the high number of tombstones with similar iconography, there is some indication that buyers could purchase ready-made or partially completed tombstones, perhaps choosing from pattern books of stock images.[23] Although these suggestions can only be hypothetical due to a lack of contemporaneous information on tombstone manufacture, this could explain the similarity between the relief sculpture for Athenian women and nurses. Furthermore, the sepulchral context is obviously not a suitable venue to recall the less laudable characteristics associated with slaves in other genres. Indeed, even the most despicable woman would not have been advertised in an unbecoming way on her tombstone, not only out of respect for her memory but, more importantly, out of respect for the public image of the family.

Yet, while Athenians doubtless felt obliged to memorialize their family-members and did so to the extent that their finances would allow, there is no other obvious reason for a slave-owner to memorialize a slave so publicly unless he or she felt true affection for her. That said, one must maintain perspective. Only exceptionally good slaves would have been memorialized in this way by exceptionally appreciative masters who could afford such stones. Moreover, there are comparatively few tombstones for wet-nurses in comparison to those for Athenians, so these are indeed extraordinary. Although they bear witness to the love and affection which could exist between slaves and their owners, only fifteen memorials for nurses have been identified out of hundreds of extant tombstones. This does not of course mean that these were the only ones, but it can at least be said that in Classical Athens it was an uncommon practice for slave-owners to erect such elaborate memorials for their slaves.

It remains to examine the inscriptions accompanying sepulchral images of nurses. In his collection of papers on the *Epigraphy of Death*, Oliver emphasizes the importance of considering sepulchral inscriptions alongside 'the monument on which it is found and the wider context in which the monument was located'.[24] Considering an inscription in isolation from the image or, alternatively, the image in isolation from the inscription, can result in only a partial understanding of the stone or even a complete misunderstanding. This is especially apparent in an examination of tombstones for wet-nurses. While sepulchral reliefs do not provide definitive evidence of their servile status, the accompanying inscriptions contribute more information. Since there are so few examples, it is imprudent to claim that there was any formula to inscriptions for wet-nurses, but there are common denominators. In the twelve examples recorded by Kosmopoulou, seven give the women's first names and their occupation as *titthê* (N1, N2, N3, N4, N8, N10, N11) and four of these also include the description *chrêstê*, a qualifier which will be discussed below (N1, N2, N3, N10).[25] A further four omit the wet-nurses' first names, giving only their occupation as *titthê* (N5, N6, N9, N12); two of these also include the description *chrêstê* (N9, N12). Two stones out of the twelve are more elaborate and include epigrams for the wet-nurses: one commemorates a woman named Malicha who hailed from the Peloponnesian island of Kythera (N4), and the other commemorates Melitta the daughter of the metic Apollodoros, who was also an *isotelês* (literally 'the bearer of equal taxation') (N7).[26] The latter case of Melitta appears to be an exception. Not only is her image and accompanying inscription more elaborate than others known for wet-nurses, none of the others are afforded patronymics, although two stones do record the wet-nurses' places of origin, identifying them as foreigners (N4, Kythera; N11, Corinth). The elaborate nature of Melitta's memorial might be explained by the fact that her father was not a slave but a metic, which strongly suggests that Melitta was also free. Since her father's name and honorary status are duly noted, it is further probable that he helped to pay for the memorial.

I have found three more Classical Attic sepulchral inscriptions for nurses in addition to Kosmopoulou's twelve. Each provides the first names of the women (and in one case a second) and also includes their occupation as *titthê* and the word *chrêstê*. The women's names are: Sopatra Maketa, Neara and Aristopolis.[27] It is likely that Sopatra's second name, Maketa, is an ethnic identifying the woman as Macedonian.

Out of a total of fifteen extant tombstones for nurses, nine include the word *chrêstê*. When used in relation to the nurses, it probably meant something like 'useful' or 'serviceable'.[28] Clearly, this was a suitable epithet for a slave; the masculine form, *chrêstos*, has also been found as a slave name.[29] In the sepulchral context, the adjective *chrêstê/-os* is frequently found in inscriptions for individuals of uncertain origin and is sometimes accompanied by a single, slavish-sounding name (or place-name) such as Lyde ('the Lydian'), Phrygia ('the Phrygian'), Syros ('the Syrian'), or Ctesion ('Possession').[30] As a result, it has been argued that in Attic sepulchral inscriptions, it is a 'Standard-Epitheton der Sklaven'.[31] In some instances, *chrêstê/-os* also describes more than one person on a single stone, as in the case of the inscription *Tertia Auphidia Aristion chrêstos chaire* ('Tertia, Auphidia, Aristion, [were] serviceable, farewell').[32] Inscriptions from other parts of Greece provide further evidence of the association between the word *chrêstos* and slaves. On a fourth-century tombstone from Thasos, a shepherd named Manes (a relatively common name for slaves; see Chapter 1.3) is commemorated as *chrêstos tais despotais* ('serviceable to his masters').[33] In view of this, it is possible that the single word *chrêstê/-os* on Attic tombstones was simply a shortened version of this longer epithet.[34] The connection is also found in Athenian literature. In a fragment from a play attributed to Menander, a slave suggests that being considered *chrêstos* is something that slaves strive for (KA VIII.1006.13).[35] This use is also seen in tragedy when Medea's nurse implies that it is the *chrêstoi douloi* ('useful slaves') who worry about their masters' misfortunes (Eur. *Med.* 54).

Four of the fifteen tombstones in question do not name the recipients. The women are simply called *titthê*, and in one case *teitthê* [*sic*?].[36] Since it was not uncommon for women of all statuses to be identified by single names on tombstones, it has been suggested that *titthê* was a given name and therefore need not denote servile status, let alone an occupation.[37] Two of the stones, however, also include the word *chrêstê* which, as discussed above, suggests that the women were slaves. It is further unlikely that free women would be given a name indicating a servile occupation, or any occupation for that matter. Even if this were a given name, it would be much more suitable for a slave, in the same sense as the name Paideusis ('Educator of Children'), which clearly associates the recipient with child-rearing (N10: the full inscription is *Paideusis titthê chrêstê*).[38] In short, while tombstones for nurses bear witness to the affection that masters and mistresses could have for their slaves, they also emphasize the strong connection between slavery and work and the master's appreciation for what was conceivably the most important virtue of the slave: usefulness.

Although examples of funerary epigrams on tombstones for nurses are exceedingly rare (only two have been preserved in the available evidence, one for the metic Melitta, above), the idea of the useful barbarian slave wet-nurse was preserved by Hellenistic epigrammatists, who composed fictive poems inspired by such epitaphs. These too are rare, but considering that such poems were composed by at least three different poets, they might have been rather more common than the preserved texts would lead us to believe.[39] In a mixed metre example by Theocritos, a Thracian wet-nurse is commemorated by her (former) charge Medeios (Epigram 20; 11 G-P = *A.P.* 7.663).[40] At the beginning of the poem, the woman is referred to as 'The Thracian'. In the second line, her name 'Cleita' is given, and in the fourth line it is said that she 'nourished the boy' (*ton kôron ethrepse*), which establishes her occupation as a wet-nurse. The poem ends with the words: 'She will always be called *chrêsima* ("useful")'.[41] Throughout, the reader is made aware of Cleita's servility, beginning with her barbarian identity and ending with the word *chrêsima*, which recalls the epitaphic slave epithet *chrêstê* seen on Classical Attic tombstones. In this context, the word must surely have the same sense of 'usefulness'. As Bruss writes, 'The poem begins and ends with reminders of Cleita's station in life: she is a slave.'[42] The final words are particularly fitting, since epigraphic evidence also indicates that the masculine form *chrêsimos* was used as an actual name for slaves.[43] Moreover, the name Cleita is rarely attested and is perhaps meant to recall the Homeric noun *kleos* ('glory'), which in turn recalls the memorable nurse of Homer's *Odyssey*, Eurycleia (see below).[44] As the epitaph as a whole and particularly the final words make clear, however, the glory of Cleita (and Eurycleia for that matter) was not that of a Homeric hero but rather that of a useful slave who was to be remembered first and foremost for her faithful service.[45]

Before moving onto the next topic, it is worthwhile to consider briefly sepulchral representations of the nurse's male counterpart: the *paidagôgos*. This word means literally 'leader of children' but in the context of slavery is often rather misleadingly translated as 'tutor'. Slave *paidagôgoi* were primarily in charge of attending to boys, which included not only taking them to and from school (Pl. *Lysis* 208c), but also more general minding duties, such as at athletic competitions (Ant. 3.2.7). They might also have responsibilities beyond the male children and be asked to serve the adult members of the household in various other capacities, such as conveying messages (Hdt. 8.75). There is even evidence that such slaves continued to be companions to their masters after they reached adulthood (e.g. Daos in Menander's *Aspis*). Although this type of slave appears relatively frequently in Athenian literature, in contrast to wet-nurses, there are fewer sepulchral commemorations for *paidagôgoi*. Five tombstones have been found bearing the designation *paidagôgos*, along with the recipient's first name, one of which sounds particularly slavish (Cteson; see above).[46] Another name, Attis, has been found four other times for slaves in Athenian inscriptions.[47] Like wet-nurses, the inscriptions do not make it explicit, at least to a modern viewer, that these men were slaves. The inclusion of an occupation in the inscriptions, however, strongly suggests that they were not Athenian citizens. Moreover, unlike wet-nurses, there is no evidence in the Athenian literature that free persons served in the capacity of *paidagôgoi*. Indeed, there was some discussion amongst both Greeks and Romans regarding the prudence of putting slaves in charge of influential young boys.[48] Yet this practice persisted for centuries, doubtless due in no small part to the reluctance of free men to take on such demanding and servile work for any length of time. As Plato writes, 'Of all the wild beasts, the boy is the most difficult to manage' (*Laws* 808d). Suffice it to say that some masters also felt enough affection for their *paidagôgoi* to honour them with memorials, although evidently less often and less elaborately than wet-nurses.

3. The Good Slave

Part II. The appearance of slaves on tombstones for their masters or mistresses

There is no question that the details of sepulchral relief imagery vary. As Johansen observed, while the images 'at first sight appear immediately intelligible to any observer', they suddenly become much less so 'at the moment one tries to explain them'.[49] There are, however, recurrent gestures and themes, which illustrate that these stones were not meant solely for aesthetic purposes but were intended to convey messages to the viewer. The challenge for the modern viewer, of course, is in decoding them. The following discussion will examine clues suggesting servile status, such as clothing, gesture, activity, and position or height of one figure in relation to others. Although none of these in isolation can identify a figure conclusively as a slave, the combination of two or more can help to support a case for identification.

As discussed in Chapters 1 and 2, Greek artists used height to show status as well as age and this also seems to have been true for figures on tombstones. While some figures are clearly children, such as those shown clinging to the knees of the deceased, reaching out to them, or sitting crumpled in grief under a chair, there is a great number of small-statured figures who are shown assisting the deceased. It is possible that these are simply young 'servant-maids', as Clairmont assumes.[50] Such small servant-figures also appear, however, on tombstones for children, where they are significantly and unrealistically shorter than the memorialized children standing beside them. Moreover, many of these small servants have mature bodies which seem incongruous with their height. One such example is seen on a tombstone for a boy named Deinias who, judging by his plump, childish body, looks like a toddler.[51] To the right of Deinias stands a male figure holding a flask under his left arm. He is about half the height of Deinias and looks like a miniature man. Because of the placement of Deinias' hand upon the figure's head it is likely that he represents the boy's personal servant, perhaps his *paidagôgos* (there are other such examples of figures with their hands placed upon the heads of servants).[52] His height clearly does not suggest his age in relation to Deinias but rather his status, as does the placement of Deinias' hand upon his head. Moreover, the fact that the boy does not return the figure's gaze but looks out towards the viewer further suggests his lowly status. There exists a similar stone for a young girl named Demainete (see Fig. 3). To her right stands a female servant nearly half her size wearing a long-sleeved chiton and holding a bird. Although the servant is looking up at Demainete, Demainete looks with a smile at a smaller bird she is holding. In addition to denoting status, it might be argued that the

reason for such differences in height between the deceased and the
slave was to identify the recipient more easily. If there are only two
figures on a stone, one's eyes are naturally drawn to the larger, taller
figure. Yet, when the deceased is shown standing beside an adult figure
who is not assisting him or her, there is no significant difference
between their heights. On the contrary, the two are often dressed
similarly and share in mutual expressions of loss and grief (see below).

Another possible way of delineating slaves on tombstones is attire,
particularly the *sakkos* ('head scarf') and the aforementioned long-
sleeved chiton often worn by female servants on Attic tombstones.[53]
Sakkoi in particular are not typically worn by memorialized women or
obvious family members, such as those involved in the gesture of
dexiôsis. While there is the occasional occurrence of a free woman
wearing a *sakkos,* they are significantly more common on female servant-
figures. Attic vase-painting provides a number of examples of more
elaborate *sakkoi,* which are worn by prostitutes, who were also presumably slaves.[54] On the other hand, when a female servant is not wearing
a *sakkos,* her hair is sometimes shown cropped.[55] Although cropped hair
was associated with mourning, memorialized figures or their family
members are not typically shown with cropped hair on tombstones,
perhaps because this hair-style was suggestive of servility (cf. Eur.
Elek. 107-8, where Orestes mistakes his sister for a slave in part
because of her close-cropped hair).[56] It is noteworthy that cropped hair
is likewise only shown on servile figures on pots, even in scenes of
mourning (see Fig. 6). Due to its association with the Skythians,
moreover, the bowl-cut, or *skaphion*, might also have been considered
indicative of barbarianism.[57] At any rate, it was almost surely considered unbecoming on free women. By contrast, long hair was seen as a
sign of noble birth at least for men.[58] This is expressed by Peisetairos in
Aristophanes' *Birds*, when mistaking the Poet for a slave he says:
'You're a slave, even with that long hair?' (Ar. *Birds* 911).[59]

Other ways of distinguishing servile figures are by the activity they
are engaged in and their association with other figures on the tombstones. Importantly, there appears to be a general lack of direct contact
between servants and the deceased. While servants are typically shown
looking up at their masters or mistresses expectantly, their gaze is not
returned. This is exemplified by the tombstone for Demainete, although
it is also seen on many other tombstones. Moreover, aside from holding
out objects, servants do not touch or reach out to the memorialized
figures with their hands, although they do sometimes express their
sorrow by touching their own faces (as we shall see shortly, this type of
solitary sorrow is also expressed by loyal slaves in Greek tragedy). On
the other hand, figures who do not seem to be assisting the memorial-

ized are often seen in the act of *dexiôsis* or otherwise touching or leaning against the deceased man or woman and making eye contact. Perhaps more than any other, these differences between the depiction of servants and other figures underscore the position of the slave *vis-à-vis* the master. While the slave is expected to provide loyal service, and even to feel sorrow at the passing of his or her master or mistress, only free persons are shown sharing in mutual and reciprocal expressions of affection and loss. This is illustrated, for instance, on a tombstone showing a seated woman in *dexiôsis* with a young man.[60] In between them stands a female servant wearing a *sakkos* and holding a box. While the deceased woman and the young man gaze into each other's eyes, the servant does not make eye contact with either of the individuals but looks off to the left.

One of the more common types of tombstone reliefs depicting servants show female figures holding out boxes to their mistresses. These are perhaps counterparts to the so-called 'mistress and maid' scenes on Attic lekythoi.[61] The boxes held by the servants were conceivably meant to represent jewellery containers, which express the perceived wealth and beauty of the recipient (as were mirrors, which women are also sometimes shown holding). This type of scene is demonstrated by a late fifth-century tombstone for a woman named Hegeso, who is shown choosing something, perhaps a necklace (the relief is now unclear), from a box held by a female figure wearing a long-sleeved chiton and a *sakkos* (Fig. 10).[62] A similar example is seen on a tombstone for the daughter of a man named Democles (the woman's name is not fully preserved) (Fig. 11).[63] The stone depicts a grown woman holding what might have been a ring, and in front of her stands a female figure, about half the height of the woman, holding a box.[64] Although both the memorialized woman and the servant wear a long-sleeved chiton, the woman also wears a mantle, which suggests that she is rather better dressed. She also does not wear a *sakkos* on her head. Moreover, while the servant gazes at her mistress, with her hand to her cheek in an expression of sorrow, her mistress looks past her.

Another commonly shown type of assistance is infant care. One example, now in the Louvre, shows a crowded family scene, in which two female servants appear in the background: one wears a *sakkos* and holds a box. She also has her hand to her eye as if wiping away a tear. The other has short, cropped hair, and holds a small infant. Both of the servants wear the long-sleeved chiton (Fig. 12). In the foreground are two women in *dexiôsis* and a young child. While the three figures in the foreground look at each other, the two servants look out towards the viewer. Another tombstone, now in a private collection, shows a female servant wearing a *sakkos* and a long-sleeved chiton holding an infant

Fig. 10. Attic grave naiskos, *c.* 400 BC.

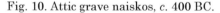

Fig. 11. Attic grave naiskos,
Athens, *c.* 380 BC.

in front of a seated woman, who looks past both of them.[65] In other cases, however, the deceased mother looks sorrowfully at the infant in the servant's arms but again, never at the slaves.

Although they appear much less frequently, there is a male counterpart to the mistress/female-servant scenes found on many Attic tombstones. While memorialized women are typically shown with female servants who hold boxes or infants, memorialized men are shown with male slaves who assist them with flasks and/or strigils. In the absence of wives or children and in view of the athletic beauty of the subjects, this type of sepulchral image appears to memorialize young, unmarried men. One particularly interesting example shows a young, unclothed man named Theomnestos holding a strigil and leaning against a column (Fig. 13). To his left stands a small, dwarf-like male figure who must surely represent a slave. The male servant holds an aryballos ('oil-flask') in his left hand and has a cloak, presumably

Fig. 12. Attic grave naiskos, *c.* 325 BC.

Fig. 13. Attic grave naiskos, *c.* 325 BC.

belonging to the youth, thrown over his shoulder.[66] What is particularly interesting about this image is that the male servant is so clearly non-ideal. This contrasts with sepulchral images of female servants, who, even when smaller and slavishly attired, are in no way physically unattractive.[67] Perhaps aware that this type of non-ideal depiction was unusual in the sepulchral context (in contrast to pot-painting, as seen in the previous chapter), the sculptor appears to have made some attempt to cover the servant's body with the flask, which he holds in front of himself. The cloak draped over his left shoulder also hides part of his body. Clairmont suggests that some of the details of the figure's physiognomy, such as a fold across his cheek and a possible furrow in his forehead, suggest that the artist actually meant to depict a dwarf.[68] The figure's non-ideal physique, however, might simply have been intended to draw a stark contrast with the youthful and athletic perfection of the memorialized man. A similar example shows a youthful, naked man leaning on a staff in full frontal view (Fig. 14).[69] To his left stands a male servant in three-quarter view, holding an aryballos

105

Fig. 14. Attic grave naiskos, *c.* 325 BC.

while he looks up at his master, as if awaiting his order. The stocky body of the servant yet again draws a contrast with the idealized, athletic body of the youth. The servant's non-ideal body is further emphasized by the placement of his right arm across his own body, as if to hide his imperfection. There are several other similar examples of memorials depicting small male servants holding clothing, flasks and strigils for athletic youths. While the youths' idealized bodies are the focal point of the images, however, the servants' bodies are obscured by the items they are holding, by their arms, or by their hands, sometimes partially covering their genital area.[70]

In short, even a relatively brief examination of figures in tombstone reliefs suggests that the sculptors developed a number of ways to

106

3. The Good Slave

differentiate between slaves and free persons. Considering recurrent elements in imagery showing servile figures, such as the types of service rendered (e.g. slaves holding boxes, infants, flasks or strigils), height differences between the slave and the deceased, type of clothing, and the general lack of direct body and eye contact between slaves and their masters, it might even be said that there existed a kind of sepulchral language consisting of a series of symbols which could be utilized to distinguish between slave and free.

What tends to be overlooked in studies of Greek tombstones is why slaves were included with free persons at all. Judging from the number of Attic reliefs showing only the deceased and a single slave, it appears that for many Athenians it was considered even more important to show slaves than family members. The most readily apparent reason for the inclusion of servile figures on tombstones was to express and to publicize the accoutrements of wealth and leisure, which the deceased enjoyed during his or her lifetime. Tombstones were public monuments, typically situated in open view along roadsides, and so the images on them were quite simply advertisements of the elite status of the individual and, by extension, the family to which he or she belonged. The very appearance of slaves on tombstones *de facto* emphasizes the freedom and comparative superiority of the deceased and their family members, which were essential distinctions in slave-holding societies such as Athens. The inclusion of slaves on these monuments might be compared to other 'animate property', such as horses, which were also reflective of wealth and status. For instance, on a tombstone from Athens, a horse is shown in the background standing between two figures in *dexiôsis* – while the horse turns its head towards the man, the two figures in the foreground look at each other (Fig. 15). Moreover, the items held by servants on tombstones, such as jewellery boxes, strigils and oil flasks, attest both to the wealth and leisure of the memorialized individuals and, more broadly, to the importance of beauty which, as discussed in the previous chapter, was a virtue primarily associated with the elite. For Athenian women, beauty is established by adornment (e.g. jewellery), while for Athenian men it is established by athleticism, which itself is associated with the *kaloika-gathoi*. Thus, such imagery not only reinforces the idea of the loyal and industrious, yet inferior and objectified slave, by contrasting slaves and their masters in this way it also expresses the importance of wealth and beauty and, above all, status in Greek society. By including slaves on Greek sepulchral monuments, the Greeks were not merely reflecting an everyday reality – the image of the slave allowed them, and by extension the viewer, to reflect upon the quintessentially Greek values of freedom, beauty and virtue.

Fig. 15. Attic grave naiskos, mid to late fourth century BC.

2. Good domestic slaves in Athenian tragedy

Centuries before tombstones for nurses even appear, loyal domestic slaves played important, even central, roles in Athenian tragedy. Their usefulness as confidantes to their masters, and more usually, their mistresses is reflected also by their usefulness to the plots, where they are often pivotal to the movement of the action, setting in motion events which sometimes prove to have tragic consequences. This section will focus primarily upon the figure of the *trophos* (the word commonly used in tragedy for 'nurse'), although there will also be consideration of other household slaves.[71] This section is not intended to be a thorough examination of all slaves in Athenian tragedy. Through the use of a number of examples, it will consider how tragedy illustrates and explores the paradoxical relationship between the master and the faithful household slave, whose desirable qualities, such as constancy, intimacy and usefulness, could lead both to a very close relationship with the master, and to undesirable results.[72] It is above all the slave nurse who exemplifies the complex nature of the master-slave relationship and who served as a conduit through which the poet could signal the tragic characteristics of the heroes and heroines, such as their weakness in the face of disaster and even, to a certain extent, their fragile authority over their own slaves.

The prototype: Homer's Eurycleia

Before examining the nurse in Athenian tragedy, however, it is useful to consider briefly Eurycleia, Telemachos' nurse in Homer's *Odyssey*, who is a precursor to the tragic slave nurse (at 1.435, it is said that Eurycleia *etrephe*, 'nursed', Telemachos when he was young). It is generally assumed that Eurycleia is a slave. For one thing, she is called a *dmôiê* ('slave'), which, as discussed in Chapter 1, was also an archaizing word used for slaves in Greek tragedy (*Od.* 1.435). Moreover, although the extent to which the Greeks of the mid-eighth century defined freedom and unfreedom remains a matter of dispute, the words *eleutheros* and *doulos* appear several times in Homeric epic. This suggests that the Greeks of the mid-eighth century understood the dichotomy of freedom and slavery, although it is in no way clear whether the concept of slavery at this time was equivalent to that which existed centuries later. What is clear is that Eurycleia was purchased by Laertes, Odysseus' father, and that she was in a 'dominated and exploited position *vis-à-vis* [her] superiors'.[73] Even if her status was not equivalent to a chattel slave of the fifth and fourth centuries, she has much in common with a chattel slave and will henceforth be referred to as a slave for the purpose of this discussion.

The existence of important domestic slaves in Greek literature is usually taken as direct evidence of their importance in Greek society. As stressed repeatedly in this book, however, representations are not merely or even primarily reflections of reality. Characters like Eurycleia, or (as we shall see) Cilissa, or Phaedra's nurse, do not represent the typical nurse in Greek households any more than heroines such as Penelope or Clytaimestra represent the typical Greek woman. While some nurses might have enjoyed comparatively more authority and influence than the average slave (as attested by the handful of grave-stones for nurses examined above), there are genre-related reasons for their important roles in Greek literature which can be traced as far back as the early stages of oral poetry. It is possible, as Karydas contends, that the authority that Eurycleia exercises over Penelope and the female domestic staff is influenced by that of a *chorêgos* ('chorus leader'), whose existence seems to have been presupposed by the time of Homer: 'Although we see her in a role that has become separated from the ensemble of *khoros*-members, she nevertheless maintains the characteristics of authority derived from the hierarchical relationship between leader and members of the archaic Greek *khoros*.'[74] Moreover, because Eurycleia's speech features 'praise and blame, boasts and commands', and is agonistic in character, it has been compared to the 'speech-acts' of Homeric heroes, such as those of Achilles and Odysseus.[75] Authority and agonistic speech are certainly not the types of characteristics typically given to servile figures in Homeric epic, which focuses almost exclusively upon members of the elite.

Eurycleia, therefore, is no average slave, even as Homeric slaves go, but is primed from the very outset to have a vital role in the epic. Her advanced age and cleverness are repeatedly stressed, as is her especially close relationship with Telemachos, and later Odysseus.[76] Her very name, meaning 'woman of broad fame', indicates her importance, as does the fact that she is given not one patronymic, which in itself is extraordinary for a slave, but two, the names of her father and grand-father (1.429, 2.347, 20.148). The only other slave whose patronymics are recorded is Eumaios (15.413-4), who likewise has an important role as Odysseus' devoted swineherd.[77] There is some indication that both Eurycleia and Eumaios originated from aristocratic families, which might help to explain their often decidedly unslavish natures. This is also made explicit by Eumaios' account of his lineage (15.403-84) and is implied by Eurycleia's grandfather's name, Peisenor, which sounds aristocratic.[78]

That said, Eurycleia's primary purpose is to serve and it quickly becomes evident that her good qualities are indispensable to her heroic masters, and to the broader story. Eurycleia is not only a trusted slave who watches over Odysseus' house and storeroom (2.344-7), she had also been responsible for Telemachos' *paideia* ('early education and care') and as such is the only person to whom he turns for help in his preparations for the search for his father. Since Telemachos' expedition represents his journey from boyhood to manhood, Eurycleia, as his nurse, is the ideal character to assist him. Her devotion to him is so strong that she even agrees to keep his voyage secret from his own mother, Penelope. Although Eurycleia vociferously and tearfully laments Telemachos' decision to go on such a dangerous journey, she dutifully obeys her master. This slavish obedience contrasts with Penelope's reaction, who after hearing of Telemachos' departure claims that only over her dead body would he have departed (2.361-80).[79] Eurycleia is clearly aware of her betrayal of her mistress and the possibility that she might suffer death for it as a result (4.743-4). Later on, she will similarly betray Penelope when she does not reveal Odysseus' identity to her (19.491-4).

Eurycleia's primary importance, therefore, are to serve as an instrument of action and duty to her male masters. As Thalmann writes, 'Slaves in the *Odyssey* are portrayed for their masters' sake, not for themselves, and everything they do or say serves that purpose.'[80] Through her help in preparing the way for Telemachos, Eurycleia propels the action towards the *Telemacheia* (Telemachos' search for his father), which is as central to the story of the *Odyssey* as Odysseus' *nostos* ('return'). Her cleverness and loyalty are directly useful to her masters and to the plot. She is, quite clearly, a useful slave. On the other hand, she also represents less than laudable qualities characteristic of slaves when she twice deceives her mistress and plots with Telemachos. Although there are grounds to forgive her deceit of Penelope – after all, the gods willed Telemachos' journey and Odysseus physically threatens her by grabbing her throat – she is nevertheless responsible and even seems to enjoy her complicity.

Less defensible, perhaps, is her joyful, gloating cries over the bloody carnage of the suitors (22.407-8) and her 'cackling' laughter as she hurries to tell Penelope of Odysseus' homecoming and the suitors' deaths (23.1).[81] Importantly, even though her feelings are understandable given the protracted unacceptable behavior of the suitors and the majority of the female servants (Eurycleia is, after all, one of the *good* slaves), her unrestrained, and rather discomfiting delight at Odysseus' grisly reordering of his house is offensive to her superiors. When Telemachos hears her cries of joy upon seeing the dead suitors, he orders her not to rejoice out loud because 'it is not the law of god to glory over slain men' (22.412). Penelope likewise bids Eurycleia not to 'boast with loud laughter' after hearing her report of the dead suitors (23.59).[82] By associating Eurycleia with such behaviour and admonishing her for it, her masters (male and female) are made to appear more restrained, reverent and civilized, while Eurycleia's unrestrained, emotive, vociferous reaction is more aligned with what we see of slaves, in particular barbarian slaves, in Classical literature.

Eurycleia is also opinionated and unafraid to stand up to her superiors or to offer unsolicited advice. When Penelope finds out about

Telemachos' departure, Eurycleia openly, even proudly, admits her part in the plot and then orders Penelope to bathe, put on clean clothes, and pray to Athena (4.750-2). Penelope silently complies. There are also several instances where she gives Odysseus advice, which he immediately disregards, only to take it later on. In Book 19, for instance, Eurycleia offers to provide the names of the disloyal and immodest female slaves and Odysseus responds by telling her that he will find out their names himself (19.496-502). He later asks her to bring the women to him (22.431-2).[83] Even when he speaks to her with harsh words or threatens her with violence, she continues to offer advice or counter his suggestions, as if she does not believe that he would actually harm her. It is this type of interplay between slave and master which illustrates their interdependence, providing Eurycleia with a degree of authority and influence which is rather surprising in a slave, but not unexpected given her longstanding role in Odysseus' household.

In short, although Eurycleia is one of the good slaves, she is also subject to behavior typically associated with slaves in Classical literature, namely scheming, deceit, lack of restraint, and self-importance. In Homer, however, both her good and bad characteristics are as serviceable to Telemachos and Odysseus as they are to the epic: the plot moves forward and everything turns out well for the masters. The success of this character in her relationship with her masters, however, will not be the rule in tragedy.

The slave nurse in Athenian tragedy

While it is true that nurses in Athenian tragedy often 'appear in a most favourable light: shrewd, knowledgeable, loyal defenders of the house, confidantes and advisors of wives and children, dependable runners of errands', like Eurycleia they are hardly ideal.[84] Although the next notable slave nurse does not appear until two centuries later, Cilissa in Aeschylus' *Libation Bearers*, there are striking similarities between Cilissa and Eurycleia, as well as important differences. Like Eurycleia, Cilissa is loyal to her charge, Orestes, almost to a fault. Her loyalty and love for Orestes lead her not only to disobey Clytaimestra by not relaying the proper message to Aigisthos, she also takes part in a plot which eventually leads to the destruction of the *oikos* (although, to be fair, this is no longer Agamemnon's *oikos* but Aigisthos'). Karydas contends that because of her vocal criticism of Clytaimestra and Aigisthos, Cilissa 'actually *invites* the intervention of the Chorus on behalf of Orestes'.[85] As we shall see, however, this is not all together true.

Cilissa's part is much smaller in comparison to Eurycleia's and later tragic nurses, yet it is crucial to the play. Her importance is initially signalled by the fact that she has what appears to be a name, at least in the sense that Thraitta and Skythes were also slave names; later tragic nurses are simply called *trophos* ('nurse'). Although her speech does not differ considerably from that of the other characters (this would be unsuitable for tragedy: see Chapter 1), her 'name' signals that she is of foreign origin: she is quite literally 'the Cilician' and is therefore presumably of Asiatic descent (ancient Cilicia was in the southern coastal region of Asia Minor). The most markedly noteworthy part of her performance is her rather lengthy account of her care of Orestes when he was an infant (749-63). Her detailed description of what the Greeks considered menial work seems extraordinary for the genre of tragedy, to the extent that some scholars have seen it as a corruption of the text. There are, however, examples of similar speeches by menial characters in Athenian tragedy, so this type of speech is not novel.[86] Cilissa's speech has several possible purposes in the play: for one, it characterizes her as an 'ordinary person' by contrasting her servility with her better-born masters.[87] It also helps to explain the reasons for her great affection for Orestes, whom she raised from an infant, as well as for her great suffering for herself, and for the demise of her master's *oikos*, which will become a typical lament of loyal household slaves in Athenian tragedy. More significantly, perhaps, her detailed account of Orestes' infancy humanizes him, creating sympathy for the now grown hero of the play, who is about to commit the hubristic act of matricide.

What is of particular note for the present study is the disloyal way in which she speaks about her superiors, and the fact that she turns against them at the mere suggestion of the Chorus. These are characteristics we shall also see in later nurse characters, who are selective in their loyalties. Cilissa's loyalties clearly rest with her former charge and she is easily 'corrupted' (in quotes because it depends upon one's view) by the Chorus' suggestion, or rather command, to tell Aigisthos to meet the palace 'guests' (one of whom is Orestes) without the protection of his spearmen (770-3). Her betrayal of Clytaimestra's message results in Orestes quickly and easily disposing of the unprotected Aigisthos.

Similar to Eurycleia, Cilissa shows disobedience to her mistress, allying herself with the male side of the family, which is now solely represented by Orestes. One of the main differences between Cilissa's and Eurycleia's portrayal is that Cilissa's loyalty and love for Orestes underscores Clytaimestra's infamous corruption, which causes Clytaimestra to turn against Agamemnon, and then her own son. Clytaimestra is represented not only as a bad wife, but also as a bad mother. The contrast between the loyalty of the nurse and the corruption of the mistress, however, is more broadly representative of the disordered world of tragedy, where slaves sometimes behave as free persons should, and free persons sometimes behave basely and immorally, rather like slaves (this will be more fully expressed in Euripides' plays; see Chapter 4.1). Orestes emphasizes his mother's corruption once again during his final confrontation with her, when he bluntly reminds her that 'after giving birth to me you hurled me out into misery' (913), a description which draws a direct contrast with the nurse's account of her own loving and attentive rearing of Orestes.

Cilissa's, as well as the Chorus', role as an instrument of action also deserves mention: slaves are not only useful to other characters in the plays, they are useful to the plays themselves. Although Cilissa's part is relatively brief, without her help Orestes would probably not have been successful in killing Aigisthos. Moreover, it is the Chorus of slave women who orchestrate the plot to change Clytaimestra's message and conspire with Cilissa, and it is they, if anyone, who are responsible for corrupting her. Indeed, without their intervention, Cilissa would have dutifully obeyed her mistress and the play would have had a very different ending. As we shall see, corruptible, plotting, scheming household slaves will continue to be a feature in several later plays and reveal a great deal about not only perceptions of slaves, but are suggestive of the fear that masters perhaps felt towards domestic slaves who were a little 'too close for comfort'. While these kinds of characteristics were clearly suitable for this type of figure, moreover, they were also highly useful to the plots.

Not long after the production of Aeschylus' play, a nurse character appears in Sophocles' *Women of Trachis* (she is also the only Sophoclean nurse).[88] Like Cilissa's, her part is not lengthy, yet she is similarly opinionated and she gives advice to her mistress, Deianeira, which propels the plot. What is particularly interesting here is that Sophocles seems acutely aware, almost self-conscious, about having the nurse, a 'slave' (*doulê*) as she describes herself, give advice to her mistress: 'If it is just (*dikaion*) for perceptive slaves (*gnômaisi doulais*) to instruct free persons (*eleutherous*) ...' (52-3). Without waiting for permission, she then goes on to advise Deianeira that she should send her son, Hyllos, to ask after his father Heracles. The apparent novelty of the existence of 'perceptive' slaves, as well as of allowing such slaves to voice their opinions and then receiving their advice is further flagged by Deianeira's response, which is directed towards Hyllos, almost as if in surprise: 'Even the words (*muthoi*) of the low-born fall well. This woman is a slave (*doulê*), but her speech (*logon*) seems free (*eleutheron*)' (60-3). The stress that Deianeira gives this brief exchange not only emphasizes the perceived differences between free persons and slaves (i.e. slaves are not *supposed* to speak well or to give good advice on such matters), more importantly here, it also spotlights Deianeira's weakness, in the form of passivity and inaction. What is further noteworthy is that it is the nurse who has to remind Deianeira that it is shameful for a son not to inquire after the whereabouts of his father. This kind of advice is in line with the nurse's role as the giver of *paideia*, which included teaching appropriate behaviour. It is tempting to think that here the audience was also meant to recall Homer's Telemachos, who set out on a dangerous journey to find his father. In both cases, it is the nurse, not the mother, who is integral to the scenario.

The topsy-turvy world of Athenian tragedy, where slaves sometimes act like free persons and free persons like slaves, is further emphasized by the relationship between Phaedra and her nurse in Euripides' *Hippolytos*. Out of the three major tragedians, Euripides appears to have been particularly interested in the nature of slavery and his plays are replete with representations of slaves (of particular interest was the question of natural versus conventional slavery, which will be discussed in the next chapter). Almost immediately following Phaedra's appearance onstage, her nurse tells her to sit still, urging her to be calm and reminding her that she is not the only mortal to have had to endure such trouble: 'It is necessary for all mortals to endure hardship' (207). These words are in response to Phaedra's desire to remove her head covering, letting her hair fall loosely around her shoulders. Since she is evidently out in the open, in full view of onlookers, exposing her head would be exceedingly immodest, particularly for a woman of her status. After Phaedra expresses her desire to drink from a spring, the nurse more sternly tells her not to say such things, particularly 'before the crowd' (212-14). Eventually, Phaedra regains her senses and is ashamed, asking her nurse to cover her head once again.

Euripides provides a similar scene in *Andromache*, when Hermione is chastized by her nurse for throwing off her veil and loosening her gown to bare her breasts (825-32). Similar to Phaedra's nurse, she also reminds her: 'God-sent misfortunes come to all mortals at one time or another' (852-3).[89] This type of interchange between a sensible slave and a comparatively insensible mistress also reflects an exchange between Hippolytos and one of his servants (*therapôn*) at the outset of the *Hippolytos*. Although his role as a *doulos* is not made explicit, he is part of a group of *therapontes* who are required to make Hippolytos' meal and rub down his horses (108-13). He also prays to Aphrodite in words 'as befit slaves (*doulois*) to speak' (115). Here the servant, via a Socratic-style dialectic, reminds Hippolytos that he should make sure also to honour Aphrodite and not spurn her in favour of Artemis (101). When Hippolytos refuses to heed the servant's warning, the latter states: 'I wish you luck, and the good sense you need!' (105).

Both Hippolytos and Phaedra are therefore initially portrayed as lacking in sense and both are given good advice by perceptive slaves, which is initially ignored. It is important to keep in mind, however, that the advice given by these slaves is precisely the kind of advice one would expect from slave *paidagôgoi* and nurses, who, as stated above, were responsible for the *paideia* of their charges. In both cases, the slaves appear to be much older. We might assume that Phaedra's nurse raised her, which would explain the closeness of their relationship. Hippolytos' servant, similarly, blames Hippolytos' rashness upon his youth (114-15). Yet the emphasis that both exchanges place upon their master's/mistress' behaviour also foreshadows the tragedy that is about to take place. As stated at the outset to this section, tragedians used slave characters as conduits through which to expose their master's or mistress' shortcomings, which could lead to disaster.

For all Phaedra's nurse's initially good, practical advice, however, her later advice is catastrophic, ostensibly because she oversteps her boundaries by advising her mistress in matters she has no right to. Although her intentions are good (she wishes to spare her mistress from grief and possible suicide) she sets about trying to convince Phaedra not to withstand Aphrodite's designs and retain her modesty, but rather to give in to her desire for her step-son Hippolytos. It would now appear that this rhetorically talented slave has gone from a good slave to a bad slave who transgresses her role and takes advantage of her emotionally wrought mistress, like the proverbial devil on one's shoulder, whispering into one's ear. She even twists Phaedra's desire to remain modest by arguing that it is *hubris* to try to best the gods, one of whom (Aphrodite) has devised her desire for her step-son (474-5). Phaedra responds with a criticism of such rhetoric, typical of Euripides' time when sophistic argumentation was under attack, claiming that it is such *kaloi logoi* ('adorned phrases') which destroy entire cities and homes (486-7). The nurse then asks Phaedra: 'Why speak so high and haughty (*semnomutheis*)?', not a particularly surprising accusation from such a lowly source (490). After listening to the nurse's argument once again, Phaedra calls her words *deina* ('terrible') and urges her not to utter such 'dreadfully shameful speech' (*aischistous logous*) (499), a response that will be reflected shortly thereafter by Hippolytos, who likewise calls the nurse's words *deina* (604). Although Phaedra urges her nurse not to continue 'speaking well' (*kalôs*), in her weakened state she is eventually convinced. Finally, Phaedra utters her doom that the nurse will be too wise (*lian sophê*) for her (518). After Phaedra relents, the nurse sets about planning how to make a love-match. She does not, however, appear to be terribly imaginative. After leaving Phaedra, she goes directly to Hippolytos and tells him about Phaedra's passion for him (601-10), setting off a chain of events which results in the deaths of both Phaedra and Hippolytos. The nurse's behaviour would seem to be suitable for a slave since, as discussed in Chapter 1, one of the primary characteristics associated with slaves is gossip and the inability to keep private information to themselves.

Before moving on to the nurse in Euripides' *Medea*, which is my final example, it should be noted that the extant *Hippolytos* might be a revised (or alternate) version of an earlier play on the same subject by Euripides.[90] In the non-extant play it is often assumed that it was Phaedra who approached Hippolytos, although this is not at all clear from the available evidence.[91] The nurse, on the other hand, 'may have tried to restrain her mistress's passion, rather than encourage its expression'.[92] At any rate, in the extant play, the nurse is the villain, while Phaedra is portrayed as the hapless victim of her goddess-induced passion. If our play is, indeed, the revised version of a less popular play, it is tempting to think that one of the reasons the extant play was successful (it won first place as part of a trilogy) is precisely because it was simply more acceptable, or perhaps more expected, for the slave, rather than Theseus' wife, to behave badly.

The nurse in Euripides' *Medea*, a play written a few years before *Hippolytos*, provides a more positive representation of loyal slaves. The nurse dominates the first two hundred lines and is even more central to conveying the story to the audience than either Cilissa or Phaedra's nurse. We might recall here Karydas' observation that the nurse character at times appears in a similar role to a *chorêgos* in that she informs the audience of the plot as well as reflects upon household events. Medea's faithful *trophos* knows her mistress well and is concerned primarily with her emotional state as well as with the safety of Medea's children. Like all tragic nurses, the *oikos* and the fate of her superiors are her central concerns, not only because she cares for her charges but also, more selfishly, because her fate is tied up with that of her masters'. This is clear when she states: 'The misfortunes of masters also fall badly to useful/loyal slaves' (54-5). The word she uses to describe slaves like herself is *chrêstos*, which, interestingly, was later to be reflected on tombstones commemorating slave nurses. After hearing from the *paidagôgos* that Medea and her children are to be exiled from Corinth, she replies: 'We are destroyed then, if we should add this new trouble to the old one' (78-9). Her use of the second person plural ('we') implies that this is not only a misfortune for Medea and her children, but also, once again, for the household slaves.

The conversation between Medea's nurse and *paidagôgos* is particularly revealing and draws an intriguing contrast between the two. Insofar as the nurse is emotional, the *paidagôgos* is pragmatic. When the *paidagôgos* hears the nurse's lament, he criticizes her for complaining to herself while her mistress is left unattended (49-52). After the nurse hears his news, moreover, she laments Jason's disloyalty to his family and worries about their future. Indeed, the nurse reflects the concerns of Medea. The *paidagôgos*, on the other hand, coldly and rather pessimistically criticizes the nurse for being so naive and, in doing so, is more reflective of Jason's character in the play: 'Is it only now you know that every man loves himself more than his fellow creature?' (85-6). Yet there are also similarities between the two slaves. As can be expected considering their roles, both are dedicated to Medea's and Jason's children and worry about their well-being. While the nurse seems also to care about Medea, however, the *paidagôgos* calls Medea a *môros* ('fool'). Yet he is also well-aware that slaves should not speak this way about their masters (61-2). A little later, the nurse reflects this concern when she refuses to go so far as to wish Jason ill because 'he is my master' (83). Nevertheless, similar to such slaves in other tragedies, both are clearly critical of their superiors and unafraid to voice their opinions to each other. Both, moreover, gossip about Medea's and Jason's affairs, although the nurse is knowledgeable about the affairs of the inner *oikos* and the *paidagôgos* about external affairs. The *paidagôgos* is clearly aware that he should not be gossiping about his masters (he hesitates at first and then later urges the nurse to keep what he says to herself), but with little prompting he divulges to the nurse what he has heard. The nurse immediately responds by telling the children what kind of father they have.

In short, the characters of both the nurse and the *paidagôgos* convey a great deal about Greek perceptions of household slaves. Their roles within and their close relationship to the tragic household reflect a reality that at least the slave-holding members of the audience could relate to. As we have seen, it was the nurse and the *paidagôgos* who were most often commemorated in death and who are referred to as *chrêstê/-os*. Yet, in the *Medea* as in the other tragedies discussed above, these slaves also represent a paradox intrinsic to the master-slave relationship. The more useful a slave is and the closer they are permitted to become with their superiors, the greater the risk that they will betray them. While there are several similarities between the representations, most importantly every one of them represents, above all, a distrust of slaves. Although slaves were considered able to dispense conventional wisdom pertaining to their roles as the providers of *paideia*, if they are permitted too much involvement in the affairs of free persons, one can expect disaster. Perhaps this is why the *paidagôgos* Daos in Menander's *Aspis* urges Smicrines not to involve him in 'free matters' (*ta tôn eleutherôn*), which he defines as pertaining to

property, weddings, and family relationships (200-4). As we shall see in
the final chapter, the consequences resulting from permitting slaves
too much authority are part of a broader conversation not only about
the nature of slaves but also the proper way to manage them.

Good slaves in other genres

A number of parallels might be drawn between the loyal domestic slave
of tragedy and similar representations of such slaves in other genres.
Greek comedy exaggerates the melodramatic characteristics of the
nurse for comic effect. This is illustrated by Simiche in Menander's
Dyscolos and her vociferous lamentations. Although her status as a
nurse is not made explicit in the play, Simiche's character is clearly
based upon tragic nurses, who so often lament their masters' situations
and report on tragic household events. One can imagine how humorous
it would have been to see this poor, old, longsuffering slave rushing onto
the stage crying repeatedly, 'O unlucky! O unlucky! O unlucky!', after
she had mistakenly dropped her master's bucket and mattock down the
well (Men. *Dysc.* 574). Even her name recalls a 'noise-maker' (a
simikion was a musical instrument with thirty-five strings; her speech
is also compared to piping, 880). Getas, Sostratos' slave, emphasizes
her tiresome lamentations when he says, 'Now, just jump in (the well)
yourself!', then further aggravates the situation by urging her, not
completely in jest considering Cnemon's temper, to, 'Run, poor woman
(*ponêra*), run! He will murder you!' (576-87). The adjective *ponêra* is
well chosen since, as discussed in Chapter 1, it connoted characteristics
associated with the underclass, such as baseness, cowardice and powerlessness. A little later, Simiche again dashes out of the house, this time
shouting: 'Who will help? O poor me, who will help!' (620-1). Now it is
her master who has fallen into the well. Although Sicon, the cook, also
makes fun of the situation, urging Simiche to drop something heavy on
Cnemon's head, Simiche remains staunchly loyal to her master. In the
same way as the nurse in Sophocles' *Women of Trachis*, who urges
Deianeira to have her son Hyllos inquire after the whereabouts of his
father, Simiche eventually convinces Gorgias to help his step-father.
Recalling the nurse's role as the provider of *paideia*, she even scolds
Cnemon for refusing to accompany the family to Pan's shrine and
warns him that he will come to harm as a result of his impiety (874-8).
Her comments here are all the more humorous because Cnemon is
neither young nor her charge but a grumpy old man.

As mentioned at the outset of this chapter, slave nurses and other
domestic slaves' proximity to the affairs of the household and to the
family members themselves gave them a special sort of power not

enjoyed by other slaves. This is made clear by Greek drama with its loyal household slaves and is also evident in other sources, such as oratory. When slaves are referred to in the forensic speeches, it is usually as witnesses to events, as 'the eyes and ears of the household'.[93] Lysias' first speech, *On the Murder of Eratosthenes*, illustrates a scenario between a female slave, her mistress, her mistress' lover (Eratosthenes), and her mistress' husband (Euphiletos), which is the kind of story we might see in Greek tragedy. In this speech, Euphiletos is defending himself against a charge of illegal homicide. As part of his defence, he recounts a story he says he learned from his wife's *therapaina* ('handmaiden'), who he says he had threatened with torture unless she revealed the truth to him. According to the slave's story, she had taken part in a plot with Eratosthenes, who aimed to have an adulterous relationship with Euphiletos' wife. Having been convinced by Eratosthenes to help him, she had frequently acted as a go-between for the adulterous couple (19-20). After hearing this, Euphiletos had the slave woman wake him the next time Eratosthenes was in the house, upon which the couple were caught in the act and Eratosthenes was killed by Euphiletos. This, at least, is Euphiletos' version of the story. On the other hand, the accusation against Euphiletos alleges that he sent the slave woman to fetch Eratosthenes, perhaps under the pretence that Euphiletos' wife wanted to see him. When he arrived, Euphiletos killed him (37-8). According to Greek law, while it was justifiable to murder someone who was in the act of adultery with one's wife, it was unacceptable to kill a man who had not been caught in the act, hence Euphiletos' stress upon having caught his wife and her paramour together.

Regardless of the truth of the matter, this speech provides a powerful insight into how slaves who had special access to one or more members of the family could be used by their superiors in household intrigue. In this case, the *therapaina* was used by three people: her mistress, Eratosthenes, and Euphiletos. Of course, there is no way of knowing for sure what exactly her involvement was, nor how willing she was, but there is a strong undercurrent of her corruptibility and culpability in this sordid affair, which the jury was expected to believe. In line with drama, this speech emphasizes both the extent to which slaves could become involved, quite literally, in household affairs, and illustrates how slaves might take sides, being loyal to one of their superiors while being disloyal to another.

This kind of relationship between slave and master is not exclusive to ancient Greece. The use of domestic slaves as go-betweens for mistresses and their lovers is also a common theme, for instance, in the evidence from the great plantations of the eighteenth and nineteenth centuries American South. Since this period yields significantly more information about slavery than ancient Greece, it might help to illuminate further the Greek situation. In his discussion of 'Life in the Big House', Genovese provides excerpts from several letters and other sources detailing female slaves' involvement in their mistress' secret romances, which he views as a consequence of the cloistered lives led by many wealthy women of the time: 'In a society that demanded female chastity and feared sexual scandal ... loyal and discreet allies among the household servants became the *sine qua non* of romance.'[94] In ancient Greece, elite women were likewise cloistered, spending much of their time in the household without their husbands (as Euphiletos himself notes) and it is not unlikely that rendezvous such as that which Euphiletos describes took place. At any rate, the jury was expected to believe the story, which reveals a distrust not only of slaves but also of wives.

Representations of the close relationship which could develop between household slaves and their mistresses also reveal what Genovese describes as the 'reciprocal dependency of slavery'. Masters and mistresses depended upon their slaves as much as the slaves depended upon their masters and mistresses, in some ways even more so. It was no easy task to replace a good domestic slave, who had not only been a longstanding and trusted member of the household, but knew all of the family's affairs and secrets. This gave such slaves a sort of power and authority which could put their owners in a rather awkward position. In Lysias' speech, the *therapaina* had information about her mistress' personal life which even her mistress' husband was unaware of. Like the nurses of Athenian tragedy, her loyalty to her mistress was so strong that her own master had to threaten her with physical violence to force her to reveal the truth. If permitted too much independence and power, some slaves might even forget their inferior position, if only momentarily, and speak back to their masters. We have already seen examples of this in the character of Eurycleia. Phaedra's nurse, moreover, does not always speak to her mistress as an inferior but tells her what she should and should not do, as if she were an equal. Inevitably, the Greeks were well aware of the dependency of masters upon their slaves and sought to mitigate this, in part, by constructing derogatory images of slaves, which advertised them as naturally inferior.

It is noteworthy that the figure of the female domestic slave, and the nurse in particular, was at least as powerful an image in American slavery as it was in ancient Greece. Where the Greek evidence provides us with prominent nurse characters in drama and touching memorials for slave nurses, American slavery has its 'mammy', who was both a literary figure as well as the recipient of elaborate memorials and epitaphs. As Genovese writes, 'No figure stands out so prominently in the moonlight-and-magnolias legend of the Old South.'[95] The very idealism of this image in both contexts is what makes it suspect, as does the negative reaction of African-Americans to the image of the mammy.[96] Although she was a real enough figure in American slavery, she has been mythologized to suit the ideals of the master-class, who fashioned the lives of real women 'and simplified them into their preferred versions of a historical stereotype'.[97] Even with an abundance of evidence in contrast to what remains from ancient Greece, it is no easy task to separate the woman from the legend. The mammy, like the Greek nurse, was often the first to receive new-borns, the first to nurse them, and the first to teach them to walk and talk. She was also responsible for teaching them proper behaviour which, paradoxically, contrasted with the expectations of those of her own status. In the same way as Greek slave nurses are shown urging their mistresses towards behaviour appropriate for elite women, mammies are sometimes shown forbidding their white female charges to do things like enter the kitchen, which was viewed as the domain of the slave.[98] The mammy, much like the Greek nurse, was 'the perfect slave – a loyal, faithful, contented, efficient, conscientious member of the family who always knew her place'.[99] She is a simple woman, devoted to her masters, and accepting of her position as a slave, even loving her white charges more than her own children. She is exactly the type of slave who justified the institution of slavery. In this way, 'the mammy was a servant ... of writers who wished to describe slavery as a humane institution'.[100]

Of course, the story of slavery is much more complex than such saccharine representations would have us believe. What we do not tend to see in the Greek evidence is the ambivalence or even aggressive behaviour towards masters that American slavery reveals. The letters and journals of Southern plantation owners not infrequently express a fear that slaves might harm them. Poisoning, in particular, was feared. Yet, while such things did, indeed, occur, they do not appear to have been very widespread. A number of interviews with former domestic slaves more commonly illustrate an ambivalence or even happiness at the grief or deaths of masters and mistresses. A slave woman named Delia Garlic states that she was glad to see her master and mistress cry because 'dey made us cry so much.' Another slave named Annie Hawkins states that she and her sister both 'natchally laughed' when they passed by their master lying in his coffin. She adds, 'Why shouldn't we? We was glad he was dead.'[101] In contrast, since only one side of slavery is yielded by the Greek evidence, we are largely restricted to what masters wanted to admit to. While it was acceptable to depict domestic slaves exhibiting desirable and undesirable qualities which justified the institution of slavery and the enslavement of certain people, it does not appear to have been acceptable to depict a wholly disloyal slave who would gloat over the death of his or her master or mistress, or intentionally cause them harm. As seen in the examples from Greek tragedy discussed above, even slaves who betrayed their mistresses or masters had what they believed to be the best interests of the household at heart. Even comic slaves, who are frequently depicted as tricky, petulant and critical of their masters, are rarely 'openly rebellious'.[102] One of the things we learn when comparing the Greek evidence to that from more modern slave societies is the extent to which representations of slaves in the Greek sources are selective and emphasize, above all, the attitudes and concerns of the master-class.

3. The collectible nurse

The final section of this chapter will consider visual representations of nurses in terracotta figurine-art. A number of nurse figurines have been found in Athens and in other Greek settlements, primarily in Boeotia, which was a centre of figurine production. While their relatively wide distribution is likely due in part to their inexpensive material and manufacture, which made them available to a broader audience, it is also reflective of the popularity of the image of the nurse. In line with the dates of most terracotta figurines, the majority of extant nurses date to the late Classical and early Hellenistic periods, when 'the purely secular art' of figurine-manufacture was developing.[103] By this time, figurines tended to be made from moulds and appear to have been utilized primarily as household ornaments and children's toys. Although figurines of old women holding infants are sometimes thought to represent nurse characters from Greek comedy, it is unclear whether they should be categorized with the popular genre of theatral terracottas. Certainly, the nurses' heavy faces, with their prominent brows, noses and mouths, are reminiscent of the grotesque comic mask associated with slaves and slavish characters. Yet the naturalism of their features, in contrast to the unrealistic distortion of the comic mask, would seem to argue against this categorization. They are more likely curiosity figurines, like the 'black boy asleep' and the 'fat woman'.[104]

For the purposes of this study, what is most interesting about these figurines is the physical features they highlight: the broad, heavy, wrinkled yet kind faces, and the large, flabby, hunched bodies with thick arms and hands (redolent of hard work), all features which are further emphasized by the tiny children they hold (Figs 16 and 17).[105] While it is not surprising that nurses, or any slave for that matter, would be represented as physically non-ideal, the emphasis is clearly

Fig. 16. Terracotta from Tanagra, Boeotia, *c.* 325 BC.

upon matronly features. This reflects not only what was conceivably a reality – it is, above all, the older and most trusted of slaves who would be chosen for this type of work – these figurines also emphasize precisely the types of features one can imagine owners would want in such slaves. The more aged and unattractive a nurse was, the more she might be expected to focus upon her important duties. For instance, nowhere in Ischomachos' lengthy list of the desired attributes of his head 'housekeeper' (*tamia*) does he mention beauty.[106] Instead, he emphasizes that she should be temperate in eating, drinking and sleeping, modest with men, industrious, have a good memory, be eager to please, loyal, caring, eager for improvement of the estate and just (Xen. *Oec.* 9.11-13). Indeed, youth and beauty might be thought to make her rather more distracted by and less modest with men.

3. The Good Slave

Fig. 17. Terracotta from Tanagra, Boeotia,
late fourth century BC.

While conducting comparative research into the image of the American slave mammy, it struck me, quite unexpectedly, how similar visual representations of the mammy are to the Greek nurse figurines. Although there would naturally have been a significant amount of human variation amongst real slave nurses in both contexts, the prominent features of the manufactured versions are large breasts, bulky, large-hipped matronly bodies, and rather masculine facial features and arms. As Manring states in the context of the American mammy, writers and artists 'took the lives of real persons and simplified them into their preferred versions of a historical stereotype'.[107] The stereotypical image of the mammy is perhaps best exemplified by the figure of Aunt Jemima, the icon for the famous American pancake mix (Fig. 18).

Fig. 18. Aunt Jemima advertisement for sheet music,
Saxx Music Co., *c.* 1899.

Although this image was not used in advertising until after abolition, the picture of a strong, happy, matronly, loyal slave woman was primarily intended to appeal to those who were reluctant to give up the concept of an idealized household slave who embodied the positive characteristics most sought after and cherished by slave-owners. In ancient Greece, of course, abolition never occurred, but the desire to depict these important figures in a way which recalled fond memories of loving, hard-working, matronly nurses must have been equally attractive, regardless of how realistic such images were in practice. In both cases, these images served the needs of the master-class, who wanted to believe in the idea of such slaves.

It is further noteworthy that both societies 'Other' these women. In the context of ancient Greece, the 'Othering' is primarily accomplished by depicting the nurses' bodies as non-ideal, which clearly contrasts with the more beautiful children they are assisting. While we cannot claim on the basis of the available evidence that these women were supposed to represent barbarian slave nurses, they do fit into the category of the 'ugly slave'. In other genres, however, slave nurses are indeed depicted as foreign (one might recall red-figure images of tattooed slave nurses, such as Geropso, Fig. 7). Although this can only be conjecture, these figurines, like other terracottas, were likely painted and it cannot be ruled out that tattoos might also have appeared on their bulky arms or perhaps elsewhere. Aunt Jemima, on the other hand, is 'Othered' primarily by her exaggerated foreign attributes, namely her dark skin and her African-style turban, which was explicitly associated with African slave women (Fig. 18). Although in reality Africans exhibit a range of skin tones, the earliest images of Aunt Jemima depict her with skin which is virtually black, which makes a stark contrast to her white masters (and her intended audience/market). Her red lips and white teeth only further emphasize her dark skin tone and give her a rather frightening, barbaric appearance (Fig. 19).[108] Although the location of emphasis with regard to ancient Greek and American slave-holders thus reveals one of the differences between the two slave systems (e.g. the Greeks did not take their slaves from only one region), it does not diminish the fact that in both cases, it was important to 'Other' the nurse and that this was done in similar ways.

Fig. 19. Aunt Jemima and Uncle Moses
Salt and Pepper Shakers, *c.* 1950.

War Captives and the Natural Slave:
Euripides and Aristotle on Slavery

Introduction

There is little doubt that the Greeks accepted slaves as a worthwhile, necessary, and even natural component of human society, comparable to domesticated animals and other 'animate tools', which, in the pre-industrialized world were similarly considered necessary for civilization. This does not mean, however, that there was no conversation about what sorts of people could be justly enslaved, how they should be procured, or how they should be managed. Although there was never any serious discussion of abolition, the Greeks nevertheless developed certain rudimentary parameters of acceptability for slavery. As discussed in earlier chapters, at least from the period of Solon and increasingly thereafter there was a general abhorrence at the idea of Greeks enslaving Greeks, and more especially, citizens enslaving fellow citizens. It was viewed as much more acceptable to enslave barbarians, who Greek ideology typically considered inferior (it need hardly be said that ideology and reality do not always intersect and the real situation was often another matter).

Yet the Greeks' acceptance of slavery as a necessary institution did not preclude the possibility of pity or empathy for those enslaved, barbarian or Greek. This doubtless resulted in part from the Greeks' knowledge of the precariousness of freedom, a state which a people engaged in almost constant warfare knew could never be taken for granted. One of the most intractable tenets of ancient war was the *nomos*, or custom, that the vanquished were the rightful property of the victors (cf. Xen. *Cyr.* 7.5.73; Arist. *Pol.* 1255a6-7). There was a long tradition of empathy for the victims of war dating at least as far back as Homer, when the strict barriers between Greek and barbarian did not yet exist. The Homeric view of the tragedy of war and its victims seems to have influenced depictions of the Trojans centuries later. In the 460s, Polygnotos, the artist responsible for the Painted Stoa at Athens, focused upon the suffering of the Trojans as part of his mural. This monumental wall painting is described by Pausanias, who indicates that the focus of the scene was not the sack of Troy but the

aftermath (1.15.1-3). Subsequent to the Persian Wars, the sack of
Athens was sometimes compared to the sack of Troy, which seems to
have led to a resurgence of interest in the suffering of the victims of
war.[1] Although many today assume that the Parthenon was the most
well-known building in Athens (as it is today), the Painted Stoa was
more easily accessible and frequented than the Parthenon and conceivably held a greater influence over Athenian writers and artists.[2]

In the fifth century, the increasingly brutal, lengthy, and personal
Peloponnesian War, which caused widespread suffering throughout the
Greek world, conceivably also had some effect upon the literature
produced during this period, although the extent to which it did has
been the subject of much debate. Parallels have been drawn between
some particularly harsh events, notably the Melian and Sicilian disas-
ters, and Euripides' depiction of the captive Trojan women in the
Troades.[3] Even if there has been some exaggeration of the possible
parallels between the Peloponnesian and the Trojan Wars, as Croally
argues, 'there is no reason to think that a play obviously concerned with
the effects of war should not make the spectators think of a war'.[4]

Since war captives in Greek tragedy tend to be depicted very differently from slaves portrayed in other genres, a consideration of this type
of representation has been held in reserve until more popular ideas
about slaves could be addressed. This chapter will begin with an
examination of war captives as they are portrayed in Euripides' Trojan
War plays (*Andromache*; *Hecuba*; *Troades*). Even though heroines,
such as Hecuba, Andromache, and Polyxena, suffer what might be
considered a threefold disability (they are not only slaves, they are also
barbarian and female), this did not preclude them from having a
nobility of character, which often stands in direct opposition to other
representations of slaves. As we shall see, the reasons behind
Euripides' depiction of war captives are complex and multifaceted.
What does seem clear is that he was responding to a contemporaneous
discussion about the roles played by nature in the formation of one's
character. In particular, there is a pervasive questioning of polarities,
such as Greek/barbarian, noble/ignoble, and free/slave. While it was
easy enough to develop a strong ideological polarity between barbarian
and Greek in the immediate aftermath of the Persian Wars, the
Peloponnesian War seems to have problematized this distinction because now the enemy was from within. Perhaps as a reflection of this,
'Euripides' Trojan War, like the Peloponnesian War, makes the identification of Greek as against barbarian problematic'.[5] As is
characteristic of Euripides' plays, we are left with more questions than
answers: who is the barbarian and, more importantly, who is the slave?

While Euripides questions polarities, Aristotle a century or so later seeks to identify, explain, and finally justify and reinforce them. The second part of this chapter will examine Aristotle's explanation of natural slavery, which encompasses many of the overlapping ideas explored in previous chapters, such as physiognomy, environmental determinism, barbarianism, and elite prejudices against manual labourers. Although by the time of Euripides it is clear that the Greeks were making distinctions between who was and was not suited to slavery, it was not until a century later that Aristotle categorized slaves as either 'slaves by convention' or 'slaves by nature'. With Aristotle, the idea of the natural inferiority of certain people and their suitability to slavery thus took the form of a single, if not exactly coherent, argument. There is a veritable mountain of literature on every aspect of Aristotle's discussion, from issues with 'difficulties, inconsistencies, and downright contradictions inherent in Aristotle's theory of natural slavery', to its relationship with slavery as it actually existed, to the natural slave's use and abuse by later apologists (particularly those of the American South).[6] This section does not seek to provide a systematic survey of the scholarship on Aristotle's natural slave but rather to explore the extent to which Aristotle assimilated ideas about slaves which had existed for at least a century before him in order to construct an argument which was essentially a recipe for an ideal (and imaginary) type of slavery.

4.1. War captives in Euripides' Trojan War plays

The noble female war captive

One of the most striking differences between the Trojan war captive in Greek tragedy and other representations of slaves is that lineage is an important part of the war captive's character. This contrasts with what we find in other sources. With exceptions such as Homer's Eurycleia and Eumaios, who as I argued in Chapter 3 are not average slaves, the family origins of slaves are hardly ever acknowledged. As a rule, slaves do not merit recognition of their ancestry, which would impart to them more humanity than was constructive for the institution. As we saw in Chapter 1, name-changing and the separation from kith and kin were deemed necessary in erasing a slave's personal and individualistic identity, supplanting it with the singular identity of 'slave'. The sources tend to reflect this lack of a complex identity by representing slaves as two dimensional, sharing only in characteristics, whether negative or positive, which were expedient for slavery. The heroines of Euripides' Trojan War plays, however, repeatedly emphasize their former free status and royal pedigree, lamenting their present state as slaves, which they consider especially cruel precisely because it is so strange to them. The Trojan princess Polyxena laments that even uttering the unfamiliar (*ouk eiôthos*) word *doulê* makes her long for death (*Hec.* 357-8) and later stresses that she is ashamed to be called a slave even among the dead (551-2). Andromache similarly contrasts her previous status as a woman from 'the freest house' (*eleutherôtatôn oikôn*) with her current state as a slave in Greece (*And.* 12-13). Her interaction with Hermione further attests to the idea that nobility and lineage can transcend slavery. Andromache is traditionally portrayed as an ideal wife who knows her place, while Hermione, as the daughter of Helen, famously does not. Andromache refers to Hermione's mother as a *philandria* ('man-lover') (229-30) and even blames Helen for the death of Achilles (248). It would seem that Andromache's womanly intelligence is attributable to her upbringing and lineage, while Hermione's lack of wisdom and modesty is attributable to hers. In short, these plays seem to stress the persistence of the nature of nobility, even under such trying circumstances as slavery. Once again, these women are not just any slaves. Although slaves are often represented as disgruntled with their state (particularly in comedy), the war captive alone prefers death to slavery. This is exemplified by Polyxena when she urges Hecuba: 'Mother, do not oppose me in word or deed, but advise me to die before suffering a shame unworthy of me' (Eur. *Troades* 372-4; cf. *Hec.* 367-78). By contrast, the Phrygian Slave in Euripides' *Orestes* is more typical of dramatic slaves, clearly (and cowardly) preferring slavery to death: 'Every man, slave or not, delights in seeing the daylight' (1523). The stark difference between the war captive and other types of slaves helps to explain why it is only the war captive who is given a leading role in Greek tragedy.

In spite of this, however, the primary concern of the war captives is not their loss of freedom as we might expect. Although they are slaves, they are also women and so they do not have or expect the same degree of freedom as men. There is a general conflation between the concerns of the Trojan captives and other women, which is particularly noticeable in their frequent references to marriage. As Goff notes, their preoccupation with marriage 'eloquently illustrates the absence of freedom that characterizes the lives of all women, not just Trojan slaves'.[7] Even though Andromache, as Neoptolemos' 'spear prize', recognizes that the sexual relationship between her and Neoptolemos is that between a master and a slave, the Chorus refers to it as a marriage (*And.* 14, 123-4). As seen above, Andromache even portrays herself as a better 'wife' than Hermione (207-31); it is implicit that she is also a better 'wife' to Neoptolemos, in part because he chooses her bed over Hermione's and because she has borne him a son while Hermione has given him no children. What Andromache stresses above all, however, is that she is modest and obedient, surely not the typical qualities associated with slaves, while Hermione, with her tantrums and overall bad behaviour, is not (234-55). Andromache's perfection as a wife is the primary reason why she was so desirable in the Greek camp. As Croally argues, she 'conforms perfectly with male ideological prescriptions'.[8] The captive women's consistent focus upon feminine concerns thus signals another important difference between the war captive and other slaves; while gender plays an integral role in how the Trojan women are depicted, gender is not equally essential to other slave representations. In particular, while other types of slaves tend to share similar qualities regardless of whether they are male or female, the Trojan women's concerns are specifically feminine and are tied in with their nobility.

Since women were not as a rule given the option to choose their husbands, the Trojan women's allocation by men to men also bears an unavoidable similarity to the lot of all women. They are particularly concerned with whether their new masters are a good 'match', much as a woman might be concerned with what sort of man she is to marry. For instance, the Chorus of captive Trojan women wonder to which Greek heroes' beds they will be assigned (*Troades* 203-4). Similarly, Hecuba complains about her allotment to Odysseus, who she views as 'vile' and 'lawless' (he is, after all, partly responsible for the death of many of her family) (*Troades* 285-7). Yet, although the Trojan heroines sometimes seek to soften their situation by using the language of marriage to describe their relationships with their captors, the plays make it clear that the relationship can be no more than a perversion of marriage, a factor which further emphasizes the women's tragic circumstances. In a lament which has been described as a 'conflation of a wedding hymn and a funeral dirge', Cassandra imagines that Hades will be her 'bridegroom' in death, and she also portrays her relationship with Agamemnon as a marriage (*Troades* 357-9, 445).[9] Although Cassandra's wording might be explained by her madness, this type of language is not exclusive to her and is more likely meant to be a source of comfort or, at the very least, was intended to be ironic.[10] One of the women's greatest concerns, however, is the negation of their elite status as the wives of royalty. After the fall of Troy, Polyxena laments that she can now only look forward to being a servant in a royal house, her bed defiled by a 'slave bought from who knows where' (*Hec.* 365-6).

Polyxena's desire for her body to be left untouched by her Greek captors further suggests the importance of retaining sexual modesty, particularly for unmarried women (*Hec.* 547-52). The heroines' concern for sexual modesty is perhaps one reason why they describe their enslavement in terms of marriage, which was an easier pill to swallow than slavery. Indeed, sexual modesty appears to have been considered particularly important for elite women. Writing around the same time as Euripides, Herodotos seems to make a distinction between females who were protected from rape and those who were not. In his explanation of the Pelasgians' removal from Attica, he states that the Pelasgians had assaulted the Athenians' daughters when they were fetching water from a spring near the Pelasgians' settlement.[11] Importantly, he adds that at this time in Athenian history, there were no servants to do this type of work (6.137). Since fetching water continued to be a female task in the Classical period, Herodotos was likely referring to the daughters of elite Athenians, who would have had slaves to do this work for them and whose chastity was presumably easier to protect. What this also indicates is that slaves were not considered worthy of the same type of protection. Although free women and slaves 'appear to be interchangeable as workers', this account reveals that they were not sexually interchangeable and further, that elite women had more protection from sexual assault than other women.[12] The Trojan heroines' lack of protection from assault is surely one of the foremost reasons why they claim to feel slavery more harshly than others.

We are reminded repeatedly in these plays that the Trojan war captives are not just any slaves, but retain the nobility of their rank even under the yoke of slavery. They might even be considered what Aristotle would later define as conventional (rather than natural) slaves. Although he does not use such descriptions, Euripides seems well aware of the distinction between natural and conventional slavery, and includes both types of slaves in his plays. Andromache implies this distinction when she complains that she was thrown into slavery 'undeservedly' (*And.* 99). The word she uses, *anaxiôs*, signifies that she considers herself unworthy of slavery, which implies that there were some who were worthy of it. The difference between the two types of slaves is demonstrated well by the contrast between Andromache and her former maidservant, who is more typical of slaves seen in drama, and can be considered one of the 'good slaves' discussed in the previous chapter. Although both Andromache and the maidservant are slaves, as Andromache herself laments when she recognizes the woman as her *sundoulos*, 'fellow slave' (*And.* 64), Andromache's maidservant continues to recognize Andromache as her *despoina* ('mistress'): 'Mistress, I do not avoid calling you this name, since I thought it fitting in your house when we lived in the land of Troy' (56-8). The maidservant, who is suitably nameless, further conforms to the usual role of the loyal household slave when she acts as an informant to her mistress, telling her of the disaster which is about to befall her, and then again when she acts as Andromache's messenger. As a good slave, she proves to be the most loyal of the messengers sent to Peleus, succeeding in her task to summon him where other slaves have failed.

The implication here is that a change in one's status does not necessarily produce a change in one's nature: in particular, even well-born barbarians can retain their free souls, regardless of whether their bodies are enslaved. While this idea is most prevalent in Euripides' plays, it also appears in a fragment from Sophocles: 'The body is slavish but the mind is free' (Fr. 854).[13] The theme of freedom and slavery is particularly prominent in Euripides' *Hecuba,* which 'constitutes one of the underlying and unifying elements', to the extent that the words *eleutheros* and *doulos* 'occur more than twice as often in *Hecuba* as in any other extant play of Euripides'.[14] There is also a significant emphasis upon the volatility of fortune, whereby the undeserving (i.e. the nobly born) are just as subject to being cast into slavery as those who are more deserving of it (i.e. the lowly born). Andromache reflects the words of Herodotean Solon when she says that no one should be called fortunate until he has died and the end of his life is known (*And.* 100-3; Hdt. 1.32). She is clearly referring to herself in this passage. Hecuba similarly reminds Odysseus that she too was once fortunate (*eu-tuchountas*) but all her happiness was taken from her in a single day (*Hec.* 284-5). The idea that one's freedom can be taken from them in a single day recalls Homer's expression *doulion hêmar* ('the day of slav-ery'), found in the *Odyssey*.[15] Hecuba makes it clear that she is referring to the upper classes when she warns Odysseus, from her own experi-ence, that the ruling class (*kratountas*) might one day end up being ruled themselves. Likewise, the ghost of her son, Polydoros, reasons that Hecuba suffers so much precisely because she had enjoyed such prosperity and brought about the envy of 'one of the gods' (57-8). The common Greek trope that the gods are jealous of human prosperity is also reflected in Herodotos' *Histories,* most notably in his narrative on Solon (1.29-33) but also in his story of Croesus, who rejected the words of Solon and challenged 'the gods in their traditional role as dispensers of goods and evils to men' (Hdt. 1.33).[16]

In short, the Trojan heroines suffer all the more because, in the Greek mind, it is the lofty who were thought to fall hardest when disaster hits. While some scholars have read such depictions of the plight of those captured in war as sympathy for slaves, it should be stressed, once again, that Euripides depicts a certain kind of slave, whose enslavement is unnatural, 'an accident of fate'.[17] The contrast between different types of slaves in a single play, such as that between Andromache's maidservant, who seems to be naturally suited to slav-ery, and Andromache, to whom slavery is unnatural and strange, makes a strong distinction between the two types of slaves. It seems to deny the possibility that certain people could ever truly be slaves – even if their bodies are enslaved, their souls remain free, an idea which must have brought a sense of comfort in a harsh world. Through his representation of enslaved Trojan women, Euripides was able to explore the idea that undeserving people might find themselves enslaved through warfare. Although Greeks, including Plato and many other elite members of Greek society, also suffered enslavement through war, piracy or kidnapping, it was much less offensive to depict barbarians suffering this fate. Moreover, as noted earlier, the Trojan war captives had long been a popular subject in Greek literature and art and so were a suitable and familiar subject for tragedy. Once again, however, we must not read these depictions as sympathy for all slaves. As with any slave representation, the depiction of the noble war captive was primarily intended to serve the needs of the master class. As Rabinowitz argues, 'Even if individuals were enslaved as a result of war or raid, they would not necessarily be called slaves because to do so would mean acknowledging that men of the highest rank could be sold into slavery.'[18] As we shall see shortly, this idea is discussed by Aristotle, who seems to claim that slavery is relative: since some people are noble everywhere, even if they are taken in war, they cannot justly be called slaves (*Pol.* 1255a22-40).

The slave speaks: polarities questioned

It has been stressed elsewhere in this book that representations of slaves can reveal much about how the Greeks viewed themselves. By inverting slave ideology, one can go some way in reconstructing what was considered ideal in Greek society: freedom, beauty, intelligence, civilization – all of which contribute to the concept of 'Greekness'. In his characteristic way, Euripides turns all of this on its head, forcing the audience to confront their notions about the meaning and nature of such dichotomies as freedom and slavery, Greek and barbarian, human and animal, even male and female, sometimes all in one character. The ultimate setting for a consideration of these polarities is the tangled aftermath of the Trojan War, where 'the normal ideological ordering of society' has been all but shattered.[19]

In tragedy, and in Euripides' plays in particular, the chaotic aftermath of war allowed both women and slaves a voice not permitted under normal circumstances, providing the audience with an unusual, and doubtless rather unsettling, insight into the 'Other' not found in other genres. Through her words and actions, it is the slave herself who questions the meaning of freedom and slavery: in her response to

Agamemnon's deference to his army, Hecuba famously laments: 'There is no mortal who is free!' (*Hec.* 864). Everyone, even a king, is a slave to something. Yet, now released from the constraints of her former status as a wife and queen, Hecuba appears more free than Agamemnon, successfully plotting the death of Polymestor with no fear of recourse. As Hecuba herself makes abundantly clear, a person who has lost everything has nothing left to lose. This is in contrast to Agamemnon, whose status as the widest-ruling king in Greece ironically forces him to defer to the wishes of the people if he is to retain power. Croally notes that other free characters are sometimes similarly compromised.[20] Cassandra, for instance, refers to the Greek messenger Talthybios as a *latris* ('servant'), while Talthybios himself admits that he conveys his message to Cassandra 'unwillingly' (*Troades* 710). Although the status of messengers in ancient Greece was hardly enviable and so Cassandra's opinion of him is not surprising, even Zeus is said to be servile to Aphrodite, a portrayal which 'questions the confident use of the free/slave polarity' (950).[21]

Although such examples might compel the audience to question whether freedom exists at all, it is not completely true, as Scodel asserts, that 'freedom does not appear in tragedy'.[22] As far as Hecuba is concerned, slavery has given her a sense of freedom she did not enjoy previously. Her partial release from the expectations of a wife and mother is surely one of the reasons why Hecuba sometimes exhibits a much more masculine intelligence and behaviour than we might expect from a woman.[23] This is most evident in her rhetorical prowess.[24] While many reasons for Hecuba's rhetorical skill in the *Hecuba* are possible, it is at least partly attributable to the fact that she has lost the most out of all the Trojan women, including her status as a wife and, arguably, even to some extent her gender.[25] Unlike the other Trojan captives, she is well past her sexual prime and so is considered useless for sexual or child-bearing purposes. Therefore, while her enslavement has released her from the normal concerns of an individual of high-standing (unlike Agamemnon), her lack of any future as a wife and mother has also to a certain extent released her from the concerns of womanhood. She famously speaks with the men as though she is on equal terms with them, to the extent that her heroic speech is virtually indistinguishable from that of the men she converses with.

Yet, in contrast to the seemingly immutable nature of nobility discussed in the previous section, Euripides also explores the idea that a noble nature might be compromised under certain circumstances. During the course of her eponymous play, Hecuba gradually loses grip on her own humanity, which culminates not only in the blinding of Polymestor, but also in the brutal slaying of Polymestor's innocent children, an act which is often compared to Medea's slaying of her own children: while both women feel that they acted out of necessity, they also rejoice in the violence of the act, much as Eurycleia rejoiced in the slaying of the suitors in Homer's *Odyssey*.[26] Although Hecuba's savage actions at the end of the play point to the idea that the savagery of war can brutalize anyone, they might also be indicative of a transition, from war captive to a more typical slave representation, in which she is unable to control her barbarous, slavish urges. This transition is further emphasized by the location of the play, 'the marginal region of the Thracian Chersonese, where Asia turns into Europe'.[27] The psychological and finally physical transformation of Hecuba is particularly interesting, as it suggests that one's natural inclinations are not immutable, that through conditioning a person might fundamentally change from a civilized human being to a more animalistic, inhuman, slavish creature. Indeed, Polymestor prophesies that upon her death Hecuba will become a 'bitch' with fiery eyes (*Hec.* 1265). It has been argued that her metamorphosis represents the 'mutability of mortal fortunes', a prominent theme in Euripides' plays, yet it might also signify to some extent the dehumanization that one undergoes in the transition from free to slave.[28] Even though the epic hero is also sometimes monumentalized with immortality upon his death, Hecuba's immortalization as a bitch 'belongs to shame and monstrosity'.[29]

Another parallel between slaves, barbarians and animals is found in the *Troades*, although here it is denied. Andromache states that not even a mare who has been separated from her mate 'drags the yoke easily', even though the mare is merely a brute beast lacking in speech and useless by comparison (670-2). This contrast would seem to imply that she, Andromache, is certainly not a speechless, unreasoning subhuman creature. By contrast, we have seen elsewhere in Greek literature that barbarians and even war captives might be compared to beasts, particularly with respect to language (or lack of it). As discussed in Chapter 1, for instance, Clytaimestra has trouble understanding Cassandra and compares her speech to the twittering of a swallow (Aesch. *Ag.* 1050-1) and there are similar comparisons in Aristophanes and Herodotos (see Chapter 1.2). Granted, Andromache's words are those of a barbarian slave, but Euripides does seem to be responding to and perhaps questioning ideas which were popular at the time and can be found in earlier tragedy.

In short, we certainly do see in Euripides' plays the more usual image of the world 'divided into two irreconcilable groups'; yet, as Saïd argues, Euripides' presentation of barbarians is often more nuanced than other representations.[30] While the opulence of Troy is frequently reiterated in the plays, as is the Trojans' barbarian ethnicity,

Euripides' plays also at times imply that this simplistic division is 'both incorrect and unhelpful'.[31] In line with Hippocrates, Aristotle, and even Thucydides, Euripides seems to acknowledge gradations of barbarianism. Polymestor is conceivably more barbaric and animalistic than the Trojan women in his comparison to a *tetrapodon*, a word he uses to describe himself, and then again when he threatens to consume the women's flesh and bones like a 'wild beast' (1070-2). The idea of the unparalleled brutality of the Thracians is also seen in Thucydides, who portrays the Thracians as the most barbaric of barbarians. In 'some uncharacteristically personal reflections', Thucydides comments upon the slaughter of schoolchildren by Thracian mercenaries, which he saw as one of the worst crimes of the war (7.29).[32] Hecuba, similarly, implies that the anger of all Thracians is characteristically harsh when she refers to Polymestor's 'boiling and most unconquerable Thracian rage' (1054-5). Euripides, via Hecuba, seems to be drawing upon the idea of the brutish Thracian seen in many other sources, while at the same time implying that she is different, perhaps even that she is a civilized and intelligent Asiatic (see Chapter 2.1 for a discussion of these ethnographic and geographic Greek stereotypes).

Moreover, although some Greek characters, such as Odysseus and Hermione, recall Greek prejudices about uncivilized barbarians, the Trojan women retaliate by demonstrating their own civility and at the same time call into question the Greeks'. While Euripides is clearly aware of prevalent ideas about barbarians, in the same way that he is aware of more typical representations of slaves, he also invites his audience 'to look at them with a critical eye'.[33] It is his barbarian characters who often voice Greek prejudices, as illustrated, for instance, when Medea tells Jason that his marriage to her, a barbarian woman (*barbaron lechos*), 'would be a dishonour to you in old age' (*Med.* 591-2). Moreover, it is Hecuba who voices a stark distinction between the Greeks and the barbarians when she states that 'the barbarian race (*to barbaron ... genos*) will never become a friend to the Greeks, nor could they' (*Hec.* 1199-201). By putting such words in the mouths of barbarians, Euripides challenges the perceived differences between Greeks and barbarians, compelling the audience to consider whether they are natural or conventional. Indeed, Hecuba illustrates herself as benevolent and pious, in contrast to the Greeks, when she reminds Odysseus that she let him go free when he was caught spying on the Trojans and he supplicated her for mercy (*Hec.* 239-47). Even more powerfully, she challenges the Greeks' 'cleverness' (*sophisma*) in religious matters when she questions their sacrifice of a woman (Polyxena) at the tomb of Achilles, 'a place where the sacrifice of a bull is rather more fitting' (261). Human sacrifice is usually associated with barbarians but here, as elsewhere in these plays, the Greeks appear more barbaric than the Trojans.

Euripides was clearly challenging and tampering with the justification of polarities such as slavery and freedom, nature and convention, Greek and barbarian, but what exactly compelled him to do so at this point in time remains a matter of dispute. It is generally assumed that he was responding to contemporaneous intellectual debates, which are identified with 'a heterogeneous group of thinkers called the sophists'.[34] But what of other current events? Are the largely sympathetic representations of war captives a 'pacifist's prayer for peace', as some scholars have argued?[35] Are they meant to problematize and criticize Athenian and Spartan conduct during the Peloponnesian War, or even Athenian imperialist ideology? Do they reflect a general sympathy for the victims of warfare dating at least as far back as Homer? With the exception of the first possibility, the answer is likely a combination of the above. The first possibility, that of pacifism, seems as unlikely as the idea that Euripides was an early abolitionist.[36] Greek culture was both a warrior society and a slave-holding society; a questioning of certain elements of warfare or slavery does not signal a call for pacifism or abolition, no matter how much one might desire to see this in the evidence. To be sure, the Greeks were largely unable to remember a time when they did not have chattel slaves – even the utopian polities of Plato and Aristotle included slaves. As we shall see shortly, Aristotle's concept of natural slavery likewise does not call for an end to slavery but rather offers a justification of a certain kind of slavery (natural) and an implicit criticism of another (conventional). Yet, there is no doubt that Euripides' presentation of the war captive often invokes sympathy and pathos. This is not only suitable for the genre of tragedy, which characteristically invites the audience to contemplate suffering and, more particularly here, the agony of war, it also invokes sympathy for a certain kind of suffering, namely that of the nobility when they are struck low. In short, even though Euripides challenges Greek stereotypes and includes a number of important slave characters in his plays, his perspective is elitist and driven by an ideology which served the master-class.

4.2. Aristotle's natural slave

Outside the vacuum

Where Euripides questions the justification of pervasive ideological polarities, such as Greek/barbarian and slave/free, Aristotle reifies, defends and explains them, arguing that in human society there exist those who are born masters and those who are born slaves. Aristotle claims that one way to resolve questions about the justice of the enslavement of war captives is to define who is naturally suited to slavery and who is not; that is, if a Greek is conquered in warfare and enslaved, his subjection would be unjust because he is by nature free. On the other hand, if a barbarian is conquered and enslaved, his subjection would be just because he is by nature a slave (*Pol.* 1254b16-19). For many scholars, Aristotle's discussion of natural slavery in the first book of the *Politics* has served as the starting (and sometimes end) point for an examination of Greek ideas about slavery. Judging by the primary position of the master/slave dichotomy in his discussion of the essential unions of mankind (along with male/female, husband/wife, and father/children), it is clear that Aristotle saw the master/slave pair as integral to human society. Indeed, rather than beginning his treatment of the fundamental unions with a discussion of male and female, as might be expected, he begins with the words: 'First let us speak of master and slave' (1253b14-15). Yet Aristotle is not concerned so much with slavery as with politics. In order to define who should rule, he must also determine who should not rule, hence his primary interest in the ruler and the ruled. Once Aristotle defines these, he is free to 'engage in the real business of politics'.[37] In other words, the importance of a natural and political hierarchy to Aristotle's *Politics* presupposes the importance of arguing for the existence of, and defining, the natural slave. Since it is on the grounds of clarifying his political theory that Aristotle seeks to attain 'some better treatment [of the union between master and slave] than presently exists', his discussion of natural slavery should not be considered a defence of slavery *per se*, but should be viewed, rather, as providing support for his political theory (1253b16-18). The natural slave has practical significance to the treatise, which is concerned with the practical knowledge of politics. In short, although Aristotle does indeed provide the most comprehensive analysis of slavery extant from ancient Greece, his discussion of slavery should not be considered either exhaustive or definitive.

As demonstrated most notably by Euripides, questions relating to slavery were being discussed well before Aristotle's time. Aristotle himself recognizes this when he refers to 'those who take the opposite view' (1255a3). Unfortunately, he does not describe what exactly this view consisted of or who was a proponent of it.[38] Alcidamas, a student of Gorgias, is most often cited as a possibility. Aristotle refers to him elsewhere and seems to have assumed in the *Politics* that the sophist's position on slavery was so well known it need not be restated (cf. *Rhet.* 1373b2-3). The scholiast on the *Rhetoric* claims that Alcidamas argued: 'God has left everyone free; nature has made no one a slave.' This statement, however, has proved to be problematic. Although it is sometimes taken as the earliest explicit criticism of slavery, since it is part of Alcidamas' *Messeniaca*, it is likely a reference to the Messenians (helots), and so to fellow Greeks.[39]

Judging by Aristotle's counter-attack on those who take the opposite view to him (1253b15-23), namely that slavery is unnatural and morally unjustifiable, there was clearly an opposition to which Aristotle was responding, however, it is exceedingly difficult to pin down any known person from ancient Greece who was a critic of the institution of slavery. It is generally believed that he was responding to a small group of intellectuals, or sophists, who were 'marked by sceptical inquiry into traditional beliefs and practices'.[40] In this context, a questioning of slavery might have been little more than a sophistic exercise. Something similar might also be said of Euripides' plays where, as we have seen, even sympathetic portrayals of slaves should be understood within the context of the characters in question and the requirements of the genre. As Aristotle argues, the best tragedies are those that arouse the emotions of 'pity or fear' (*Poetics* 1452b), both of which are well-represented by depicting the enslavement of the Trojan women. Not only was slavery never seriously challenged in the Greco-Roman world, the previous chapters have shown that slavery was, on the contrary, widely accepted and, judging by the typically derogatory and two-dimensional representations of slaves, the Greeks by and large sought to justify slavery by representing slaves in a very restricted and self-serving way, namely, as physically, intellectually, and morally inferior to their masters. It might even be argued that other Greek representations of slaves are no more realistic than Aristotle's, as they are all self-serving. As slave-holders, the Greeks had no real interest in depicting the reality of slavery and, unlike the slave-holding American South and other later slave-societies, we lack evidence from the slaves themselves.

So, what does Aristotle's natural slave have in common with representations of slaves in other sources? As stated above, Aristotle was not particularly concerned with the reality of slavery so much as with the topic of politics and, more specifically, different types of rule. This does not mean, however, that he was unaffected by popular ideas about slaves and slavery which had pervaded Greek thinking for centuries before him. Yet some scholars argue that Aristotle's representation of natural slavery should be separated out from slavery as it actually existed in the Greek world – any overlap of ideas should not be viewed as a 'false consciousness': 'The theory does not explicitly or otherwise pretend to be a theory directly or indirectly concerned with contemporary slavery.'[41] By the same token, Millett sees the overlap, such as the idea that barbarians are slaves by nature, as part of a conscious method of persuasion meant to win over his audience, in the same way as a court speech: 'Essential to the persuasive process is Aristotle's grounding of his philosophical exposition of slavery in realities familiar to his audience.'[42]

While there is little doubt that Aristotle's work is grounded in its socio-cultural context (he was, after all, part of a culture and so can hardly be deemed unaffected by his intellectual, artistic and social surroundings), the overlap between his discussion of slavery and ideas found in other sources was almost surely more influenced by ideology than familiar, empirical realities. Aristotle himself seems well aware that the real situation was much more nuanced, yet he explains that he is concerned primarily with free people ('natural masters') who are 'in the best state of both body and soul' (1254a). This, in turn, implies that he is primarily concerned with the *ideal* natural slave, and further, that he also recognized this type of person probably did not exist (or was very rare). In order to produce a 'theory', he had largely to ignore the complexity of the real situation, which has left his treatment of slavery open to a significant, and perhaps rather unfair, amount of criticism.

One example of the influence of popular ideology upon Aristotle's work is his connection between slaves and barbarians. Millett claims that, 'Here, at least, Aristotle's thinking represented a reality of Athenian slavery.'[43] As we have seen, Athenian sources do often associate slavery with barbarians and, since barbarians were generally considered inferior to Greeks, they were thought to be the quintessential slaves. Yet, determining whether the *majority* of slaves in Greek city-states were, in fact, non-Greek is not so easy. It is often assumed, based upon representations of slaves in Greek literature and art, that most slaves were non-Greek, however, the evidence for an overwhelmingly foreign ethnicity of actual slaves is problematic and inconclusive. As evidence for the barbarian ethnicity of most slaves, Millett refers to Theopompos, who allegedly wrote that the Chians were the first of the Greeks to use non-Greek slaves (6.265b-c).[44] Although this certainly does indicate that the Greeks used foreign slaves (which is not in dispute), it does not imply that the *majority* of slaves in the Greek world were barbarians. Another source of evidence for the foreign provenance of Greece's slaves are slave names and ethnics recorded in inscriptions, yet this also proves problematic. While some inscriptions, such as the Attic Stelai (*IG* I³ 421-30), include foreign ethnics along with several of the slaves' names, the majority of inscriptions do not.[45] This means that we must rely upon the names themselves to identify ethnicity, which creates a number of issues, not least the use of a name as evidence for ethnic origin (see Chapter 1.3). An even more difficult issue, however, is that out of the hundreds of extant names found for slaves in the inscriptions the vast majority are Greek and so give no indication of foreign ethnicity. This does not mean that all slaves with Greek names were Greek, but based upon this type of evidence it is exceedingly difficult to demonstrate that the *majority* of slaves in Greek city-states were, in fact, barbarians. Although it is unlikely that by the Classical period Athenians enslaved their fellow Athenians, they might well have used other Greeks as slaves – indeed, there is some epigraphic and literary evidence to support this (cf. Thuc. 3.68, 4.48, 5.84-116).[46] In short, while Aristotle was to a certain extent reflecting an empirical reality when he made his natural slave barbarian, this identification was useful for his argument that some people were naturally suited to slavery and, considering his contention that barbarians were too slavish to rule themselves properly, likely was more influenced by Greek ideology than with what he saw around him (1252b; cf. Eur. *Iph. Aul.* 1400).

One of the primary reasons why Aristotle thought that barbarians were naturally suited to slavery was because of their geographical and climactic environments, which he considered unsuitable for the development of natural masters. In an argument reminiscent of Hippocrates' *Airs*, and more indirectly with Hecuba's opinion of Thracians discussed in the previous section, Aristotle sees climate and location as integral to the formation of the human character. In Book 7, regions with cold climates (i.e. parts of Europe) are said to produce people who are spirited but deficient in intelligence and skill, while people reared in warmer climates (i.e. parts of Asia) are said to have skill and intelligence but are lacking in spirit. Europeans inhabiting colder climates are said to be comparatively free because of their spiritedness, yet they lack the capacity to rule their neighbours. On the other hand, Asiatics, because of their servile natures, are said to be naturally predisposed to being ruled and living like slaves (1327b24-9). In short, neither are natural masters, and so they are natural slaves. Not surprisingly, the role of natural master is reserved for the Greeks who, because of their intermediate geographical location, have the spiritedness, intelligence, and skill necessary to rule themselves and others (1327b29-34). As we saw in Chapter 1, this sounds a great deal like the Aristotelian *Physiognomonica*, which considers the inhabitants of too cold or too hot climates as physically and/or intellectually deficient. The idea that deficient (i.e. non-Greek) regions produce 'culturally deformed' people might even be extended to monsters and date back to Homer, who situates the primitive cyclopes in a land far from Greece, where they live in caves and have no laws, government or agriculture.[47] It is no coincidence that the Greeks connected both monsters and deficient human beings (i.e. slaves and barbarians) with foreign lands, since both were considered to be comparatively crude and uncivilized.

Aristotle's perception of Asiatic barbarians as slavish is also likely influenced by the view, which became increasingly popular in the decades following the Persian Wars, that the Persians in particular were soft and slavish. As seen in earlier chapters, this idea is used to great comic effect by Aristophanes, but can also be found in the works of fourth-century writers such as Xenophon, Plato and Isocrates. Xenophon, in his *Cyropaedia*, accuses the Persians of *malakia* ('softness') and argues that, in line with the general Persian populace who 'follow their leaders', the Persian elite were becoming 'ever more cowardly' (8.15, 27). Similarly, Isocrates in his *Panegyricos* accuses the Persians of being 'better trained for slavery than our own *oiketai*' (4.150) and Plato claims that later Persian rulers were coddled by 'women and eunuchs' (*Laws* 695a). In each of these cases, the decline of Persian culture is connected with the Persians' tyrannical form of government, which in the Greek mind made everyone, save the ruler, subject to one man.

Although Aristotle, unlike these writers, is not explicit that he is thinking specifically of Persians when he discusses foreign government, his contention that non-Greeks suffer from inferior systems of government which facilitate their perceived slavishness might be related to ideas about the Persian monarchy which were popular in the fourth century (Aristotle was not Athenian, but he lived in Athens and was clearly influenced by Athenian ideology). He argues, for instance, that barbarian governments are inferior to those found in Greek city-states because they are pseudo-tyrannical; that is, the subjects are willing but the ruler governs 'according to his own fancy' (1295a10-17). On the other hand, he posits, 'no freeman willingly endures such a government' (1295a22). Since 'the excellence of a citizen must be relative to his constitution', if a state has an inferior form of government then the citizens of that state must also be inferior to the same degree (1276b30-2).

These sentiments are also found in the fourth-century Athenian political speeches. Isocrates claims: The soul of a state is nothing other than its *politeia* ... and thus each person fares in accordance to the constitution under which he lives' (2.14). This, in turn, reflects the idea in Plato's *Menexenos* that *politeia* 'is the nurse of men' (238c). The Athenians by and large equated their own particular *politeia* with freedom, while they equated with slavery subjection under one ruler, the antithesis to democracy. Hyperides, in the political context of the funeral speech, explains that: 'There cannot be complete happiness without *autonomia* ("independence"). For men to be happy, they must be ruled by the voice of the law, not the threats of one man' (6.25).[48]

Similarly, Demosthenes, in a speech against oligarchies, argues that: 'The few can never be well-disposed to the many, nor those who covet power to those who have chosen a life of equality' (15.18). Because the Persians, and later the Macedonians who were the primary inspiration for such fourth-century rhetoric, did not rule themselves individually but were subject to kings, even those who were in fact very powerful, as were both the Persians and the Macedonians, were nonetheless depicted as no better than slaves. In view of this ideology, it is no wonder that Aristotle insisted barbarians are all slavish and have an inferior type of government. As stated above, this idea had practical significance to his political treatise.

Another area where Aristotle's concept of the natural slave appears to be influenced by Greek ideology is his conflation of slaves with manual labourers more generally. Like most other Greek sources, Aristotle's work is elitist and views all labourers as slavish. Aristotle's ideal *polis* is governed by those who have *euporia* ('plentiful resources'), which presumably means wealthy men who do not have to work for a living (1329a19-20). On the other hand, the *banausoi* ('craftsmen') and others who are said to have no share in virtue are denied a share in governing the state (1329a20-2). Earlier on, Aristotle had argued: 'The multitude of *banausoi* and market-place people' live an 'inferior life' because their occupations have 'no share in virtue' (1319a26-9). Indeed, 'the best form of state,' Aristotle asserts, 'will not make a *banausos* a citizen' because 'no man can practice excellence who is living the life of a *banausos* or a hired labourer' (1278a8, 21-2).

As discussed in Chapter 2, the idea that craftsmen are slavish is not uncommon in Greek sources. In some respects, Plato anticipates Aristotle here. For instance, the Stranger in the *Statesman* asserts that no one working in a servile position, and this includes all labourers, should have a share in ruling, an argument with which the Platonic Socrates agrees (289c-290c). This is in line with Plato's ideal polis in the *Republic*, where labourers, who are said to have strong bodies 'sufficient for toil' but weak minds, are the lowest order of the city and do not take part in its governance (371e). The desire to exclude labourers from politics to some extent draws upon the 'science' of physiognomy, which connected the state of the body with the state of the mind. As discussed in Chapter 2, Greek ideology reasoned that if a person spent the majority of his time performing menial labour, both his body and his mind would suffer, which would consequently make him unworthy for statesmanship.

It is worth noting once again that Aristotle's natural slave is stooped and strong with a stunted mind – like a domesticated animal, the natural slave has reason sufficient only to perform his necessary tasks

145

and nothing more (1254b28-31). Greek art likewise illustrates this 'hierarchy made visible on the body', where both labourers and slaves are shown squatting or sitting on the ground: if the 'athlete's body is upright, as Aristotle says the bodies of free men should be, the labourer's body is doubled over, folded in two'.[49] These ideas about labourers and their conflation with views of slaves rely heavily upon elite prejudices against those who had to work for a living. It was evidently difficult for men whose physical activity was confined to athletic pursuits and who were privileged with the time, leisure, and finances to enjoy a higher education, to imagine that someone lacking the means to develop equally their bodies and their minds could rule as well as they. The point seems to be that 'just as the grape will not flourish if deprived of viniculture, neither will a human being achieve full command of his potential for reason' if deprived of the appropriate environmental, cultural and political factors.[50] As discussed in Chapter 2, there was a strong differentiation made between the pursuits of the elite and those of labourers and slaves. Although labourers and slaves have strength, their strength is menial and not to be extolled. The upper classes should also be physically fit, but their fitness is confined to the sphere of elite pursuits, namely athletics, while their minds are trained in philosophy and politics. Aristotle also associates them with other 'bodily excellences' such as beauty, health, and even stature (*megethos*) (Arist. *Rhet.* 1.5.4; cf. *Pol.* 1255b35-7).

One might parallel these ideas with images of free men on tombstones, where they are sometimes shown as comparatively taller and more beautiful than their servants (see Chapter 3.1). This type of visualization is founded not only in a social and economic hierarchy but also in the idea that those who spend their lives occupied in menial pursuits manifest their inferiority physically. Since these perceptions are rooted in ideology, their empirical reality is a moot point. The Greeks must have recognized that not all labourers were slaves, but the fact that many Greeks took pay for their work and undertook the same types of occupations as slaves (such as crafts, trade and hired help) made them as good as slaves in the eyes of those to whom they provided their services.[51] Some sources, such as the Old Oligarch, claim that the common people looked like slaves due to their clothing and general appearance, which suggests that labourers dressed alike regardless of their status (Ps. Xen. *Ath. Pol.* 1.10).[52] While free labourers did in practice take part in the governance of the democratic state, political theorists, notably Plato and Aristotle, pointedly denied them this right in their utopic *poleis* and thus reflected an elitism and prejudice frequently found in classical sources (cf. Pl. *Statesman* 289e-290a; Arist. *Pol.* 1278a22-4, 1319a20-31, 1329a20-5). As the Old Oligarch writes, 'In every land, it is the best element who is opposed to democracy' (Ps.-Xen. *Ath. Pol.* 1.5).

Another area where Aristotle converges with popular ideology is in his conflation of slaves and animals. Although he differentiates between human beings and lower animals (*thêriou*), the latter of which he associates primarily with the use of the body (*Pol.* 1254b16-19), he seems to struggle with determining to which category slaves belong. While he recognizes that slaves are not merely brute beasts because they can at least apprehend reason, whereas animals are subservient only to feelings, he also argues that slaves are *like* domestic animals ('our animals') insofar as both provide necessary bodily service (1254b25-8). It would seem, then, that he saw slaves as not quite human and not quite animal, but somewhere in between, and that he considered the formation of the slave as attributable both to nature and to nurture, or 'use'. Yet, he seems to lean towards nature when he argues (infamously) that because a slave, unlike a free person, is 'capable of belonging to another' and of being used like an animal, nature *wants* to distinguish physically between free and slave, essentially making the slave 'look the part' of a service animal – i.e. strong and stooped (1254b21-31).

As was discussed in Chapter 2, the difficulty in defining and categorizing the slave would seem to lie not so much in the intrusion of reality (i.e. that slaves are human beings and as human beings do not necessarily conform to the ideology) but rather in the institution of slavery itself. While political theorists such as Aristotle wanted to recognize slaves as 'animate tools' (*empsuchon organon*: Arist. *Pol.* 1253b28-9; *NE* 1161b4) or animals, to the extent that Aristotle thought that slavishness should manifest itself physically, as slave-owners themselves they also wanted slaves to have the types of human qualities which were desirable, indeed necessary, in slaves: trustworthiness, loyalty, and enough reason to perform their tasks well. This is why Aristotle's natural slave is both animalistic and human.

A complementary source is Plato's *Laws* in which views of slaves and their corresponding treatment are discussed. Where Aristotle sees animalistic and human components in every natural slave, however, Plato separates them into different types of slaves. In Book 6, the Athenian states that there are two minds about slaves: some masters consider their slaves to be better and more trustworthy than their own sons, while others claim that, because the soul of a slave is not sound (*hugiês*), slaves should be trusted by no one (776e). While the former treats his slave well, which presumably means that he treats him humanely, the latter treats his slave as though he has the nature of a brute beast and accordingly goads and whips him (777a). Although

147

Plato's *Laws* represents two different types of slaves and masters, when combined they make the ideal slave and the ideal master. What might be called the extreme positive view, namely that slaves can be good and be the preservers of their master's households, fulfils the master's wish of a loyal, trustworthy and useful slave. This view also incorporates a master who seems to recognize that by treating his slave well, his slave will serve him well. The extreme negative view, on the other hand, fulfils the master's desire that the slave deserves to be treated like an animal because he is subhuman and in doing so, the master necessarily reminds his slave (and himself) of the slave's animalistic subservience. Both views reinforce and justify slavery as a useful institution which relies upon people who are naturally suited to slavery. Indeed, just as ideally in every slave there should be qualities which make him useful and suited to slavery, every master should treat his slave humanely and like an animal, since the slave is both human and animal. When viewed in this way, Plato differs little from Aristotle, since both incorporate the human and animalistic components of the slave.

As we saw in Chapter 1, the very names given to slaves reflect this dichotomy: while some slaves might be given names that denigrate them, such as those referring to foreign ethnicity, animals, or slavish occupations, others might be given names denoting characteristics desired in slaves, such as loyalty, goodness, self-control or preservation. Furthermore, as seen in Chapter 2 and 3, Greek art represents dichotomous views of slaves: sometimes slaves are shown as ugly, short or tattooed, while other times slaves are hardly distinguishable from their masters, identifiable only by their menial, but loyal, service. Neither view is normative or realistic, but rather illustrates an ideology that pervades all the genres. While Aristotle's adherence to this ideology has been seen as a failing in an otherwise brilliant thinker, we must not underestimate the fact that Aristotle was himself a slave holder, in a slave society, speaking to what was surely an audience of elite slave owners much like himself.[53]

In short, although Aristotle's concept of natural slavery is in no way definitive, it is important in part because it provides the only comprehensive treatment of slavery which has survived from ancient Greece. Over the course of only a few pages, Aristotle's discussion of the natural slave neatly encapsulates, reinforces, and even embraces ideas about class relations, pseudo-science (physiognomy and environmental determinism) and Greek cultural and political superiority which are usually only found scattered amongst other written and artistic sources from ancient Greece. Aristotle, therefore, brings us full circle – he might be one of the latest sources for ideas about slaves from the Classical period, but he nevertheless upholds what had been the status quo for at least a century before him. The very fact that he insisted upon the idea that some people were naturally suited to slavery, even while recognizing that nature often fails in her task of making obvious distinctions between slave and free, and even in the face of seeds of criticism about the justification of slavery, illustrates how important this concept was to Aristotle and, in his view, to the ordering of Greek society. In Athens, at least, the fact that Aristotle readily accepted 'within the family a form of power that [he] considered an aberration in the *polis* ... namely, tyrannical or despotic power' is a potent and revealing manifestation of the importance of slavery in ancient Greece.[54]

Notes

Introduction

1. Unlike the City Dionysia, which was held later in the year during the sailing season and was thus attended by more foreigners and foreign delegates (especially during the period of the Athenian Empire), the Lenaia was a smaller festival attracting primarily, if not exclusively, those who were already resident in Attica. See Sommerstein (2002), 6-9 for a discussion of the Lenaia.

2. For the Athenian cult of Sabazios and the god's Asiatic origin, see Sommerstein (1983), 152.

3. For a comprehensive treatment of barbarians in Greek drama, see Hall (1989a); Long (1986).

4. For the origins and worship of Sabazios in Athens, see Long (1986), 30-2, 35-6, 39-41, 46-7. Cf. Sommerstein (1983), 152-3.

5. Demosthenes (18.258-60), for instance, uses Aeschines' mother's alleged association with this cult to tarnish her and her son's reputations.

6. See Fragiadakis (1986) for a comprehensive list of slave names found in ancient Greek sources. Although there are a number of names indicating foreign origin, there are many more which are Greek. For the difficulty in determining origin based upon names, however, see Chapters 1 and 4.

7. Finley (1959), 150.

8. See Pritchett (1956), 276-8 for a discussion of the prices of slaves recorded on the Attic stelai. Pritchett concludes that the average price for a slave in these inscriptions was 174 drachmas. When compared to fourth-century literary references, the cost of slaves recorded on the Attic Stelai is 'somewhat lower'; however, as Pritchett points out, the literary references are not only later, they are also to skilled artisans, who seem to have commanded significantly higher prices (up to 1000 drachmas for a skilled slave; see Xen. *Mem.* 2.5.2). At any rate, if the average worker's income was one drachma per day in the fifth century (based upon the Erechtheion Accounts), even 174 drachmas was a high price to pay, especially when the cost of maintaining the slave is also taken into account. For the difficulties in determining average wages in ancient Athens,

see Loomis (1998), 233-4, who argues that one drachma per day seems high for the fifth century, but rather low for the fourth century. For a comparison between slave and free hired labour, see Silver (2006), 257-63.

9. Campbell (1985), 15.

10. Campbell (1985), 15.

11. See above, n. 8.

12. Andreau (2002), 129.

13. Joshel and Murnaghan (1998), 2.

14. Finley (1998; originally published in 1980).

15. The best comparative study of slavery to date is Orlando Patterson's *Slavery and Social Death*.

16. For a discussion of the difficulty of defining 'ideology', see Strauss (1990), 101-3.

17. Goff (2004), 9-10.

18. Goff (2004), 10.

19. See duBois (2003), ch. 5 for a discussion of 'Slavery as Metaphor'. Translation adapted from Dubois.

20. Although Herodotos and Aristotle appear to have spent a great deal of time at Athens, their focus is not restricted to Athens but often includes other Greek *poleis*, and Greek culture more generally.

1. The Language of Slavery

1. Finley (1960), 146; Garlan (1988), 20.

2. There is a great deal of dispute about the date of the Xenophontic *Athenian Constitution* but it was most likely composed in either the 420s or the 410s BC. For a discussion of the controversy and the internal evidence see Osborne (2004), 1-15.

3. Harvey (1988), 48.

4. Kyrtatas (2001), 1056.

5. Garlan (1988), 20.

6. For other, less common, words for 'slave', see Kyrtatas (2001), 1056-61.

7. Tovar (1972), 318-25.

8. Raaflaub (2004), 19.

9. Austin and Vidal-Naquet (1977), 44.

10. Beringer (1982), 47.

11. Raaflaub (2004), 20.

12. Raaflaub (2004), 20.

13. *Douleion eidos* (*Od.* 24.252-3); *doulê* (*Il.* 3.409, *Od.* 4.12); *doulosunê* (*Od.*

22.423); *doulion êmar* (*Il.* 6.462-3, *Od.* 14.340, 17.323). For further discussion, see Raaflaub (2004), 24-6.

14. Willetts (1967), 39-40.

15. The political concept of freedom seems to have developed later than the political concept of slavery. Raaflaub places this development in the time of Solon, when slavery, as debt-bondage, had become a major concern in Greek society. Prior to this, while the Greeks, as slave-owners, understood the loss of freedom and had a terminology to describe this, the value of one's own personal freedom seems to have been of little interest, primarily because it was taken for granted, at least by the upper levels of society who are responsible for the majority of the literature. At this time, the loss of one's freedom was relatively rare and was usually suffered by the 'silent' members of society – the women and children. From what can be determined from early Greek texts (such as Homer and Hesiod), the victors would not usually enslave the men but kill or ransom them. It was probably not until Greeks were being enslaved by each other at a rate and consistency which became alarming to a large number of people that the idea of freedom became 'a battle cry', laying the groundwork for the importance of the concept of freedom from this time on. Raaflaub (2004), 47. For a detailed discussion of the development of the concept of 'freedom', see Raaflaub (2004), 29-57.

16. For a definition of class in the context of ancient Greece, see Thalmann (1988), 4.

17. Tovar (1972), 324.

18. For a thorough discussion of Persian influence on Greek culture, see Miller (2004).

19. The idea that Persian society was in gradual decline is also found in the works of Xenophon, Plato and Isocrates, all of whom generally agree that from the time of Darius the Persians were on a 'downward slope of decadence' (Pl. *Laws* 697c). For a discussion, see Briant (2002), 193-210, who argues that this view was due more to ideology than to historical reality.

20. Cartledge (1993), 136.

21. While the context is different from the *Anabasis*, Xenophon draws a similar connection in his *Cyropaedia*, when he compares the treatment of the Persian servant class to that of animals: 'Whenever there was an expedition, [Cyrus] would lead [the servants] to water, just as he did beasts of burden' (8.1.44).

22. Garlan (1988), 53.

23. Wiedemann (1987), 13.

24. Bradley (2000), 110.

25. In Plato's *Phaedo* the adjective *andrapodôdês* ('slavish') is used similarly to express a brutish, animalistic quality. Socrates argues that virtue without wisdom is *andrapodôdês* and is not really true virtue at all but a 'painted illusion (*skiagraphia*) ... neither healthy nor true' (69b).

26. Bradley (2000), 111.

27. Bradley (2000), 110-11. See Weiler (2003), 22-4 for a discussion of slave markets.

28. See Bradley (2000), 111.

29. Daly (1961), 21-2. Daly posits that, because of the prominence of Isis in the story and its negative view of hellenic learning, the *Life* was written by a Greek-speaking Egyptian in the first century AD. See also Hopkins (1993), 11 n. 14 for a detailed list of references on the dating of the *Life of Aesop*.

30. Lissarrague (2000), 132 states that Aesop himself 'can be placed in the sixth century and his date of death in 564 BC'.

31. The section numbers and translations are from Daly (1961).

32. Burnard (2001), 325.

33. Gschnitzer (1976), 16: 'Wie *dêmotês* der Angehörige einer Gemeinde, so ist *oiketês* der Angehörige eines Hauses.'

34. The term *oikeus* is found once in tragedy, where it does suggest a slave (Soph. *OT* 756). This man is grouped with the *dmôes* in the next line.

35. An exceptional use seems to be Herodotos' reference to the Cretan Anaxilaos' 'servant' Micythos as an *oiketês*. While this man might have been a slave, he was also put in charge of Rhegion, which calls into question whether this man was actually a slave (7.170).

36. Garlan (1988), 21.

37. The word occurs fourteen times in the *Oeconomicus*. It is actually more common in Xenophon's *Memorabilia* and *Cyropaedia*, where it occurs twenty-three and eighteen times; however, the *Oeconomicus* is considerably shorter than these works.

38. For a discussion of slaves as witnesses to household events, see Hunter (1994), 85, where she argues that 'privacy was unthinkable in the Athenian household'.

39. Hunter (1994), 75.

40. Fischer-Hansen (2000), 91: The term *ergasterion* offers 'no descriptions in a physical sense, and ... is often used simply of a habitation where work of different categories was practiced, or even of just a group of workmen'.

41. See Golden (1985), 91 n. 3 for further discussion and examples.

42. See Dover (1989), 85.

43. It has been suggested by both LSJ and P. Chantraine's *Dictionnaire*

étymologique de la langue grecque III (Paris, 1974) that when *pais* is used for a son or daughter it relates to the father, while *teknon* (also 'child') relates to the mother. There is plenty of evidence, however, that this was not always the case. For references, see Golden (1985), 91 n. 1.

44. See Klees (1975), 30 n. 123.

45. Quotation from Golden (1985), 100.

46. Quotation is from Fisher (1992), 493. For a discussion of the definition of *hybris*, see MacDowell (1976), 14-31. For a thorough treatment of the topic, see Fisher (1992).

47. See Golden (1985), 102-3 for further discussion.

48. Wiedemann (1987), 25.

49. Bäbler (1998), 26.

50. Wiedemann (1987), 25: 'It might be worth bearing in mind that, given the low life-expectancy, a large proportion of slaves (as of the population at large) actually were children.'

51. Harrison (1998), 1. See also Finley (1954), especially 256-8. Cartledge (2001), 307, however, contends that Herodotos 'was more concerned to stress differences of mores and customs, especially religious and sexual'.

52. Mitchell (2007), 20 and n. 54.

53. Davies (1993), 12: Language 'created an equation between "Greek", or "Greek-speaker", and "civilized" so strong that even the Roman conquest of the Eastern Mediterranean barely broke it'.

54. Mitchell (2007), 19: 'The point was not that the Hellenes did share cultural traits, but that they thought and said that they did.'

55. Finley (1954), 257.

56. The perception that foreign languages sounded like babble was not exclusive to the Greeks. Herodotos claims that the Egyptians also called those who did not speak their language *barbaroi*, but does not provide the actual word they used (2.158.5). Harrison (1998), 1 notes further that this idea also occurs in the Arabic root *ae-ja-ma*, which means variously 'speaking incorrect Arabic, dumb, speechless, barbarian, non-Arab, foreigner, alien, Persian'.

57. See Harrison (1998), 2-4 for a discussion of Herodotos' seemingly limited knowledge of foreign languages. Themistocles, who learned Persian after his expulsion from Athens, provides a rare example of a bilingual Greek. Cf. Thuc. 1.138; Plut. *Them.* 29.3.

58. See Davies (2002) for a discussion of Greek views of dialects. Davies notes that, while non-Attic dialects are made fun of in Attic comedy, they are never compared to the sounds of animals (166). For a discussion of Greek views of primitive humans, see Gera (2003), 112 and n. 2.

59. The classic example of representing barbarian societies as the inverse of Greek is Herodotos' account of the Egyptians (2.35-6).

60. Sommerstein (1987), 307 suggests that this might be because he is talking to the swallows. Regardless, comparisons between barbarian speech and animals sounds are also found in other Greek sources.

61. Hartog (1988), 151.

62. See Gera (2003), 185-7.

63. For a discussion of the Greek diet, see Flaceliere (1965), 168-73. For a broader study of food in antiquity, see Wilkins and Hill (2006).

64. See Harrison (1998), 6-7 for a discussion of the hazy distinction between dialect and language, both of which are referred to as *glôssa*.

65. The most extensive studies to date are Hall (1989a) and Long (1986). Also useful is Saïd (2002).

66. See Colvin (1999), 49: 'Attic tragedy follows the Homeric precedent in not permitting the representation of dialect or foreign language.'

67. For a discussion of how foreigners are depicted in tragedy, see Hall (1989a), 117-21.

68. See West (1987), 277 for an examination of this unique character. Not only does he break into an *aria* instead of 'following the conventional procedures of a tragic newsbringer', he sings a monody, which is normally sung only by important characters.

69. The Skythian language seems to have been especially grating to the Greek ear. Athenaeus quotes a fragment, probably from the poet Parmenon, in which drunken speech is equated with the speech of Skythians (5.221a). See Hall (1989b), 40.

70. The word Chrysis uses is the vocative *dusmore*, which literally means 'ill-fated'.

71. For instance, Herodotos' lengthy description of Skythian burial practices (at least those involving royalty) does not refer to any vocal mourning – in fact, this description gives the impression that Skythian funerals were carried out in silence (4.71).

72. This might be partly due to the fact that the Chorus consists of old men. In Greek society, females, boys and old men were all considered susceptible to a lack of *sôphrosunê*. See McNiven (2000), 83 who argues: 'The distinction was not merely between Man and Woman, but between Man, i.e. freeborn, adult Greek (Athenian) male, and Others.' Old men might be considered Others because they are past their prime.

73. Stears (1998), 115 refers to some early Greek pots of the Geometric period, which include on their handles clay women with their arms lifted to

their heads and 'dashes of brown paint on their white-slip cheeks to indicate laceration'.

74. For further discussion, see Hall (1989a), 44.

75. Colvin (1999), 77. The slave does refer to Asiatic dirges during the first part of his speech (1390).

76. In his detailed analysis of the Attic comedies, Colvin (1999), 294 concludes that using barbarized Greek in texts 'was clearly a common and accepted feature of comic drama'.

77. For further examples, see Hall (1989b), 38-9.

78. See Hall (1989b), 39-40.

79. Hall (1989b), 39.

80. For further detail, see Colvin (1999), 290-1; Sommerstein (1994), 221; Hall (1989b), 39-40.

81. Hunter (1994), 3.

82. For a discussion of the Skythian Archers, see Hunter (1994) 145-9.

83. 'Jin, native of Guinea', Deerfield, Mass., 1732. Quoted by Dillard (1992), 62.

84. Recorded by Daniel P. Horsmanden, New York, 1741. Quoted by Dillard (1992), 63.

85. Stowe (1979), 97.

86. American colonial slave traders usually came from the lowest orders of society and were often impoverished ex-prisoners or criminals. See Martin and Spurrell (1962), xiv. The use of phonetic spelling for the words of slaves was in style during Stowe's time. This continued through to the twentieth century and is evident in transcripts of interviews with ex-slaves. For an online source of transcripts compiled between 1936-8 see: http://xroads.virginia.edu/~hyper/wpa/wpahome.html (accessed 18 December 2009). The entire collection is published by Rawick (1972).

87. For Skythian names, see Rostovtzeff (1922), 36-40.

88. Willi (2003), 219.

89. For further examples of criticism of slave speech, see Ar. *Birds* 62; *Peace* 97-8.

90. Patterson (1982), 79: 'In all societies the slave was considered a degraded person.'

91. Suda *Lex.* K 877.1: *Katachysmata*; Pollux 3.77. See also Cohen (2000), 145-6; Ehrenberg (1962), 169.

92. The literal meaning of the word *katachusma* is 'that which is poured over' (LSJ).

93. In this scene, however, Aristophanes reverses the normal order of things by having the wife offer to perform the ceremony upon the god Wealth.

94. Patterson (1982), 54.

95. See Patterson (1982), 55.

96. Pyrrhias: *IG* II^2 1553.26-7. Paideusis: Description of a wet-nurse on an Attic gravestone, 4th century BC, Athens, National Museum 378. The stone actually reads '*Paideusis titthê chrêstê*' ('Paideusis was a useful nurse'), a typical formula for slave epitaphs (see Chapter 3.1 for further discussion of tombstones for wet-nurses). Nicon of Cimon: Athenian Naval Catalogue 1.18, in Meritt (1927), 363.

97. This is discussed by Thomas (2000), 82-3.

98. For a detailed examination of this dialectic, see Baxter (1992).

99. The main inscription dates to the late fifth century, *IG* I^3 474-5, 409/8 BC, *IG* I^3 476, 408/7 BC. Cf. Lambert (2000), 157-60 for a further possible addition. I am using the line numbers published in *The Erechtheum*, Harvard University Press, 1927 (text by Caskey, Fowler, Paton, Stevens). Aeschines: 14.1.15; Apollodoros: 13.2.29; Timocrates: 14.1.1-2. For a discussion of the workmen and their statuses, see Randall (1953), 199-210.

100. The most useful resource for slave names is Fragiadakis (1986). The *Lexicon of Greek Personal Names* (*LGPN*) is also an invaluable resource and is now online at www.lgpn.ox.ac.uk/online/index.html (accessed December 2009).

101. In this speech Demosthenes also claims that Aeschines' father was once a shackled slave who worked as a schoolteacher and that Aeschines' mother had worked as a prostitute (18.129). For other, less direct, attacks on Aeschines' parents, see Dem. 19.199-200, 249, 281, which was delivered about thirteen years earlier while Aeschines' father was still alive. Aeschines makes a similar personal attack against Demosthenes when he accuses his grandmother, perhaps accurately, of having been Scythian (3.172). This kind of character assassination was a well-known technique used by orators to denigrate their opponents. For a recent analysis of character defamation in the speeches of Demosthenes and Aeschines, see Worman (2008), 213-74.

102. The adjective *glaukos* has various translations, such as 'gleaming', and can also mean 'greyish-blue'. Athena's epithet *glaukôpis* is common in Homer (cf. *Il.* 1.206).

103. Fragiadakis (1986), 41.

104. As per Fragiadakis (1986).

105. Ehrenberg (1962), 172.

106. Braund and Tsetskhladze (1989), 122.

107. While slaves are identified by their first names alone, citizens are identified by their first names and patronymics or demes in the genitive. Metics

are identified by their first names and are said to be 'living in' their demes (rather than belonging to them).

108. Two of these citizens were painters, which was an occupation often associated with slaves, foreigners and the lower class generally. Cf. *LGPN* 400.

109. Daos in Menander's *Aspis* refers to himself as Phrygian (206). Strabo, however, argues that this name is Dacian (7.3.12). The name Syros is similarly ambiguous and might refer to the Cycladic island or to the Levant.

110. Naval Catalogue, *IG* I^3 1032 (*IG* II^2 1951), 408/7 BC. For references, see Fragiadakis (1986), 371-2.

111. Fragiadakis (1986), 358-9.

112. DeVries (2000), 340 and n. 8.The feminine version, Mania, was similarly popular for female slaves and is found in both literary and epigraphic evidence; it was also the name of the Dardanian wife of the satrap Zenis, from whom she took over the governorship of Aeolis (Xen. *Hell.* 3.1.10). See DeVries (2000), 340 and n. 7. Cf. Bäbler (1998), 250-60.

113. Sommerstein (1987), 287: 'The slave's nature matches his name.' See also Bäbler (1998), 158 n. 732.

114. See Wrenhaven (forthcoming, 2012).

115. See Braund and Tsetskhladze (1989); Finely (1962).

116. Fragiadakis (1986), 47: 'Nach dem Wunsch des Besitzers und Namensgebers sollen die Namensträger die Personifizierung von Tugenden und guten Eigenschaften sein.'

117. Fragiadakis (1986), 49-50.

118. Ehrenberg (1962), 172.

119. Aristoboulos: *IG* II^2 1951.137; Aristoboule: *SEG* XXI 97.16.

120. *IG* II^2 1951.137, *c.* 400 BC.

121. Cf. Hom. *Il.* 2.763, *Od.* 9.432, 14.414.

122. Burnard (2001), 325.

123. Burnard (2001), 325. According to this study, in the inventories from 1753, only twelve out of 2,221 slaves had two names.

124. Dickey (1996), 232. She also points out, however, that most servile characters depicted in Greek drama, where the majority of the evidence for address is found, were probably meant to represent slaves and so there was no need to make such a distinction (231-5).

125. Dickey (1996), 232.

126. Dickey (1996), 233.

127. This might be compared, once again, to Burnard's conclusion that slave-owners in eighteenth-century Jamaica 'fostered such [onomastic] distinc-

tions in order to further their belief that blacks were inferior – more like animals than Anglo-Europeans': Burnard (2001), 328.

128. This might be compared to the word *Cyclops*, which is what Odysseus calls Polyphemos after he demonstrates his barbarianism by devouring some of Odysseus' comrades (Hom. *Od.* 9.347, 364). In contrast, in Homer Greeks are never addressed as 'Achaean' or 'Argive'. Dickey (1996), 175-6.

129. Dickey (1996), 233.

130. Dickey (1996), 233.

131. For a discussion of titles used in Greek texts, see Dickey (1996), 90-104.

2. The Body of the Slave

1. Quoted by Genovese (1976), 78.

2. Isaac (2004), 41.

3. Genovese (1976), 3.

4. Thalmann (2011), 78.

5. Isaac (2004), 154.

6. For a discussion of the origins of Physiognomy, see Tsouna (1998), 177-9. The description 'physiognomic consciousness' is borrowed from Evans (1969), 5, etc.

7. Thalmann (1988), 1.

8. Thalmann (1988), 6.

9. For an alternative view, see van der Eijk (2005), 236, who argues that similar ideas are expressed in a number of Aristotle's works. For arguments in favour of Physiognomy being an ancient science rather than a pseudoscience, see Isaac (2006), 150 and no. 376.

10. Evans (1969), 6.

11. For the translation of *dianoia* here as 'mental disposition' see van der Eijk (2005), 236. Van der Eijk argues that the author of the *Physiognomonika* deals primarily with 'moral dispositions and characteristics' and only rarely refers to 'intellectual capacities'.

12. See the collection of essays in Joshel and Murnaghan (1998).

13. Joshel and Murnaghan (1998), 1.

14. Joshel and Murnaghan (1998), 3.

15. Isaac (2004), 151.

16. Isaac (2004), 153.

17. Hesk (2000), 222; cf. 219-27.

18. Cf. The definition of *tapeinos* in LSJ.

19. My use of this designation follows Thomas (2000), 76.

20. The dates of Hippocrates' corpus have been the subject of a great deal of debate and range from about 430-400 BCE. For the date of Hippocrates' works, especially *Airs* and its in relation to Herodotos' *Histories*, see Thomas (2000), 24-5.

21. This kind of rhetoric is particularly evident in the Attic epideictic speeches. Isocrates, for instance, associates *malakia* with the Persians, whom he saw as culturally and politically degenerate and slavish (*Pan.* 4.149-50; *Phil.* 5.124).

22. If Herodotos did think that there was a strong connection between environment and character, one would think that he would also have stated that Greece produces the best people. See Isaac (2004), 59, who argues that 'some commentators have made too much of this'; and Thomas (2000), 75: Herodotos' ideas 'both conflict with and complement the theories of his contemporaries'. For the argument that Herodotos considered *nomos* ('custom') more important than environment, see Thomas (2000), 102-34.

23. Although there are traces of environmental theory in Herodotos, these ideas 'are not of central importance and they are not used in any systematic way so as to establish a hierarchy of peoples and their values.' Isaac (2004), 60.

24. Thomas (2000), 102.

25. Thomas (2000), 110.

26. Isaac (2004), 69.

27. Galen *QAM* 57.11-3. Quote from Boys-Stones (2007), 95.

28. Boys-Stones (2007), 98.

29. Unlike *Airs*, however, Herodotos gives a generally more varied and positive description of the Scythians and, above all, does not assimilate their characters and form to their land and climate (as stated above, however, this does not mean that he did not have this in mind).

30. For example, in Lysias 1.18, the master asks his slave to choose between punishment, that is, whipping and the mill, or telling the truth.

31. Bradley (2000), 112.

32. For a detailed study of the development and use of *kalos kagathos – kalokagathia*, see Bourriot (1995). But see Fisher's (*JHS* 119, 1999) and Cairns' (*CR* 47, 1997) reviews, both of which to varying degrees question Bourriot's methodology and conclusions. For a discussion of the idea that *kalokagathia* was a 'class label', see Dover (1994), 43-5.

33. Quote is from Golden (1998), 33.

34. Dover (1994), 41-2.

35. For an examination of Greek athletic facilities, see Harris (1979), 136-50.

36. For a recent argument in favour of the idea that democratic Athens

fostered inclusion of the lower classes in formerly elite pursuits, see Fisher (2008), 208-12.

37. Greek literature provides several references to the large appetites of athletes. See Golden (1998), 157-8. Nevertheless, it has also been argued that although the games may have started as an elite pursuit, with the advent of hoplite warfare and the need to train in groups, people of the lower classes also began to take part in athletic competitions. Cf. Tzachou-Alexandri (1989), 32. Yet aside from the fact that hoplites can hardly be considered members of the lower class, Golden (1998), 27 argues that 'the usual sports of the gymnasium and the competitive festivals were just not very well designed as preparation for hoplite warfare'. In a fragment from Euripides' *Autolykos*, for instance, a character questions the usefulness of skills such as wrestling, sprinting and discus throwing in the context of warfare (fr. 282N.[2]).

38. Tzachou-Alexandri (1989), 32-3; Forbes (1945), 33-4.

39. The idea that sophists were simply 'professional teachers' was popularized by Plato and is discussed in several of his dialectics, where such men are severely criticized for taking payment for philosophical instruction. The accuracy of Plato's depiction of the sophists, however, continues to be a subject of debate. For a recent discussion, see Wallace (2007), 215-37.

40. Weiler (2002), 11-28.

41. The meanings and uses of the word *kakos* has inspired a great deal of discussion. For a variety of examinations of *kakos* as it relates to 'the discourse of badness and evil', see Sluiter (2008).

42. Sluiter (2008), 10 n. 26.

43. Cf. Arist. *Ath. Pol.* 28. 1-5. Here Aristotle argues that where previously the Athenians had been led by the better sort of citizens (who he refers to as *kaloi kagathoi* at 28.5), after Pericles died, Athens was increasingly led by men such as the loud-mouthed and (allegedly) base-born demagogue Cleon.

44. Sluiter (2008), 10 n. 26.

45. This is one of the definitions given in LSJ.

46. For a discussion of the meaning of these terms in Theognis, see Greenhalgh (1972), 196-8.

47. Weiler (2002), 14.

48. Fisher (1998), 70.

49. For a discussion of ideology versus reality in the context of female labour, see Brock (1994), 336-46.

50. Athens, *c.* 420 BC. Now held by the British Museum, GR 1805.7-3.183 (Sculpture 628).

51. Golden (1998), 147.

52. 'Hephaestus stands outcast midst the wonders he has made.' Golden (1998), 147.

53. Burford (1972), 72-3.

54. See Thalmann (1988), 16 n. 41, 25.

55. Bremmer (1992), 16-17. With the introduction of the phalanx, however, 'there was no longer room for heroes asserting themselves by striding ahead' (17).

56. This continued to be the ideal in later periods. Bremmer (1992), 20 remarks that 'in late antiquity an orderly (*kosmion*), quiet (*hemeron, hesukhon*) and leisurely (*skholaion*) but not sluggish gait is the cultural ideal of pagans and Christians alike'.

57. Bremmer (1992), 19.

58. A good example is a red-figure cup by the Foundry Painter, *c.* 490-480 BC, Athens. Antikensammlung, Staatliche Museen, Berlin. This cup shows several men at various stages of statue production, while three leisured men stand watching. For a recent discussion of this cup, see Thalmann (2011), 78-80.

59. This was the case for Euxitheos (Dem. 57.31, 35), who found himself having to defend his citizenship. The accusations of spurious citizenship were partially based upon the fact that Euxitheos' mother once sold ribbons in the marketplace and worked as a wet-nurse, both occupations associated with, though not exclusive to, slaves (see Chapter 3.1). Similarly, a person's right to citizenship was sometimes questioned because they had a foreign accent, name, or ancestor. Cf. Dem. 18.129, 22.58, 61; Is. 3.12-3; Lys. 30.1, 5, 13.8. In not one of these cases, however, were the accusations formally brought as part of the indictments.

60. See Duckworth (1936), 93-102. Cf. Csapo (1987); Stace (1968), 70.

61. Davidson (1998), 43. Cf. 36-69 for a lively discussion of drinking in ancient Greece.

62. Belfiore (1986), 424. In this same work, however, Plato also discusses some benefits of drunkenness, which appear to be restricted to adults over forty years of age.

63. Lissarrague (2000), 111 and n. 22.

64. Davidson (1998), 47.

65. Davidson (1998), 47.

66. Murray (2002), 144.

67. For laws against citizen-women consuming wine, see Murray (2002), 143.

68. Quote from Davidson (1998), 53.

69. Jordan (1985), 156 n. 11. The word *kapêlos* is rather broad in meaning and can refer either to a general retailer or to a taverner, although in comedy it tends to refer to a taverner. See Davidson (1998), 53 and n. 26. Retailers, on the other hand, are usually described by what they sell, such as a *sêsamopôlês* ('sesame-seller'), *ichthuopôlês* ('fish-seller'), etc.

70. *Catalogi Paterarum Argentearum, IG 2^2* 1553-78 and *Agora* I 3183, 4763, 5774, 5893 and 5927. For commentary, consult Lewis (1959), 208-38 and (1968), 368-80. See also Westermann (1946), 92-104. Retail occupations are common in these lists, which are typically believed to record freed slaves (now metics) and their occupations. See Tod (1950), 3-26.

71. Murray (2002), 142.

72. Attic red-figure *kylix* attributed to the Onesimos Painter, *c.* 500 BC, J. Paul Getty Museum, Inventory #86.AE.284; Attic red-figure *kylix*, attributed to the Brygos Painter, *c.* 480 BC, Martin von Wagner-Museum no. 479.

73. Sutton (2000), 193.

74. For slaves' and labourers' clothing, see Stone (1981), 176; Pipili (2000), 154.

75. *SEG* 27.261 ll. 27-9. For a translation, see Hubbard (2003), 85 2.28. Cf. Gauthier and Hatzopoulos (1993).

76. Harrison (1998), vol. I, 37-8; Todd (1993), 107. While this law is referred to in several forensic speeches, there are no known cases in which a man was actually indicted on the charge of prostitution.

77. Sumner (1979), 267.

78. Aristotle, for instance, states that the Cretans do not allow slaves to take part in gymnastic exercises (*Pol.* 1264a 21). Cf. Crowther (1992), 38-9; Bonfante (1989), 555-6.

79. Harrison (1998), vol. 1, 163.

80. Simms (1988), 68.

81. See Simms (1988) for a discussion of the cult of Bendis in Attica.

82. For the alternate view, see Cohen (2000), 138-40. His case, however, appears rather overstated and does not take into account the frequent oratorical tool of tarnishing the reputation of one's opponent by claiming that he is a slave.

83. Murray (2002), 140-1; Fisher (2002), 126-9; Todd (1993), 270.

84. For the distinction between a *graphê* and a *dikê idia* (usually shortened to *dikê*), see MacDowell (1986), 57-61.

85. Murray (2002), 145.

86. Although there are only two known cases in which a person was indicted on a charge of *hubris*, Cohen argues that there are 'approximately five-hundred occurrences of *hubris* or its cognates in the principle surviving Athenian prose authors'. Cohen (2000), 162.

87. In this case, Conon was not actually charged with a *graphê hubreôs*. Ariston explains that due to his youth and inexperience, he had chosen to indict Conon on a private suit for injurious treatment, *dikê aikeias*, although he had grounds to bring against him the more serious charge of *graphê hubreôs* (54.1).

88. Fisher (2002), 128-9.

89. For a discussion of the various legal protections available to slaves, see Harrison (1998), vol. 1, 167-72. With the possible exception of slaves who were living apart from their masters (*chôris oikountes*) or public slaves (*dêmosioi*), slaves would have had to rely upon citizens to bring charges for them. The only avenue open to slaves to protect themselves from cruel treatment appears to have been the right to take refuge at 'the Theseion or the altar of the Eumenides on the Areopagos', where they could entreat a third-party to purchase them (172).

90. The evidential torture of slaves was also a feature of Roman law, although by late antiquity this was extended to all but the wealthiest citizens. See Wiedemann (1981), 168-70.

91. Genovese (1976), 25.

92. For similar views, see Dem. 29.5, 45.61-2, 52.22; Is. 8.12 (cf. Dem. 30.37); Ant. 1.12, 6.25.

93. Ober (1996), 26: 'Athenian masses responded vigorously and readily to any comment with which they took issue.' Cf. Harding (1987), 29; Ober (1989), 133. For a discussion of the jury, see Todd (1990), 146-73.

94. For a chart detailing challenges of *basanos* in the Athenian forensic speeches, see Hunter (1994), 93-4. Cf. Mirhady (2000), 53-74; Todd (2000), 33; Gagarin (1996), 9.

95. Headlam (1893), 1-5; Gagarin (1996), 2.

96. Mirhady (1996), 131.

97. This problem was recognized by the Romans and led to a pre-Augustan law forbidding slaves being called to testify under torture against their masters without their masters' consent. See Dio Cassius 55.5. Cf. Wiedemann (1981), 168-9 no. 179.

98. Mirhady (2000), 54.

99. Dubois (1991), 21.

100. Plato uses *basanos* four times to mean a 'test': *Laws* 957d4, *Epin.* 991c4, *Ep.* 313d2, 355c7. *Basanos* may also have been used on free foreigners. See Lys. 13.59.

101. Carey (1988), 244-5.

102. Hesk (2000), 26. Cf. Thuc. 2.39. In some cases, however, lies are more acceptable. See Hesk (2000), ch. 3 for a discussion of the 'noble lie' (*gennaion pseudos*), 'when certain situations make lying a moral necessity' (152).

103. For a discussion, see Hall (1997), 113.

104. Golden (1985), 101-2. From ancient to modern times, wives have also been subject to corporal punishment from their husbands. See Genovese (1976), 73-5.

105. Patterson (1982), 2.

106. Patterson (1982), 3.

107. For the illegality of torturing citizens, see Andoc. 1.43 (The decree of Scamandrios).

108. Rawick (1972), 59. Although this statement was made in the context of a discussion of the antebellum South, it also applies to the context of ancient Greek slavery.

109. For further references to the whipping of slaves, see Ar. *Lys.* 1240, *Frogs* 501, *Knights* 1228; Xen. *Mem.* 2.1.16; *Law of the Docimastai,* Rhodes and Osborne (2003), no. 25, ll. 13-16. The bristle-whip (*hustrichis,* lit. 'porcupine') was probably made of pig-bristles and could also be used for torture. Cf. Sommerstein (1985), 168 l. 746.

110. Dubois (1991), 52.

111. Although there is a significant amount of evidence for the sexual use (and abuse) of slaves from a variety of Roman sources, the Greek evidence is relatively sparse and largely anecdotal or indirect. For a discussion of the sexual abuse of slaves in the context of Apuleius' *The Golden Ass,* see Bradley (2000), 115-25. For the sexual abuse of Roman slaves more generally, see Kolendo (1981), 288-97.

112. Sommerstein suggests that 'the bosoms of women running errands in the fields' might also refer to female slaves sent on errands. Cf. line 1146, where Syra, a female slave, is sent to call another slave, Manes, home from the fields. Sommerstein (1985), 158.

113. For this translation, see Dubois (2003), 105.

114. See Sutton (2000), 196 fig. 7.7 for the image. We might also recall how the sons of Conon and their fellow revellers are said to have emptied chamber pots over the heads of the serving slaves at the fort in Panactum (Dem. 54.4).

115. Johnson and Ryan (2005), 4. For images showing the rough treatment of prostitutes at symposia, see Wrenhaven (2009), 375-8.

116. Omitowoju (2002), 6.

117. Finley noted something that is still true today: Although the sexual availability of slaves 'is treated as commonplace in Graeco-Roman literature from Homer on ... only modern writers have managed largely to ignore it, to the extent that the fundamental research remains to be done'. Finley (1980), 95-6.

118. 'Slaves of both sexes were often pinched and pummelled during the symposia.' Percy (1996), 117. Cf. Dem. 54.4-5.

119. Attic red-figure pot, attributed to the Hegesiboulos Painter, classical. New York Metropolitan Museum, 07.286.47. For the image, see Dover (1989), R295. Cf. Xenophanes of Colophon, who writes that one of the slaves' duties at symposia was to place plaited crowns upon the revellers' heads. For the poem, see Stewart (2008), 168.

120. For a discussion of homosexuality as 'in part an institution of transition from the subordinate and quasi-servile status of boyhood to the status of adult free citizen', see Golden (1984).

121. See Golden (1984), 313-16. For the Greek terminology, see Davidson (2007), 38-50: 'The elegists imply that *charis* is characteristic of relations with boys precisely because, as autonomous subjects, they are free to favor or to return generosity, and cannot be pinned down' (45).

122. The same, however, cannot be said of Archaic pot-painting, which presents a number of images of homosexual and heterosexual sex.

123. For the 'discouragement of male prostitution of free citizens' and the *graphê hetairêseôs*, see Harrison (1998), vol. I, 37-8.

124. See Cohen (2000), 169-71.

125. Dover (1989), 32-3.

126. See Dover (1989), 97.

127. See Sutton (2000), 183-91 for an examination of the relationship between the Other and sexual acts considered shameless, such as masturbation, fellatio and anal intercourse.

128. For a discussion of this image, see Keuls (1985), 285-6.

129. Sutton (2000), 184 n. 19.

130. Stewart (2008), 150.

131. Stewart (2008), 150.

132. Boardman (2001), 168.

133. For a discussion of the relatively high cost of decorated pots, see Boardman (2001), 157-64.

134. Lewis (2002), 5.

135. Lewis (2002), 75.

136. Johnston (1991), 214-15. For further examples of images and vessel shapes aimed at a foreign (Etruscan) market, see Osborne (2001), 278.

137. Boardman (2001), 236. See also Osborne (2001), 280-3, 90.

138. Spivey (1991), 132.

139. Spivey (1991), 133-4.

140. Boardman (2001), 156. Boardman has found evidence that some potters might have hired out sets of vessels to be used on occasions, such as at

symposia. Vessels from these sets might then have been sold on later, perhaps at a discounted price.

141. Boardman (2001), 247.

142. Bundrick (2008), 8.

143. *c.* 340 BC. Boston Museum of Fine Arts, 03.804.

144. For a detailed examination of the various meanings of nudity and nakedness in Greek literature and art in isolation and in comparison with other ancient cultures see Bonfante (1989), 543-70.

145. Quote from Bonfante (1989), 544.

146. Cf. *c.* 460 BC Attic red-figure oinochoe attributed to the Chicago Painter. Boston Museum of Fine Arts, 13.196. For a photo, see Castriota (2000), 445 fig. 17.1.

147. Red-figure plate by Paseas. New Haven, Yale University Art Gallery 1913.169. For the image and a discussion, see Bonfante (1989), 560. There are other representations of this same scene where Cassandra is not depicted as abnormally small. An example is a red-figure kylix by the Codros Painter (440 BC) now in the Louvre (Inv. G. 458).

148. Athens National Museum 934. For a drawing of the relief, see Clairmont (1993), 0.930 (Plate vol.) and the accompanying description (Cat. vol. 1). The inscription, *IG* II.2 7816, reads 'Deinias Ôathen [*sic*]', who was evidently of citizen family. Other members of his family appear on a loutrophoros (2.852 = *IG* II.2 7825).

149. Although there are instances of Greeks enslaving other Greeks, by the fifth century, at least, these appear to have been exceptions to the rule. Herodotos, for example, expresses surprise that the Lesbians once enslaved the Arisbians 'even though they were blood-relatives' (1.151). For a discussion of the foreign sources of Greek slaves, see Cartledge (1993), 136-40.

150. Bérard (2000), 409.

151. Oakley (2000), 245.

152. See Oakley (2000), 239 fig. 9.6 for a similar example of a black female servant and her mistress.

153. In his study of 'stigmata' in the ancient world, Jones (1987), 145-6 finds that tattooing 'was associated above all with the Thracians' and gives several literary and iconographic examples. Another notable representation is a fifth-century Attic red-figure skyphos depicting Heracles and his Thracian nurse Geropso, who is shown with prominent tattoos on her face, arms and feet. Attributed to the Pistoxenos Painter, *c.* 460 BC. Schwerin, Kunstsammlungen, Staatliches Museum 708. For the image, see Tsiafakis (2000), 374 fig. 14.4.

154. There is some evidence that the Greeks adopted penal tattooing from the Persians. In Greek society, it was used as a way to punish and mark out runaway slaves. See Jones (1987), 146. In Aristophanes' *Birds*, a runaway slave is referred to as a 'multi-coloured grouse' (760-1). Cf. Aristophanes *Lys.* 330-1 for another references to tattooed (female) slaves.

155. For a detailed discussion of the identification of slaves in comic theatrical art, see Wrenhaven (forthcoming, 2012).

156. For a discussion of the stereotypes attributed to courtesans, see Glazebrook (2006), 126-30. Cf. Wrenhaven (2009), 373.

157. There was, however, a discrepancy between the 'Big House of the legend' and 'the Big House of reality', where manners appear to have been more important in making the domestic slaves 'more presentable to upper-class white society' than light skin. See Genovese (1976), 327-8.

158. Athens, fourth century, terracotta.

159. Weiler (2002), 23-4.

160. Pericles allegedly commented when he saw a slave fall from a tree: 'There's another *paidagôgos*' (Hieronymos of Rhodes ap. Stob. *Flor.* 31.121).

161. Suda s.v. *Harpokration* and Hesychus s.v. *agora Kerkopon*; Diogenes Laertius 9.114; cf. Weiler (2002), 23. The Roman equivalent might have been the so-called *teratôn agora*. See Plut. *Mor.* 520c; Garland (1995), 47.

162. Garland (1995), 46.

3. The Good Slave

1. Thalmann (1998), 27 refers to the idea that slaves are innately inferior as the 'suspicious' view, which 'sees slaves as inferior and unreliable, and therefore naturally subordinate but in need of coercion and control'.

2. Finley (1980), 105.

3. For a discussion of Athens' *dêmosioi*, see Cohen (2000), 136-7; Wiedemann (1981), 154-7. For the Scythian Archers, see Hunter (1994), 120-53.

4. The phrase *chôris oikountes* is used by modern scholars to describe slaves who were already living-apart from their masters in a quasi-free, self-supporting condition and paying their masters what was probably a monthly fee (*apophora*). Syros in Menander's *Epitrepontes* is one example (379-80). Similarly, Demosthenes mentions a slave called Lampis, who had a wife and children (34.37). See Cohen (2000), 130-2 for a discussion of these types of slaves and the related scholarship.

5. For epigraphic evidence of Attic manumission, the reader is referred to a group of late fourth-century inscriptions, the *phialai exeleutherikai* ('freed-

men's cups'). *Catalogi Paterarum Argentearum, IG* 2^2 1553-78 and *Agora* I 4763, I 5656, I 5893, I 5927 (*SEG* XXV 177-180) + I 3183 (= *Hesperia* 28, 1959, pp. 208-38) + I 5774 (= *Hesperia* 30, 1961, p. 247, no. 43) and I 4665 (= *Hesperia* 65, 1996, pp. 452-3). For the evidence that family groups were sometimes released, see Rosivach (1989), 369-70. For overall commentary on these inscriptions, consult Lewis (1959), 208-38 and (1968), 368-80. See also Zelnick-Abramovitz (2005), 282-90; Westermann (1946), 94-104. The *phialai exeleutherikai* also appear later in the Parthenon treasury lists, *IG* 2^2 1469.32-7; 1480.9-11. For a recent alternative interpretation of the *phialai* lists, see Meyer (2010), who argues that they do not record manumissions of slaves but rather prosecutions of metics for failing to pay the *metoikion* ('metic tax').

6. Pomeroy (1997), 18 refers to the *polis* as a version of the family or, more specifically, 'a family of men'.

7. Kosmopoulou (2001), 282.

8. Kosmopoulou (2001), 285. For a discussion of the terminology for wet-nurses and the various meanings, see Rühfel (1988), 43.

9. Vogt (1974), 107.

10. Thalmann (1998), 27.

11. For a discussion of barbarian, and especially Thracian, wet-nurses in Athenian art and other sources, see Bäbler (2005); Rühfel (1988), 45-7.

12. Kosmopoulou (2001), 283. An exception is a late fifth-century or early fourth-century tombstone for a copper-smelter named Sosinous, who at any rate was not an Athenian citizen but a metic from Gortyn. Cf. Clairmont (1993), 258-60, 1.202.

13. Sourvinou-Inwood (1996), 227: 'The woman with distaff' schemata seen on tombstones corresponds to the 'married woman, *gynê*, shown in her persona as spinner, that is, performing a domestic task symbolic of the desired virtues of the ideal Greek woman'.

14. Slaves are also listed with occupations on the Attic Manumissions and Attic Stelai inscriptions. For the Attic Manumissions, see above, n. 5. For the Attic Stelai (*IG* I^3 421, 426), see Pritchett (1953), 240-9, 268-79; (1956), 276-81; (1961), 23-5. Cf. Fornara (1983), 171-5.

15. For wet-nurses on tombstones and in other genres, see especially Rühfel (1988), 43-57; Bäbler (2005); Kosmopoulou (2001), 285-92. For an extensive study of classical Attic tombstones, see Clairmont (1993).

16. Kosmopoulou (2001), 287. Women could not actually be citizens, hence the quotes. The term *astos* is usually considered to be synonymous with *politês*. *But see Cohen (2000) 48, 50-63, who translates astai* as 'local persons', which refers more explicitly to the state of being an 'insider', in contrast to a *xenê*, or 'outsider'.

17. Rossi (2001), 308.

18. See Clairmont (1993), 115 and n. 10. Johansen (1951) defines *dexiôsis* as follows: 'It is a manifestation of the fundamental thought that the two parties together make up a whole, the family, which the intervention of death has failed to sunder, and that as parts of this whole they are of equal importance' (151).

19. Neils and Oakley (2003), 307; Kosmopoulou (2001), 287; Bäbler (1998), 24; Clairmont (1993), 36; Rühfel (1988), 48. For the *chitôn cheiridôtos* as originally foreign dress, see Miller (1997), 156-60.

20. Dué (2006), 155. Ferrari (1997), 8. See also Ferrari (1990) and (2002), 54-6, 73-81.

21. Kosmopoulou (2001), 306 N1.

22. Karouzou (1957); Simon (1963). Cf. Kosmopoulou (2001), 287 and nos 75-9.

23. For a discussion of 'ready-bought and commissioned' tombstones and burial vessels, see Clairmont (1993), 66-72.

24. Oliver (2000), 3.

25. Kosmopoulou (2001), 306-11.

26. For the meaning of *isotelês* and *isoteleia* and their connection with metics, see Whitehead (1977), 11-13.

27. *IG* II^2 9271, 12242 and *SEG* 26:341.

28. The term *chrêstos* was also sometimes applied to the aristocracy as a sort of class label with the intention of differentiating them from the *poneroi*, or the masses. This meaning, however, became much less common in the Classical period, when it was generally replaced by the word *agathos*. See most recently Rosenbloom (2004); Osborne (2000), 23-8. The differences between the uses of the word may also be the result of the fact that the two types of evidence are so different: the literature is 'the work of authors of outstanding genius and strongly marked individuality, while [the inscriptions] are all public documents'. Tod (1951), 183.

29. 349 BC Anaxandr. fr. 2.4 Edmonds II 46. Cf. Fragiadakis (1986), 379 no. 889.

30. Lyde: *IG* II^2 11977; Phrygia: *IG* II^2 3019; Syros x 3: *IG* II^2 12691-3; Ktesion *IG* II^2 11925. For a list of sepulchral inscriptions for people of uncertain status and origin, see *Tituli sepulcrales hominum originis incertae, IG* II^2 10531-13085.

31. Scholl (1986), 307. See also Bäbler (1998), 65-6 and n. 327; Masson (1972), 18; *SEG* 39.325.

32. *IG* II^2 10763a.

33. *IG* XII, Suppl. 453. For an Athenian reference to a slave shepherd, see Ps.-Dem. 47.57.

34. For a discussion of this stone, see Robert (1949), 152-60.

35. Kassel-Austin *PCG* VIII, fr. com. adesp. 1006.

36. Other apparent misspellings of *titthê* are *tittê* (*SEG* 21:1064) and *tithê* (*IG* II^2 12559); Kosmopoulou N2. Here the woman's name is spelled 'Synete', whereas *IG* has 'Pynete'. See Bäbler (2005), 78 and Karouzou (1957) for possible reasons for the misspelling of Pyraichme's occupation (*SEG* 21:1064).

37. For discussion and further bibliography on this topic, see Rossi (2001), 310-11 and Pfisterer-Haas (1990), 43.

38. Clairmont argues that the name Paideusis was given to the woman later in life in recognition 'of her good educational services' (1993), 222. Since masters named their slaves, it is also possible that the woman was given this name upon her purchase in anticipation of the type of service she was expected to provide.

39. See Rossi (2001), 305. For the preserved epigraphic examples, see *IG* II^2 7873 and 9112.

40. For detailed commentary on this epigram, see Rossi (2001), 313-22; Bruss (2005), 79-82. For Hellenistic poems for slaves, see Lattimore (1942), 280-5.

41. This translation is based on that of Rossi (2001), 322.

42. Bruss (2005), 81.

43. *Chrêsimos*, has been found three times as a name for slaves: *IG* II^2 1576.21-3, 330 BC; *IG* II^2 8329, Attic, Roman period; Degrassi 13.2.207, AD 44. Cf. Houston (2002), 150. In the epigraphic context, the word *chrêsima* is not found on actual funerary inscriptions but is 'reserved for explicitly political contexts'. Bruss (2005), 81 n. 89. See also Rossi (2001), 319-22.

44. For the rarity of this name, see Rossi (2001), 318.

45. For similar examples, see Callimachus' epitaph commemorating a Phrygian wet-nurse named Aischra (*AP* 7.458), and Dioscorides' rather ironic epitaph for a drunken wet-nurse named Silenis (*AP* 7.456).

46. *IG* II^2 10715, Apollodoros; *IG* II^2 10903, Attis; *IG* II^2 11932, Cteson; *IG* II^2 12433, Pausanias; *IG* II^2 12611, Simon.

47. *SEG* XXIV 163.326; in the form of Attas, *IG* II^2 1951.173; *IG* II^2 2940.5; *IG* II^2 1558 67-8. The latter is from the disputed *phialai*-inscriptions (see above, n. 9). This man was either a former slave or a metic, who at any rate might have been a freedman.

48. See Vogt (1974), 110.

49. Johansen (1951), 11. This observation was inspired, in turn, by Beazley's

remarks about the interpretation of the sepulchral imagery on the Attic white lekythoi.

50. Clairmont (1993), Introductory vol., 36.

51. Athens, National Museum 934. The image, which now only survives as a drawing, is reproduced in Clairmont (1993), Plates vol., 0.930.

52. See Fisher (1993), 8 fig. 1. For another example, see the late fourth-century tombstone for Ameinocleia, daughter of Andromenes, Athens, National Archaeological Museum (Art Resource, ART404626). This stone shows a woman with two female servants: one holding a box and the other kneeling on the floor, putting her mistress' sandal on her foot, while the mistress steadies herself by placing her hand upon the kneeling servant's head.

53. Clairmont (1993), 36. The word *sakkos* can refer both to a type of textile made out of coarse material, such as goat-hair, and to clothing made from this material, such as a head-scarf.

54. See Neils (2000), 214-17 and figs 8.5, 8.6, 8.8, 8.10.

55. There are several examples in Clairmont (1993), Plates vol., e.g. 2.151, 2.152, 2.187, 2.294a, etc.

56. Cropped hair could also be a sign of shame. Cf. Ar. *Thesm.* 836 where the Chorus Leader states that the mother of a cowardly man should be made to sit behind that of a brave man with her hair cropped in a bowl cut. Plato indicated that a person's hair and name could identify them as a slave (*Alk.* I.120b; cf. Arist. *Rh.* 1367a29ff.). Cf. Neils and Oakley (2003) 227.

57. Bäbler (1998), 24-5.

58. Cf. *Knights* 580, *Clouds* 14, *Wasps* 466. As Sommerstein (1987), 259 l. 911 writes: 'Poor men, let alone slaves, would never wear their hair thus.' Cf. Ehrenberg (1962), 97.

59. See Bäbler (1998), 24-5 who also remarks that: 'Eine Kurzhaarfrisur war für eine freie junge Frau normalerweise eine Schmach' (25).

60. Athens, Piraeus Museum 433. Clairmont (1993), Plate vol., 3.416.

61. For discussion of these disputed scenes, particularly the difficulty in interpreting the social status of the women, see Rystedt (1994); Reilly (1989); Kurtz (1988).

62. Athens, National Museum 2894. Clairmont (1993), Plate vol., 2.150.

63. Athens, Nation Museum, 4006. Clairmont (1993), Plate vol., 1.797.

64. It has been suggested that the woman holds a flower, although a ring is more likely, particularly in view of the box held by the servant. Clairmont (1993), Cat. vol. I, 447-8, 1.797.

65. New York. Collection of Shelby White and Leon Levy. Clairmont (1993), Plate vol., 1.780a.

66. Athens, National Museum 3586. Clairmont (1993), Plate vol., 1.879.

67. Himmelmann (1971), 41 also expresses surprise at the appearance of such a non-ideal figure in the sepulchral context.

68. Clairmont (1993), Cat. vol. I, 480.

69. Athens, National Museum 3702. Clairmont (1993), Plate vol., 1.935.

70. See Clairmont (1993), Plate vol., 1.880, 1.881, 1.886, 1.890.

71. Like *titthê*, the word *trophos* is usually translated as 'nurse', however, unlike *titthê*, it seems to refer more generally to a female domestic slave who served as a personal servant and companion to a person younger than herself. A *trophos* might also serve as a *titthê* ('wet-nurse'), since there is some indication that the words could be used interchangeably. See Kosmopoulou (2001), 285. In the extant examples from tragedy, however, nurses are always referred to as *trophoi* and, with the exception of Cilissa, Orestes' nurse in Aeschylus' *Libation Bearers*, nurses are associated with mistresses.

72. For a book-length study of slave nurses in Athenian tragedy, consult Karydas (1998). See also Hall (1997), 114-17.

73. The quote is from Thalmann (1998), 24. After examining all of the instances of *dmôes/dmôai*, the most common noun used for servants in Homer, Gschnitzer (1976) concludes that these figures are unfree. For a discussion of the difficulty determining the status of servant figures in early Greek literature and history, see Beringer (1982); Garlan (1988), 35-6.

74. Karydas (1998), 8.

75. Karydas (1998), 10.

76 For a list of the repeated references to Eurycleia's wisdom and age, see Karydas (1998), 61-3, tables II and III.

77. There is another possibility at 23.228, where Penelope refers to her personal maidservant as 'the daughter of Actor' (*Aktoris*). She does not give the woman's first name but she is likely referring to Eurynome, who is her 'attendant of the bedchamber' (*thalamêpolos*, 23.293).

78. Thalmann (1998), 31-2 contends that Eumaios' (and perhaps Eurycleia's) noble lineage was a way for the text to deal with his unslavish nature.

79. For further examples of the assistance of good servants in Homeric epic, see Olson (1992), 219-21.

80. Thalmann (1998), 27. Aristotle states as much in the *Politics* when he writes that it is the slave who serves the master's interest, not the other way around (1278b32-7).

81. See Falkner (1989), 124 for this translation of *kagchaloôsa* and for further discussion of the 'sadistic delight' Eurycleia takes in the murder of the suitors and the 'faithless servant women'.

82. Another Homeric example of a 'vengeful old woman' is Hecuba, particularly her comment that she would like to eat Achilles' liver in retaliation for killing her son (*Il.* 24.212-14). Cf. Falkner (1989), 124-5.

83. For further examples and discussion, see Karydas (1998), 54-5.

84. Henderson (1987), 123.

85. Karydas (1998), 65.

86. See Conacher (1987), 7. Compare with the Watchman's speech (Aesch. *Ag.* 1-39) and the Guard's speech (Soph. *Ant.* 223-77).

87. Karydas (1998), 69.

88. Although there is some dispute about whether this character was a *trophos* or a *therapaina*, as Karydas (1998), 76 n. 37 notes, her advisory and authoritative role strongly suggests that she should be interpreted as a *trophos*.

89. See Karydas (1998) 83-92 for a more detailed discussion of the 'nurse and handmaid' in Euripides' *Andromache*.

90. For an alternate argument, see Hutchinson (2004). Hutchinson suggests, in part, that the extant play might actually be earlier than the non-extant play (24-7) and that the pair might be an example of 'homonymous tragedies' (26-8).

91. For other possibilities, see Roisman (1999), 398-409.

92. Burian (2005), 201-2.

93 For a thorough discussion of references to domestic slaves in Attic oratory and the lack of privacy between such slaves and their masters, see Hunter (1993), 70-95.

94. Genovese (1976), 344.

95. Genovese (1976), 353.

96. See Kern-Foxworth (1994), 82-6 for black views of the Aunt Jemima image.

97. Manring (1998), 20.

98. Genovese (1976), 354.

99. Genovese (1976), 356.

100. Manring (1998), 18.

101. Genovese (1976), 349. Cf. Rawick (1972), 132.

102. Olson (forthcoming, 2012).

103. Vafopoulou-Richardson (1991), viii. Prior to this (i.e. in the archaic and high classical periods), terracotta figurines seem more commonly to have had a religious significance (e.g. votive offerings) and were hand-moulded.

104. See Vafopoulou-Richardson (1991), no. 27 and nos 31ab.

105. A similar example from Athens is held by the British Museum, AN355091001.

106. Although the word *tamia* need not refer to a slave, the context makes

it clear that Ischomachos is instructing his wife on the proper management of the household slaves, which is her primary duty (Xen. *Oec.* 9-17).

107. Manring (1998), 20.

108. Because of the contrast between Aunt Jemima's skin, teeth, lips, the light rings around her eyes and her very wide smile, which together give her a mask-like appearance, she has been compared to the minstrel, who was also a caricatures of a slave. See Manring (1998), 66-8.

4. War Captives and the Natural Slave

1. See Dué (2006), 99-106 for further discussion.

2. The Painted Stoa and its influence in antiquity is discussed by Wycherley (1953), 20-35.

3. For the view that Euripides' *Trojan Women* parallels events of the Trojan War with the Peloponnesian War, see especially Delebecque (1951), 245-62. For the opposite view, see Zuntz (1972), 58, who argues that 'there are no "allusions" in tragedy'. For a more measured approach, see Croally (1994), 232-4.

4. Croally (1994), 234.

5. Croally (1994), 115.

6. Quote from Millett (2007), 188. For relatively recent, detailed and useful discussions of Aristotle's theory of slavery, see Millett (2007), 178-209; Brunt (1993), 343-66. For the literature on Aristotle and the American proslavery argument, see Millett (2007), 179 n. 3.

7. Goff (2009), 51.

8. Croally (1994), 92.

9. Dué (2006), 144.

10. For a discussion and alternative explanations, see Goff (2009), 52.

11. The word 'sons' is usually edited out of this section. See Paradiso (1993), 21-6.

12. For further discussion of this passage, see Rabinowitz (1998), 57.

13. See also Eur. *Helen* 728-33; fr. 831.

14. Daitz (1971) 217.

15. For a discussion of this expression and its use in Homer, see Beringer (1982), 25.

16. Quote from Shapiro (1996), 352.

17. Rabinowitz (1998), 60.

18. Rabinowitz (1998), 58.

19. Croally (1994), 83.

20. Croally (1994), 100.

21. Quote from Croally (1994), 100.

22. Scodel (1980), 110.

23. Hecuba is not completely released from the feminine: a significant part of her speech is in the form of lamentation, which is a quintessentially feminine genre. For a detailed discussion of lament in Euripides' *Hecuba*, see Dué (2006), 117-35.

24. Women were more commonly associated with other genres of speech, such as 'gossip, seductive persuasion, lamentation, and other forms of ritual speech'. For a discussion of these feminine discursive practices, see McClure (1999), 32-68.

25. Kastely, for instance, argues that in *Hecuba*, rhetoric is placed in opposition to *bia* ('violence') and is intended to illustrate the failure of public discourse: Euripides 'places a protagonist skilled in rhetoric in a situation in which those in power, insulated from pain, cannot be reached through persuasion'. Kastely (1993), 1036.

26. For instance, see Daitz (1971), 222: 'Both pairs of innocent children were slain by dehumanized women to punish a guilty father.'

27. Hall (2000), xx.

28. The metamorphosis of Hecuba is discussed in detail by Segal (1990), 304-17.

29. Segal (1990), 309.

30. Saïd (2002), 69, 62-100.

31. Croally (1994), 112.

32. Cartledge (2001), 308.

33. Saïd (2002), 70.

34. Croally (1994), 56.

35. Quote from Dué (2006), 149. For her part, Dué sees the *Troades* 'as a questioning of imperialist ideology rather than a pacifist's prayer for peace'.

36. By the fifth century, there is evidence that some intellectuals were beginning to imagine life without slaves. Athenaeus refers to scenes from Old Comedy that describe tools and food moving on their own (*Deip.* 6.267e-70a); Plato's *Statesman* describes the Golden Age of Cronos, when the earth furnished food of its own accord; and Aristotle imagines a hypothetical situation in which tools accomplished their own work (*Pol.* 1253b35-8). These descriptions, however, are fantastical and should not be taken to reflect any serious abolitionist argument. For further discussion, see Cambiano (1987), 25-6; Garlan (1988), 130.

37. Frank (2004), 91.

38. For a discussion of these 'anonymous opponents of slavery', see especially Cambiano (1987), 22-41.

39. See Cambiano (1987), 24. Garnsey (1996), 75-6 on the other hand, argues that the statement was meant to encompass all people, not just Greeks.

40. Garnsey (1996), 77.

41. Schofield (1990), 21-2.

42. Millett (2007), 193.

43. Millett (2007), 194.

44. Millett (2007), 194.

45. The Attic Stelai have been published with a full commentary by Pritchett (1953). See also later publications by the same author (1956), esp. 276-81 and two new fragments (1961); *GHI* (1946 and 1969) no. 79. For ancient references, see Pollux 10.97; Thuc. 6.27-8; Andoc. 1.13.

46. From the Attic Stelai: Macedonia (*IG* I3 422); Melitus (*IG* I3 421); Messenia (*IG* I^3 430). Other possibilities are found in the Naval Catalogue: Arcadia; Laconia (*IG* I^3 1032).

47. Dobbs (1994), 84, 75.

48. For a detailed discussion of Attic funeral speeches, see Loraux (1986).

49. Thalmann (2011), 78, 81. See Thalmann (2011), 78-81 for a discussion of the labourer's body in Greek art.

50. Dobbs (1994), 74.

51. For a discussion of free employment in Classical Greece, see Brock (1994); Garnsey (1980), 1-29; Thompson (1982). Cf. Cohen (2000), 142-54, who argues that although some Greek *politai* took paid employment, they did not work for an employer on a continuous basis for fear of being considered slavish. This argument is difficult to believe, as it based upon a too-literal reading of the sources, which are elitist by nature. While some citizens were surely wealthy enough not to have to take paid employment and could denigrate those who did, many more would not have had the luxury of working almost exclusively for themselves, regardless of the existence of a stigma against continuous paid work espoused by the sources.

52. Some scholars have taken this statement to mean that Athens' slaves are so well-dressed they look like citizens, however, the opposite meaning is much more likely. As attested by his overall discussion, the Old Oligarch clearly views the common people as vulgar and unfit to rule, and so this statement is surely a further slight against them. Cf. Osborne (2004), 18 no. 1.10-11.

53. It can be assumed that as a member of the upper class, Aristotle himself held slaves. For evidence, one is directed to Diogenes Laertius 5.14-15, which purports to record the will of Aristotle and in which some of his loyal household slaves are freed (with various provisions).

54. Thalmann (2011), 74.

Bibliography

Journal abbreviations are based upon those
used by *L'Année Philologique*.

Andreau, J. (2002) 'Markets, fairs and monetary loans: cultural history and economic history in Roman Italy and Hellenistic Greece', in P. Cartledge, E. Cohen and L. Foxhall (eds) *Money, Labour and Land* (London and New York).

Austin, M.M. and P. Vidal-Naquet (1977) *Economic and Social History of Ancient Greece* (London).

Bäbler, B. (1998) *Fleissige Thrakerinnen und wehrhafte Skythen* (Stuttgart).

Bäbler, B. (2005) 'Fremde Frauen in Athen. Thrakische Ammen und Athenische Kinder', in U. Riemer and P. Riemer (eds) *Xenophobie-Philoxenie* (Stuttgart).

Baxter, T.M.S. (1992) *The Cratylus* (Leiden and New York).

Belfiore, E. (1986) 'Wine and catharsis of the emotions in Plato's *Laws*', *CQ* 36, 421-37.

Bérard, C. (2000) 'The image of the Other and the foreign hero', in Beth Cohen (ed.) *Not the Classical Ideal* (Leiden).

Beringer, W. (1982) '"Servile status" in the sources for early Greek history', *Historia* 31, 13-32.

Boardman, J. (2001) *The History of Greek Vases* (London).

Bonfante, L. (1989) 'Nudity as a costume in Classical art', *AJA* 93, 543-70.

Bourriot, F. (1995) *Kalos Kagathos – Kalokagathia: d'un terme de propagande de sophistes à une notion sociale et philosophique* (Hildesheim and New York).

Boys-Stones, G. (2007) 'Physiognomy and ancient psychological theory', in S. Swain (ed.) *Seeing the Face, Seeing the Soul* (Oxford).

Bradley, K. (2000) 'Animalizing the slave: the truth of fiction', *JRS* 90, 110-25.

Braund, D.C. and G.R. Tsetskhladze (1989) 'The export of slaves from Colchis', *CQ* 39, 114-25.

Bremmer, J. (1992) 'Walking, standing, and sitting in ancient Greek culture', in J. Bremmer and H. Roodenburg (eds) *A Cultural History of Gesture* (Cambridge).

179

Bibliography

Briant, P. (2002) 'History and ideology', in T. Harrison (ed.) *Greeks and Barbarians* (Edinburgh).

Brock, R. (1994) 'The labour of women in Classical Athens', *CQ* 44, 336-46.

Brunt, P.A. (1993) *Studies in Greek History and Thought* (Oxford).

Bruss, J.S. (2005) *Hidden Presences: Monuments, Gravesites, and Corpses in Greek Funerary Epigram* (Leuven).

Bundrick, S.D. (2008) 'The fabric of the city: imagining textile production in Classical Athens', *Hesperia* 77, 283-334.

Burford, A. (1972) *Craftsmen in Greek and Roman Society* (Ithaca, New York).

Burian, P. (2005) 'Myth into *muthos*: the shaping of tragic plot', in P.E. Easterling (ed.) *The Cambridge Companion to Greek Tragedy* (Cambridge).

Burnard, T. (2001) 'Slave naming patterns: onomastics and the taxonomy of race in eighteenth-century Jamaica', *Journal of Interdisciplinary History* 31.3, 325-46.

Cambiano, G. (1987) 'Aristotle and the anonymous opponents of slavery', in M.I. Finley (ed.) *Classical Slavery* (London).

Campbell, R.B. (1985) 'Intermittent slave ownership: Texas as a test case', *Journal of Southern History* 51, 15-23.

Cartledge, P. (1993) *The Greeks: A Portrait of Self and Others* (Oxford and New York).

Cartledge, P. (2001) 'Greeks and "Barbarians"', in A.-F. Christidis (ed.) *A History of Ancient Greek: From the Beginnings to Late Antiquity* (Cambridge).

Carey, C. (1988) 'A note on torture in Athenian homicide cases', *Historia* 37, 241-5.

Castriota, D. (2000) 'Justice, kingship, and imperialism: rhetoric and reality in fifth-century BC representations following the Persian Wars', in Beth Cohen (ed.) *Not the Classical Ideal* (Leiden).

Christ, M.R. (1998) *The Litigious Athenian* (Baltimore).

Clairmont, C.W. (1993) *Classical Attic Tombstones* (Kilchberg).

Cohen, E.E. (2000) *The Athenian Nation* (Princeton).

Colvin, S. (1999) *Dialect in Aristophanes* (Oxford and New York).

Conacher, D.J. (1987) *Aeschylus' Oresteia: A Literary Commentary* (Toronto).

Croally, N.T. (1994) *Euripidean Polemic* (Cambridge).

Crowther, N.B. (1992) 'Slaves in Greek athletics', *QUCC* 40, 35-42.

Csapo, E. (1987) 'Is the threat-monologue of the "servus currens" an index of Roman authorship?', *Phoenix* 41, 399-419.

Daitz, S.G. (1971) 'Concepts of freedom and slavery in Euripides' *Hecuba*', *Hermes* 99, 217-26.

Bibliography

Daly, L.W. (1961) *Aesop Without Morals* (New York and London).

Davidson, J. (1998) *Courtesans and Fishcakes* (London).

Davidson, J. (2007) *The Greeks and Greek Love: A Radical Reappraisal of Homosexuality in Ancient Greece* (London).

Davies, A.M. (2002) 'The Greek notion of dialect', in T. Harrison (ed.) *Greeks and Barbarians* (Edinburgh).

Davies, J.K. (1993) *Democracy and Classical Greece* (London).

Delebecque, E. (1951) *Euripide et la guerre du Péloponnèse* (Paris).

DeVries, K. (2000) 'The nearly other: the Attic vision of Phrygians and Lydians', in Beth Cohen (ed.) *Not the Classical Ideal* (Leiden).

Dickey, E. (1996) *Greek Forms of Address* (Oxford and New York).

Dillard, J.L. (1992) *A History of American English* (London).

Dobbs, D. (1994) 'Natural right and the problem of Aristotle's defence of slavery', *Journal of Politics* 56, 69-94.

Dover, K.J. (1989) *Greek Homosexuality* (London).

Dover, K.J. (1994) *Greek Popular Morality* (Indianapolis).

Dubois, P. (1991) *Torture and Truth* (New York and London).

Dubois, P. (2003) *Slaves and Other Objects* (Chicago).

Duckworth, G. (1936) 'The dramatic function of the *servus currens* in Roman comedy', *Classical Studies Presented to Edward Capps on his Seventieth Birthday* (Princeton).

Dué, C. (2006) *The Captive Woman's Lament in Greek Tragedy* (Austin).

Ehrenberg, V. (1962) *The People of Aristophanes* (Oxford).

Eijk, P.J. van der (2005) *Medicine and Philosophy in Classical Antiquity: Doctors and Philosophers on Nature, Soul, Health and Disease* (Cambridge).

Evans, E.C. (1969) *Physiognomics in the Ancient World* (Philadelphia).

Falkner, T.M. (1989) 'The wrath of Alcmene: gender, authority and old age in Euripides' *Children of Heracles*', in T.M. Falkner and J. de Luce (eds) *Old Age in Greek and Latin Literature* (New York).

Ferrari, G. (1990) 'Figures of speech: the picture of *Aidos*', *Mêtis* V, 185-200.

Ferrari, G. (1997) 'Figures in the text: metaphors and riddles in the *Agamemnon*', *CPh* 92, 1-45.

Ferrari, G. (2002) *Figures of Speech: Men and Maidens in Ancient Greece* (Chicago).

Finley, M.I. (1954) 'The ancient Greeks and their nation: the sociological problem', *British Journal of Sociology* 5.3, 253-64.

Finley, M.I. (1959) 'Was Greek civilization based on slave labour?', *Historia* 8, 145-64.

Finley, M.I. (1960) *Slavery in Classical Antiquity* (Cambridge).

Bibliography

Finley, M.I. (1962) 'The Black Sea and Danubian regions and the slave trade in antiquity', *Klio* 40, 51-9.

Finley, M.I. (1980) *Ancient Slavery and Modern Ideology* (London).

Finley, M.I. (1998; ed. B. D. Shaw) *Ancient Slavery and Modern Ideology* (Princeton).

Fisher, N.R.E. (1992) Hybris: *A Study in the Values of Honour and Shame in Ancient Greece* (Warminster).

Fisher, N.R.E. (1993) *Slavery in Classical Greece* (London).

Fisher, N.R.E. (1998) 'Violence, Masculinity, and the Law in Classical Athens', in L. Foxhall and J. Salmon (eds) *When Men were Men: Masculinity, Power, and Identity in Classical Antiquity* (London and New York).

Fisher, N.R.E. (2002) 'The Law of *Hubris* in Athens', in P. Cartledge and P. Millett (eds) *Nomos: Essays in Athenian Law, Politics, and Society* (Cambridge and New York).

Fisher, N.R.E. (2008) 'The bad boyfriend, the flatterer and the sycophant: related forms of the kakos in democratic Athens', in I. Sluiter and R.M. Rosen (eds) *Kakos: Badness and Anti-value in Classical Antiquity* (Leiden and Boston).

Fischer-Hansen, T. (2000) 'Ergasteria in the western Greek world', in P. Flensted-Jensen, T.H. Nielsen and L. Rubinstein (eds) *Polis and Politics: Studies in Ancient Greek History* (Copenhagen).

Flacelière, R. (1965) *Daily Life in Ancient Greece at the Time of Pericles*, tr. Peter Green (New York).

Forbes, C.A. (1945) 'Expanded uses of the Greek gymnasium', *CPh* 40, 32-42.

Fornara, C. (1983) *Archaic Times to the End of the Peloponnesian War* (Cambridge and New York).

Fragiadakis, C. (1986) *Die attischen Sklavennamen von der spätarchaischen Epoche bis in die römische Kaiserzeit* (Mannheim).

Frank, J. (2004) 'Citizens, slaves, and foreigners: Aristotle on human nature', *American Political Science Review* 98, 91-104.

Gagarin, M. (1996) 'The torture of slaves in Athenian law', *CPh* 91, 1-18.

Garlan, Y. (1988) *Slavery in Ancient Greece* (Ithaca and London).

Garland, R. (1995) *The Eye of the Beholder: Deformity and Disability in the Graeco-Roman World* (London).

Garnsey, P. (ed.) (1980) *Non-Slave Labour in the Greco-Roman World* (Cambridge).

Garnsey, P. (1996) *Ideas of Slavery from Aristotle to Augustine* (Cambridge).

Gauthier, P.L. and M.B. Hatzopoulos (1993) *La Loi Gymnasiarchique de Beroia* (Athens and Paris).

Genovese, E.D. (1976) *Roll, Jordan, Roll* (New York).

Gera, D.L. (2003) *Ancient Greek Ideas on Speech, Language, and Civilization* (Oxford).

Bibliography

Glazebrook, A. (2006) 'The bad girls of Athens: the image and function of *hetairai* in judicial oratory', in C.A. Faraone and L.K. McClure (eds) *Prostitutes and Courtesans in the Ancient World*.

Goff, B. (2004) *Citizen Bacchae: Women's Ritual Practice in Ancient Greece* (Berkeley).

Goff, B. (2009) *Euripides: Trojan Women* (London).

Golden, M. (1984) 'Slavery and homosexuality at Athens', *Phoenix* 38, 308-24.

Golden, M. (1985) 'Pais, "child" and "slave"', *AC* 54, 91-104.

Golden, M. (1998) *Sport and Society in Ancient Greece* (Cambridge and New York).

Greenhalgh, P.A.L. (1972) 'Aristocracy and its advocates in archaic Greece', *G&R* 19.2, 190-207.

Gschnitzer, F. (1976) *Studien zur Griechischen Terminologie der Sklaverei* (Wiesbaden).

Hall, E. (1989a) *Inventing the Barbarian: Greek Self-Definition through Tragedy* (Oxford).

Hall, E. (1989b) 'The archer scene in Aristophanes' *Thesmophoriazusae*', *Philologus* 133, 38-59

Hall, E. (1997) 'The sociology of Athenian tragedy', in P.E. Easterling (ed.) *The Cambridge Companion to Greek Tragedy* (Cambridge).

Hall, E. (2000) 'Introduction', in J. Morwood (ed.) *Euripides: Hecuba, The Trojan Women, Andromache* (Oxford).

Harding, P. (1987) 'Rhetoric and politics in fourth century Athens', *Phoenix* 41, 25-39.

Harris, H.A. (1979) *Greek Athletes and Athletics* (Westport).

Harrison, A.R.W. (1998) *The Law of Athens* (Indianapolis).

Harrison, T. (1998) 'Herodotus' conception of foreign languages', *Histos* 2, 1-39.

Harrison, T. (ed.) (2002) *Greeks and Barbarians* (Edinburgh).

Hartog, F. (1988) *The Mirror of Herodotus* (Berkeley).

Harvey, F.D. (1988) 'Herodotus and the man-footed creature', in L. Archer (ed.) *Slavery and Other Forms of Unfree Labour* (New York).

Headlam, J.W. (1893) 'On the *proklêsis eis basanon* in Attic law', *CR* 7, 1-5

Henderson, J. (1987) 'Older women in Attic Old Comedy', *TAPhA* 117, 105-29.

Hesk, J. (2000) *Deception and Democracy in Classical Athens* (Cambridge).

Himmelmann, N. (1971) 'Archäologisches zum Problem der Sklaverei', *Abh. Mainz Geistes- u. Sozialwiss.* 13 (Mainz).

Hopkins, K. (1993) 'Novel evidence for Roman slavery', *P&P* 138, 3-27.

Houston, G.W. (2002) 'The slave and freedman personnel of public libraries in ancient Rome', *TAPhA* 132, 139-76.

Bibliography

Hubbard, T.K. (2003) *Homosexuality in Greece and Rome: A Sourcebook of Basic Documents* (Berkeley and London).

Hunter, V. (1993) *Policing Athens* (Princeton).

Hutchinson, G.O. (2004) 'Euripides' other "Hippolytus"', *ZPE* 149, 15-28.

Isaac, B. (2004) *The Invention of Racism in Classical Antiquity* (Princeton and Oxford).

Johansen, K.F. (1951) *The Attic Grave-Reliefs of the Classical Period* (Copenhagen).

Johnson, M. and T. Ryan (2005) *Sexuality in Greek and Roman Society and Literature* (London and New York).

Johnston, A. (1991) 'Greek vases in the marketplace', in T. Rasmussen and N. Spivey (eds) *Looking at Greek Vases* (Cambridge).

Jones, C.P. (1987) 'Stigma: tattooing and branding in Graeco-Roman antiquity', *JRS* 77, 139-55.

Jordan, D.R. (1985) 'A survey of Greek defixiones not included in the special corpora', *GRBS* 26, 151-97.

Joshel, S.R. and S. Murnaghan (eds) *Women and Slaves in Greco-Roman Culture* (London and New York).

Kassel, R. and C. Austin (1995) *Poetae Comici Graeci* VIII (Berlin).

Karouzou, S. (1957) 'Epitumbia stêlê titthês sto Ethniko Mouseio', *Hellenica* 15, 311-23.

Karydas, H.P. (1998) *Eurykleia and her Successors: Female Figures of Authority in Greek Poetics* (Lanham).

Kastely, James L. (1993) 'Violence and rhetoric in Euripides' *Hecuba*', *PMLA* 108, 1036-49.

Kern-Foxworth, M. (1994) *Aunt Jemima Uncle Ben & Rastus: Blacks in Advertising, Yesterday, Today, and Tomorrow* (Westport).

Keuls, E.C. (1985) *The Reign of the Phallus* (New York).

Klees, H. (1975) *Herren und Sklaven. Die Sklaverei im Oikonomischen und Politischen Schrifttum der Griechen in Klassicher Zeit* (Wiesbaden).

Kolendo, J. (1981) 'L'esclavage et la vie sexuelle des hommes libres à Rome', *Index* 10, 288-97.

Kosmopoulou, A. (2001) '"Working women": female professionals on Classical Attic gravestones', *ABSA* 96, 281-319.

Kurtz, D.C. (1988) 'Mistress and maid', *Annali: Sezione di archeologia e storia antica* 10, 141-9.

Kyrtatas, D.J. (2001) 'The vocabulary of slavery', in A.-F. Christidis (ed.) *A History of Ancient Greek: From the Beginnings to Late Antiquity* (Cambridge).

Lambert, S.D. (2000) 'The Erechtheum workers of *IG* ii^2 1654', *ZPE* 132, 157-60.

Bibliography

Lattimore, R. (1942) *Themes in Greek and Latin Epitaphs* (Urbana).

Lauffer, S. (1955-6) *Die Bergwerkssklaven von Laureion*, 2 vols (Mainz).

Lewis, D.M. (1959) 'Attic manumissions', *Hesperia* 28, 208-38.

Lewis, D.M. (1968) 'Dedications of phialai at Athens', *Hesperia* 37, 368-80.

Lewis, S. (2002) *The Athenian Woman: An Iconographic Handbook* (New York and London).

Lissarrague, F. (2000) 'The Athenian image of the foreigner', in T. Harrison (ed.) *Greeks and Barbarians* (Edinburgh).

Long, T. (1986) *Barbarians in Greek Comedy* (Carbondale and Edwardsville).

Loomis, W.T. (1998) *Wages, Welfare, Costs, and Inflation in Classical Athens* (Ann Arbor).

Loraux, N. (1986) *The Invention of Athens* (London).

McClure, L. (1999) *Spoken Like a Woman: Speech and Gender in Athenian Drama* (Princeton).

MacDowell, D.M. (1976) '"Hybris" in Athens', *G&R* 23, 14-31.

MacDowell, D.M. (1986) *The Law in Classical Athens* (Ithaca, New York).

McNiven, T.J. (2000) 'Behaving like an other', in B. Cohen (ed.) *Not the Classical Ideal* (Leiden).

Manring, M.M. (1998) *Slave in a Box: The Strange Career of Aunt Jemima* (Charlottesville).

Martin, B. and M. Spurrell (1962) *The Journal of a Slave Trader* (London).

Masson, O. (1972) 'Les noms des esclaves dans la Grèce antique', *Actes du colloque 1971 sur l'esclavage: tenu à Besançon, les 10-11 Mai 1971*, 9-23.

Meritt, B.D. (1927) 'An Athenian naval catalogue', *AJA* 31, 462-70.

Meyer, E.A. (2010) *Metics and the Athenian Phialai-Inscriptions: A Study in Athenian Epigraphy and Law* (Stuttgart).

Miller, M.C. (2004) *Athens and Persia in the Fifth Century BC* (New York and Cambridge).

Millett, P. (2007) 'Aristotle and slavery in Athens', *G&R* 54, 178-209.

Mirhady, D.C. (1996) 'Torture and Rhetoric in Athens', *JHS* 116, 119-31.

Mirhady, D.C. (2000) 'The Athenian rationale for torture', in J.C. Edmondson and V.J. Hunter (eds) *Law and Social Status in Classical Athens* (Oxford).

Mitchell, L. (2007) *Panhellenism and the Barbarian in Archaic and Classical Greece* (Swansea).

Murray, O. (2002) 'The Solonian law of *hubris*', in P. Cartledge, P. Millett, and S. Todd (eds) *Nomos: Essays in Athenian Law and Politics*.

Neils, J. (2000) 'Others within the other: an intimate look at *hetairai* and maenads', in B. Cohen (ed.) *Not the Classical Ideal* (Leiden).

Bibliography

Neils, J. and J.H. Oakley (2003) *Coming of Age in Ancient Greece: Images of Childhood from the Classical Past* (New Haven).

Oakley, J.H. (2000) 'Some "other" members of the Athenian household: maids and their mistresses in fifth-century Athenian art', in B. Cohen (ed.) *Not the Classical Ideal* (Leiden).

Ober, J. (1989) *Mass and Elite in Democratic Athens* (New Jersey).

Ober, J. (1996) *The Athenian Revolution: Essays on Ancient Greek Democracy and Political Theory* (Princeton).

Oliver, G.J. (2000) *The Epigraphy of Death: Studies in the History and Society of Greece and Rome* (Liverpool).

Olson, S.D. (1992) 'Servants' suggestions in Homer's *Odyssey*', *CJ* 87, 219-27.

Olson, S.D. (forthcoming, 2012) 'Slaves and politics in early Aristophanic comedy', in R. Tordoff and B. Akrigg (eds) *Slaves and Slavery in Ancient Greek Comic Drama* (Cambridge).

Omitowoju, R. (2002) *Rape and the Politics of Consent in Classical Athens* (Cambridge).

Osborne, R. (2000) 'An other view: an essay in political history', in B. Cohen (ed.) *Not the Classical Ideal* (Leiden).

Osborne, R. (2001) 'Why did Athenian pots appeal to the Etruscans?', *World Archaeology* 33, 277-95.

Osborne, R. (2004) *The Old Oligarch: Pseudo-Xenophon's* Constitution of the Athenians, *LACTOR* 2 (London).

Paradiso, A. (1993) 'Erodoto, VI, 137 e la schiavitù minorile', *Métis* 8, 21-6.

Patterson, O. (1982) *Slavery and Social Death* (Cambridge, Mass. and London).

Percy, W.A. III (1996) *Pederasty and Pedagogy in Archaic Greece* (Urbana and Chicago).

Pfisterer-Haas, S. (1990) 'Ältere Frauen auf Attischen Grabdenkmälern', *Mitteilungen des Deutschen Archäologischen Instituts, Athenische Abteilung*, 105, 179-96.

Pipili, M. (2000) 'Wearing an other hat: workmen in town and country', in B. Cohen (ed.) *Not the Classical Ideal* (Leiden).

Pomeroy, S.B. (1997) *Families in Classical and Hellenistic Greece: Representations and Realities* (Oxford and New York).

Pritchett, W.K. (1953) 'The Attic stelai, part I', *Hesperia* 22, 225-99.

Pritchett, W.K. (1956) 'The Attic stelai, part II', *Hesperia* 25, 178-328.

Pritchett, W.K. (1961) 'Five new fragments of the Attic stelai', *Hesperia* 30, 23-9.

Raaflaub, K. (2004) *The Discovery of Freedom in Ancient Greece* (Chicago).

Rabinowitz, N.S. (1998) 'Slaves with Slaves: Women and Class in Euripidean

Bibliography

Tragedy', in S.R. Joshel and S. Murnaghan (eds) *Women and Slaves in Greco-Roman Culture* (London and New York).

Randall, R.H. Jr. (1953) 'The Erechtheum workmen', *AJA* 57, 199-210.

Rawick, P. (ed.) (1972) *The American Slave: A Composite Autobiography,* vol. I (Westport).

Reilly, J. (1989) 'Many brides: "mistress and maid" on Athenian lekythoi', *Hesperia* 58, 411-44.

Robert, L. (1949) 'Épitaphe d'un Berger à Thasos', *Hellenica* 7, 152-60.

Roisman, H.M. (1999) 'The veiled Hippolytus and Phaedra', *Hermes* 127, 397-409.

Rosenbloom, D.S. (2004) '*Ponêroi* vs. *chrêstoi*: the ostracism of Hyperbolos and the struggle for hegemony in Athens after the death of Pericles Parts I-II', *TAPhA* 134, 133-4.

Rosivach, V.J. (1989) '*Talasiourgoi* and *Paidia* in *IG* 2^2 1553-78: a note on Athenian social history', *Historia* 38, 365-70.

Rossi, L. (2001) *The Epigrams Ascribed to Theocritus* (Leuven).

Rostovtzeff, M. (1922) *Iranians and Greeks in South Russia* (Oxford).

Rühfel, H. (1988) 'Ammen und Kinderfrauen im klassischen Athen', *Ant.W.* 19, 43-58.

Rystedt, E. (1994) 'Women, music, and a white-ground lekythos in the Medelhavsmuseet', in E. Rystedt, C. Scheffer and C. Wikander (eds) *Opus Mixtum: Essays in Ancient Art and Society* (Stockholm).

Saïd, S. (2002) 'Greeks and barbarians in Euripides' tragedies: the end of differences?' in T. Harrison (ed.) *Greeks and Barbarians* (Edinburgh).

Schofield, M. (1990) 'Ideology and philosophy in Aristotle's theory of slavery', in G. Patzig (ed.) *Aristoteles 'Politik'* (Göttingen).

Scholl, R. (1986) 'Sklaverei in der Arbeitswelt der Antike im Lichte der verschiedenen Quellenkategorien', *Gymnasium* 93, 476-96.

Scodel, R. (1980) *The Trojan Trilogy of Euripides* (Göttingen).

Segal, C. (1990) 'Golden armor and servile robes: heroism and metamorphosis in *Hecuba* of Euripides', *AJPh* 111, 304-17.

Shapiro, S. (1996) 'Herodotus and Solon', *ClAnt* 15, 348-64.

Silver, M. (2006) 'Slave versus free hired workers in ancient Greece', *Historia* 55, 257-63.

Simms, R.R. (1988) 'The cult of the Thracian goddess Bendis in Athens and Attica', *AncW* 18, 59-78.

Simon, E. (1963) 'Ein Anthesterien-Skyphos des Polygnotos', *AK* 6, 6-22.

Sluiter, I. (2008) 'General introduction,' in I. Sluiter and R.M. Rosen (eds) *Kakos: Badness and Anti-value in Classical Antiquity* (Leiden and Boston).

Sommerstein, A.H. (1983) *Wasps* (Warminster).

Bibliography

Sommerstein, A.H. (1985) *Peace* (Warminster).

Sommerstein, A.H. (1987) *Birds* (Warminster).

Sommerstein, A.H. (1994) *Thesmophoriazusae* (Warminster).

Sommerstein, A.H. (2002) *Greek Drama and Dramatists* (London and New York).

Sourvinou-Inwood, C. (1996) *'Reading' Greek Death* (Oxford and New York).

Spivey, N. (1991) 'Greek vases in Etruria', in T. Rasmussen and N. Spivey (eds) *Looking at Greek Vases* (Cambridge).

Stace, C. (1968) 'The Slaves of Plautus', *G&R* 15, 64-77.

Stears, K. (1998) 'Death becomes her: gender and Athenian death ritual', in S. Blundell and M. Williamson (eds) *The Sacred and the Feminine in Ancient Greece* (London and New York).

Stewart, A. (2008) *Classical Greece and the Birth of Western Art* (Cambridge).

Stone, L.M. (1981) *Costume in Aristophanic Comedy* (New York).

Stowe, H.B. (1979) *Uncle Tom's Cabin* (Norwalk).

Strauss, B.S. (1990) *'Oikos/Polis*: towards a theory of Athenian paternal ideology 450-399 BC', in *Aspects of Athenian Democracy. Classica et Mediaevalia. Dissertationes* 11 (Copenhagen).

Sumner, C. (1979) *Reading Ideologies: An Investigation into the Marxist Theory of Ideology and Law* (London and New York).

Sutton, R.F. Jr. (2000) 'The good, the base, and the ugly: the drunken orgy in Attic vase painting and the Athenian self', in B. Cohen (ed.) *Not the Classical Ideal* (Leiden).

Thalmann, W.G. (1988) 'Thersites: Comedy, Scapegoats, and Heroic Ideology', *TAPhA* 118, 1-28.

Thalmann, W.G. (1998) 'Female slaves in the *Odyssey*', in S.R. Joshel and S. Murnaghan (eds) *Women and Slaves in Greco-Roman Culture* (London and New York)

Thalmann, W.G. (2011) 'Some ancient Greek images of slavery', in R. Alston, E. Hall and L. Proffitt (eds) *Reading Ancient Slavery* (London).

Thomas, R. (2000) *Herodotus in Context* (Cambridge).

Thompson, W.E. (1982) 'The Athenian entrepreneur', *AC* 51, 53-85.

Tod, M.N. (1950) 'Epigraphical notes on freedmen's professions', *Epigraphica* 12, 3-26.

Tod, M.N. (1951) 'Laudatory epithets in Greek epitaphs', *ABSA* 46, 182-90.

Todd, S.C. (1990) *'Lady Chatterley's Lover* and the Attic Orators', *JHS* 110, 146-73.

Todd, S.C. (1993) *The Shape of Athenian Law* (Oxford).

Todd, S.C. (2000) 'The Purpose of Evidence in Athenian Courts', in P. Cartledge, P. Millett, S. Todd (eds) *Nomos: Essays in Athenian Law, Politics, and Society* (Cambridge).

Bibliography

Tovar, A. (1972) 'Indo-European etymology of DO-E-RO', *Minos* 12, 318-25.

Tsiafakis, D. (2000) 'The allure and repulsion of Thracians in the art of Classical Athens', in B. Cohen (ed) *Not the Classical Ideal* (Leiden).

Tsouna, V. (1998) 'Doubts about other minds and the science of physiognomics', *CQ* 48, 175-86.

Tzachou-Alexandri, O. (1989) *Mind and Body: Athletic Contests in Ancient Greece* (Athens).

Vafopoulou-Richardson, C.E. (1991) *Ancient Greek Terracottas* (Oxford).

Vogt, J. (1974) *Ancient Slavery and the Ideal of Man* (Oxford).

Wallace, R.W. (2007) 'Plato's sophists, intellectual history after 450, and Sokrates', in L.J. Samons II (ed.) *The Cambridge Companion to the Age of Pericles* (Cambridge).

Weiler, I. (2002) 'Inverted *Kalokagathia*', in T. Wiedemann and J. Gardner (eds) *Representing the Body of the Slave* (London and Portland).

Weiler, I. (2003) *Die Beendigung des Sklavenstatus im Altertum: ein Beitrag zur vergleichenden Sozialgeschichte* (Stuttgart).

West, M.L. (1987) *Orestes* (Wiltshire).

Westermann, W.L. (1946) 'Two studies in Athenian manumission', *JNES* 5, 92-104.

Whitehead, D. (1977) *The Ideology of the Athenian Metic* (Cambridge).

Wiedemann, T.E.J. (1981) *Greek and Roman Slavery* (London).

Wiedemann, T.E.J. (1987) *Slavery* (Oxford).

Wiedemann, T.E.J. and Jane Gardner (eds) (2002) *Representing the Body of the Slave* (London).

Wilkins, J.M. and S. Hill (2006) *Food in the Ancient World* (Oxford).

Willetts, R.F. (1967) *The Law Code of Gortyn, Edited with Introduction, Translation and Commentary. Kadmos* Suppl. 1 (Berlin).

Willi, A. (2003) *The Languages of Aristophanes* (Oxford).

Worman, N. (2008) *Abusive Mouths in Classical Athens* (Cambridge).

Wrenhaven, K.L. (2009) 'The identity of the "wool-workers" in the Attic manumissions', *Hesperia* 78, 367-86.

Wrenhaven, K.L. (forthcoming 2012) 'A comedy of errors: the comic slave in Greek art', in R. Tordoff and B. Akrigg (eds) *Slaves and Slavery in Ancient Greek Comic Drama* (Cambridge).

Wycherley, R.E. (1953) 'The Painted Stoa', *Phoenix* 7, 20-35.

Zelnick-Abramovitz, R. (2005) *Not Wholly Free: The Concept of Manumission and the Status of Manumitted Slaves in the Ancient Greek World* (Leiden).

Zuntz, G. (1972) 'Contemporary politics in the plays of Euripides', in *Opuscula Selecta* (Manchester).

Index

Index

Printed in Great Britain
by Amazon.co.uk, Ltd.,
Marston Gate.